Nietzsche

This classic biography of Nietzsche was first published in the 1960s and was enthusiastically reviewed at the time. In the years that have passed, the secondary literature on this most fertile and influential of modern philosophers has expanded enormously, and yet this biography remains the single best account of the life and works for the student or nonspecialist. Long out of print, it is now reissued with its text updated in the light of recent research.

The biography chronicles Nietzsche's evolution from the pious son of a country parson to the university professor who at the age of twenty-five had already conceived the basis of his mature philosophy. The book discusses his friendship and breach with Wagner, his attitude toward Schopenhauer, and his indebtedness to Darwin and the Greeks. It follows the years of his maturity, with his struggles with ill-health; his wanderings in Italy, France, and Switzerland; his abortive affair with Lou Salomé; and his mental collapse in 1889. The final part of the book considers the development of the Nietzsche legend during his years of madness.

Into this chronicle is integrated an account of the evolution of the philosophy from *The Birth of Tragedy* to *Ecce Homo*. The ideas are discussed in clear and straightforward language. In the biography's quotations, R. J. Hollingdale, one of the preeminent translators of this philosopher's works, allows Nietzsche to speak for himself in a translation that transmits the vividness and virtuosity of Nietzsche's many styles.

This is the ideal book with which anyone interested in Nietzsche's life and work can learn why he is such a significant figure for the development of modern thought. It is understandable for those—be they students, nonspecialists, or general readers of biography—who have only the slightest acquaintance with the vocabulary of philosophy.

R. J. Hollingdale, one of the most admired translators of Nietzsche, has widely disseminated the works of this philosopher by translating eleven of his books, three of which have been published by Cambridge University Press (*Daybreak, Untimely Meditations,* and *Human, All Too Human*).

Nietzsche

The Man and His Philosophy

Revised Edition

R. J. HOLLINGDALE

PUBLISHED BY THE PRESS SYNDICATE OF THE UNIVERSITY OF CAMBRIDGE
The Pitt Building, Trumpington Street, Cambridge, United Kingdom

CAMBRIDGE UNIVERSITY PRESS
The Edinburgh Building, Cambridge CB2 2RU, UK
40 West 20th Street, New York, NY 10011-4211, USA
10 Stamford Road, Oakleigh, Melbourne 3166, Australia
Ruiz de Alarcón 13, 28014 Madrid, Spain
Dock House, The Waterfront, Cape Town 8001, South Africa

http://www.cambridge.org

© R. J. Hollingdale 1965, 1999

First published by Routledge & Kegan Paul and Louisiana State University Press 1965
Revised edition first published by Cambridge University Press 1999
First paperback edition 2001

Printed in the United States of America

Typeface Ehrhardt 10.5/13 pt. *System* MagnaType™ [AG]

A catalog record for this book is available from the British Library.

Library of Congress Cataloging-in-Publication Data
Hollingdale, R. J.
Nietzsche : the man and his philosophy / R.J. Hollingdale—Rev.
ed.
p.   cm.
Includes bibliographical references and index.
1. Nietzsche, Friedrich Wilhelm, 1844-1900. I. Title.
B3317.H557   1999
193—dc21
[B]   98-33299
                                                                  CIP

ISBN 0 521 64091 1 hardback
ISBN 0 521 00295 8 paperback

Contents

Contents

Preface to the Revised Edition

As I said in the Preface to the original edition, the purpose of this book is to outline the life of Nietzsche as concisely as seems reasonable; his philosophy is considered as a part of his life, and here too the objective is conciseness. What I try to describe is the course of his existence and his thought in their essentials.

I have subjected the book to a thorough revision in which I have corrected what I now perceive as stylistic faults, removed some passages that seem to me misguided or out of date, and amended a few statements of supposed fact which later research has shown not to be factual; but in every essential respect the book has remained the work which first appeared in 1965.

I have eliminated the appendices of the original as being superannuated and have replaced them with a Postscript which in a strictly limited way surveys the changes that have taken place in the publication, reception and appreciation of Nietzsche over the past thirty-five years (part of this Postscript was first published in *International Studies in Philosophy,* vol. XXII/2, 1990). The original bibliography belongs, of course, to an older generation of Nietzsche study, and I have substituted a new one.

All the passages quoted from Nietzsche's works and letters were newly translated for the original 1965 edition: the works are cited by title or title initials (for which see the list that follows) and chapter and/or section, which are the same for all editions; the letters are cited by date so that they can be referred to in any edition.

Little Venice,
London

A List of Nietzsche's Works

In the large body of work published under Nietzsche's name during his life and since his death it is necessary to make a distinction between his genuine 'works' (i.e. those books published by him or prepared by him for publication) and all the remaining material (i.e. *Nachlass* [material left behind after his collapse and death], philologica, juvenilia): for the former group Nietzsche is responsible, for the latter he is not, since its distinguishing characteristic is that he did not offer it to the public as his 'work'. Yet, mainly through the publication of *The Will to Power*—a compilation drawn from the *Nachlass* of the 1880s—the dividing line between these two groups has become blurred and the logical and orderly development of his philosophy obscured. If we are to attempt to trace that development we must first be clear where it is to be discovered—i.e. in the 'works'. It would also be well to fix in advance the order in which Nietzsche's works appeared, since this is obviously of importance to any consideration of how his thought developed. For these reasons I give here a chronological list of Nietzsche's works as defined above. (The initials by which they are cited in the text are given on the right.)

1. *Die Geburt der Tragödie, oder Griechentum und Pessimismus* (The GT Birth of Tragedy, or Hellenism and Pessimism). Published 1872, under the title *Die Geburt der Tragödie aus dem Geiste der Musik* (The Birth of Tragedy out of the Spirit of Music), and consisting of 25 sections, with a 'Foreword to Richard Wagner'. 2nd edn. 1874 embodies some textual changes. 3rd edn. 1886 bears the altered title given above, and is prefaced by an 'Essay in Self-Criticism': although termed a 'new edition' it is in reality a reissue of remaining copies of the two previous editions (with the title changed and the prefatory essay added). The text quoted in the present work is that of the 2nd edn.

2. *Unzeitgemässe Betrachtungen* (Untimely Meditations).

Erstes Stück: David Strauss, der Bekenner und der Schriftsteller. UI
(First Essay: David Strauss, the Confessor and the Writer.)
Published 1873. A long essay in 12 sections.

Zweites Stück: Vom Nutzen und Nachteil der Historie für das UII
Leben. (Second Essay: On the Usefulness and Disadvantage
for Life of [the study of] History.) Published 1874. A long
essay in 10 sections, with a Foreword.

Drittes Stück: Schopenhauer als Erzieher. (Third Essay: UIII
Schopenhauer as Educator.) Published 1874. A long essay in 8
sections.

Viertes Stück: Richard Wagner in Bayreuth. (Fourth Essay: UIV
Richard Wagner in Bayreuth.) Published 1876. A long essay in
11 sections. Further 'Untimely Meditations' were planned but
not completed.

3. *Menschliches, Allzumenschliches. Ein Buch für freie Geister* (Human, All Too Human. A Book for Free Spirits).

Volume One. Published 1878, comprising 638 sections ordered MA
under 9 chapters, with a dedication to Voltaire and a quotation
from Descartes 'instead of a preface'. 2nd edn. 1886 unchanged except: (i) the dedication is removed, (ii) a newly-written Preface replaces the quotation, and (iii) a poetic
postlude, 'Under Freunden' (Among Friends), is added.

Volume Two. Erste Abteilung: Vermischte Meinungen und VMS
Sprüche. (First Division: Assorted Opinions and Maxims.)
Published 1879, comprising 408 sections.

Zweite Abteilung: Der Wanderer und sein Schatten. (Second WS
Division: The Wanderer and His Shadow.) Published 1880,
comprising 350 sections enclosed within a dialogue between
the Wanderer and his shadow.

2nd edn. 1886 combines these two divisions as the 2nd vol. of
MA, the only change being the addition of a newly-written
Preface.

4. *Morgenröte. Gedanken über die moralischen Vorurteile* (Daybreak: M
Thoughts on the Prejudices of Morality). Published 1881, comprising 575 sections ordered under 5 'books'. 2nd edn. 1887
unaltered except for the addition of a newly-written Preface.

5. *Die fröhliche Wissenschaft ('la gaya scienza')* (The Gay Science). FW
Published 1882, comprising 342 sections ordered under 4 'books'

and preceded by a 'Prologue in German Rhyme: *Scherz, List und Rache'* (Jest, Cunning and Revenge—the title is from Goethe) containing 63 short poems. 2nd edn. 1887 adds to the 1st edn.: (i) a 5th 'book': *Wir Furchtlosen* (We Who Are Without Fear), (ii) an appendix, *Lieder des Prinzen Vogelfrei* (Songs of Prince Free as a Bird), containing 14 poems, (iii) a newly-written Preface. A quotation from Emerson which stood as the motto of the 1st edn. is replaced by a quatrain of Nietzsche's own.

6. *Also sprach Zarathustra. Ein Buch für Alle und Keinen* (Thus Z Spoke Zarathustra. A Book for Everyone and No One).

   Part One, published 1883, comprises 'Zarathustra's Prologue' and 22 chapters.

   Part Two, also published 1883, comprises 22 chapters.

   Part Three, published 1884, comprises 16 chapters.

   Fourth and Last Part, comprising 20 chapters, issued privately 1885; first public issue 1892 as part of the first collected edn. of Nietzsche (ed. Peter Gast).

   Parts One, Two and Three were reissued as a single vol. in 1887 without alteration or addition.

7. *Jenseits von Gut und Böse. Vorspiel einer Philosophie der Zukunft* J (Beyond Good and Evil. Prelude to a Philosophy of the Future). Published 1886, comprising 296 sections ordered under 9 chapters, a Preface, and a poetic postlude, 'Aus hohen Bergen' (From High Mountains).

8. *Zur Genealogie der Moral. Eine Streitschrift* (Towards a Geneal- GM ogy of Morals. A Polemic). Published 1887, comprising 3 essays with a Preface.

9. *Der Fall Wagner. Ein Musikanten-Problem* (The Wagner Case. A W Musician's Problem). Published 1888. A polemical essay, with a Preface, two Postscripts and an Epilogue.

10. *Götzen-Dämmerung, oder Wie man mit dem Hammer philosophiert* G (Twilight of the Idols, or How to Philosophize with a Hammer). Prepared for publication 1888, published 1889. 10 chapters with a Foreword and a quotation from Z, 'Der Hammer redet' (The Hammer Speaks), as an epilogue.

11. *Nietzsche contra Wagner. Aktenstücke eines Psychologen* (Nietzsche NCW contra Wagner. A Psychologist's Brief). Prepared for publication 1888, issued privately 1889; first public issue 1895, as part of the

Gesamtausgabe in Grossoktav, ed. Fritz Koegel. 9 short chapters, with Foreword and Epilogue.

12. *Der Antichrist* (The Anti-Christ). Prepared for publication 1888,   A
    published 1895 as part of the *Gesamtausgabe in Grossoktav.* A
    long essay in 62 sections, with a Foreword.

13. *Dionysos-Dithyramben* (Dithyrambs of Dionysus). Nine poems of   DD
    various dates, apparently arranged by Nietzsche for publication
    at the end of 1888; published in 1892 in the first collected edn.,
    ed. Peter Gast.

14. *Ecce Homo. Wie man wird, was man ist* (Ecce Homo. How One   EH
    Becomes What One Is). An autobiography in 4 chapters with a
    Foreword. (Between the 3rd and 4th chapters are 10 sections
    dealing with Nietzsche's previous works: reference in the text of
    the present work is indicated by initials: e.g. EH–J, EH–GM.)
    Prepared for publication during the last quarter of 1888 and
    partly printed; published 1908 (limited edn.), 1911 (unlimited
    edn.)

Der Wille zur Macht (The Will to Power) is cited in the text by the initials WM.

. . . a curiosity like mine is decidedly the most pleasurable of vices.—I beg
your pardon! I meant to say: the love of truth has its reward in Heaven, and
already upon earth.

(J 45)

I

1844–1869

We are . . . *good Europeans*, the heirs of . . . millennia of the European spirit: as such we have outgrown Christianity, and precisely because we have grown out of it, because our forefathers were Christians of the ruthless integrity of Christianity, who for the sake of their faith gladly sacrificed their goods and their blood, their station and their country. We—do the same. (FW 377)

1

The Child

The Protestant pastor is the grandfather of German philosophy. (A 10)

1

Nietzsche's views have always seemed so strikingly different from the background of opinion against which he grew up that they have often been thought to owe their origin to a violent reaction against his upbringing. His entire philosophy even has been seen as no more than a calculated antithesis to the tradition in which he was raised. He was the heir of a line of Lutheran pastors going back to the beginning of the seventeenth century, his father and both grandfathers were Lutheran ministers, and he lived the first five and a half years of his life in a parsonage and later in an equally pious home; and it has been argued that his subsequent irreligion is to be explained by reference to these facts. There are two main reasons for rejecting this view as an adequate explanation of the genesis of Nietzsche's thought. In the first place, no serious student today would be inclined to exaggerate the differences between his outlook and that of Christianity: the tendency today—a justified tendency, as I think—is to emphasize the conventional elements in his philosophy and its connection with that 'Protestant' tradition of inquiry of which the whole of German philosophy may be said to be a part. Secondly, the need to account for the irrationality supposed to characterize Nietzsche's thought is disappearing with the growing recognition that it is not irrational at all. The notion that his philosophy was a reaction to his environment presupposed it was founded on emotion rather than on reason: the background of emotional rebellion was called on to account for the irrationalism, the irrationalism held responsible for the violence and radical nature of the rebellion. Here again the conventional picture has had to be modified, and the temptation now is to ignore

3

rather than emphasize the element of rebellion which is undoubtedly present in his work and to emphasize rather than ignore its strong links with the past.

The more closely one studies Nietzsche's work, the less inclined one is to look outside it for an elucidation of its meaning or an explanation of its origin. The need is no longer felt to psychologize it away or to find in an oppressively orthodox home the ground from which it sprang; and when this need is no longer felt it becomes possible to take a more realistic view of what that home was like. It then becomes clear that the conventional picture is founded on a misconception here, too. The Nietzsche home was certainly an orthodox one; but the quality of that orthodoxy has been rather misunderstood. To an outsider, the Lutheran Church resembles the Anglican more than any other: it is not fundamentalist or fanatical, and not puritan. It holds a special place in the history of German culture and education: the *Pfarrhaustradition*, as it is called—the preservation and advancement of cultural enlightenment in the Lutheran parsonage—is one of the few unbroken threads in the fabric of German historical development over the past three hundred years. Those brought up in that tradition, whether they entered the church themselves or not, have played a disproportionately large part in the cultural and intellectual life of Germany, and when Nietzsche wrote that the Protestant (i.e. Lutheran) pastor was the grandfather of German philosophy he was telling the strict truth. His own home was constructed on the conventional Lutheran pattern. There is no question but that he was happy there, and he never said he had 'rebelled' against an environment which he found insupportable. Apart from his father and mother the most influential figure of his childhood and youth was his maternal grandfather, Pastor David Oehler, with whom he and his sister spent many holidays. Grandfather Oehler was a hunting parson of the old type; he possessed a large library and was musically gifted; his parsonage resembled a farm and for most of his working week he was more of a farmer than a clergyman. He was a very robust gentleman, had eleven children, died in harness at 72, and strikes one as being about as devout and other-worldly as Laurence Sterne. Like the Anglican Church, the Lutheran offered the lower orders one of the few routes to social and cultural betterment: the fact that Nietzsche's forebears took it is not evidence of exceptional piety (or necessarily of any piety at all). If the English-speaking reader thinks of the Anglican Church of the eighteenth century, in which a Swift could become dean of a cathedral, a Berkeley a bishop and even a Sterne not lose his living, he will have a fair idea of the climate of tolerant orthodoxy in which Nietzsche grew up.

Nietzsche's ancestry has been traced back to the sixteenth century. Over 200 forebears are known, all of them Germans. Few were peasants or farmers (none were aristocrats); mostly they were small tradesmen: hatters, carpenters, butchers and the like. But by the eighteenth century the families that finally converged in the philosopher were all in the Lutheran Church.

The earliest Nietzsche to enter the church was the philosopher's grandfather Friedrich August Ludwig (1756–1826), who rose to the rank of superintendent, the equivalent of a bishop. Friedrich August's mother's family were Lutheran pastors for five generations (1600–1725) and his wife's father and great-grandfather had also been in the church. He was the author of two polemical defences of Christianity in the French Revolutionary period, one of which advanced in its subtitle the belief that Christianity would endure forever. This difference of opinion notwithstanding, there is something about the grandfather that reminds us of the grandson: the extreme assertion of a threatened tradition is common to both, and there is some similarity of polemical style in their writings, although the grandfather has little of the grandson's wit and rhetorical brilliance.[1]

Friedrich August's son, the philosopher's father, Karl Ludwig Nietzsche, was born in 1813. He was destined for the church from the first and became pastor of the village of Röcken, near Lützen, and of the neighbouring hamlets of Michlitz and Bothfeld, in 1842. The following year he married one of the daughters of the pastor of Pobles, a village an hour's journey away. Franziska Oehler, the philosopher's mother, was the sixth of Pastor Oehler's eleven children. Born in 1826, she was 17 when she married Pastor Nietzsche; her education is said to have been faulty, but there is plenty of testimony to her gaiety and good sense. These may sound prosaic virtues, but they were not very much in evidence at the Röcken parsonage before she went there. Pastor Nietzsche's establishment was a quieter one than that of the farming and hunting Pastor Oehler. It was dominated by the incumbent's widowed mother, and also in residence were his two step-sisters, Augusta and Rosalie, a pair of elderly oddities, amiable, well-meaning, unmarried and mildly neurotic: they achieved posthumous fame as 'Nietzsche's aunts', the embodiment of the provincial stuffiness against which the whole Nietzschean philosophy is supposed by some commentators to be a reaction.

The new Frau Pastor was so much younger than the other members of the household it must have seemed to her she was moving from one parental home to another less agreeable, of which, far from being the mistress, she was the most junior member; when her children came along they were more her

---

[1]Friedrich August Nietzsche's books are: *Gamaliel, oder die immerwährende Dauer des Christentums* (1796), and *Beiträge zur Beförderung einer vernünftigen Denkensart über Religion, Erziehung, Unter-tanenpflicht und Menschenliebe* (1804). They afford us the only glimpse we have of an intellectual quality out of the ordinary in the Nietzsche family before the birth of the philosopher.

contemporaries than anyone else in the house. All that we know of her shows Franziska Nietzsche to have been a notably gentle and humane person. She inherited a deal of her father's love of living, and her faith, which was profound, was of that instinctive sort that expresses itself in actions rather than sermons. She was the type of Christian who cannot conceive that anyone who has been taught the gospel can ever seriously doubt its truth, and who therefore views with an indulgent eye heresies merely written in books: the only time she really quarrelled with her son was on the one occasion she thought he intended to translate his theoretical paganism into action.

A wholly unnecessary confusion has been introduced into the straightforward tale of Nietzsche's ancestry by the story that the Nietzsches were really descended from Polish nobility. According to a 'family legend', these aristocratic forebears were Protestants who fled to Germany from Catholic persecution in their homeland. Nietzsche subscribed to this story to the end of his life; as late as 1888 he wrote to Georg Brandes: 'My ancestors were Polish noblemen (Nietzky); the type seems to have been well preserved despite three generations of German mothers', and he repeated the claim elsewhere, notably in *Ecce Homo*. Brandes, who knew of Nietzsche's history only what Nietzsche had told him, gave it wide currency by repeating it in his obituary of him. The researches of Max Oehler, sometime curator of the Nietzsche Archive at Weimar, have proved—what Nietzsche's contemporaries suspected—that there is no truth in it. It was Oehler who traced the 200 ancestors referred to, and who established that they all bore German names, even the wives' families. According to Richard Blunck,[1] Nietzky is not a Polish name, while Nietzsche is an exceptionally common one throughout central Germany, in this and cognate forms (e.g. Nitsche, Nitzke). Like many common surnames, it derives from a common forename, in this case Nikolaus (Nicholas), which, abbreviated to Nick and assimilated with the Slavic Nitz (pronounced Nitsch) became Nitsche and then Nietzsche. It is obvious that Nietzsche made no investigation of his ancestry, and his reference to 'three generations of German mothers' seems a piece of pure invention. Why he wished to believe that a family of Lutheran parsons had Polish noblemen for their forebears cannot be determined with certainty, but my own feeling is that he wanted not so much to be thought aristocratic as to be thought Polish: that is, his propagation of the legend was part of his campaign against Germany, 'Europe's flatland', the nation with 'every great crime against culture for the last four centuries . . . on their conscience' (EH—W 2), and who, moreover, had bought only 170 copies

---

[1]Richard Blunck: *Friedrich Nietzsche. Kindheit und Jugend* (Basel, 1953), p. 16.

of *Human, All Too Human* during its first year of publication and whose reaction to the first three volumes of *Zarathustra* had been so cool that no publisher would risk handling the fourth. He had spent the ten years up to 1888 in producing a succession of works which should in all reason have established him as the leading figure in German literature and philosophy of his time; but nothing of the sort had happened; he had encountered silence and indifference; and his just anger at this treatment toppled over in his last year of sanity into blind, unreasoning hatred. He would now allow the Germans nothing but their crimes. No one, he said, had ever written the German language as well as Heine and Nietzsche, and Heine was a Jew and Nietzsche—was a Pole.

2

Nietzsche was born on the 15th October 1844, at Röcken. His birthday was also that of the reigning king of Prussia, of whom Pastor Nietzsche was a great admirer, and he was named Friedrich Wilhelm after the king. Pastor and Franziska Nietzsche had two further children: a daughter, Elizabeth, who was born on the 10th July 1846, and a second son, Joseph, who was born in February 1848 and died in infancy.

The parsonage in which the young Fritz spent the first five years of his life was in the heart of the countryside. Surrounded by farms, it was itself a farm of a kind, with an orchard behind and a farmyard in front. Beyond the farmyard was a flower garden, and separated from this by a hedge was what seemed to the child a paradisean spot: four ponds, full of fish and surrounded by willow trees. It was here he spent most of his time during the summer. The nearest town, Lützen, half an hour away, was a very sleepy place that woke up only for the annual fair, a visit to which provided the only occasion many of the inhabitants of Röcken had for leaving the village from one year's end to the other. The town, which lies in Saxony-Anhalt in what was formerly East Germany, is still only a small place; in Nietzsche's day it stood in a completely rural area, surrounded by villages for which it provided a market and 'capital'.

It is perhaps unnecessary to say that the revolutionary outbreaks of 1848 and 1849 made little mark on Röcken. Nietzsche records in *Aus meinem Leben*[1] that he saw wagonloads of cheering men, whom he took to be rebels, careering

---

[1]This document was written between the 18th August and the 1st September 1858, just before Nietzsche left home to become a boarder at Landesschule Pforta. He wanted to set down all he could remember of his childhood before leaving it behind.

with banners flying along the road past the parsonage. Pastor Nietzsche is known to have deplored the uprisings as acts of base ingratitude towards his beloved king, and it may be recalled that the gravamen of Wagner's offence in participating in the Dresden revolt of May 1849 was held to lie in the ingratitude it displayed towards the king of Saxony, who had rescued him from poverty by making him a conductor at the royal opera house.

But all this was of no concern to the infant Fritz. The uneventful life, the changeless progression of days in which all that varies is the weather, the secure home apparently destined to endure forever, is the element of infancy, and it was the element in which Nietzsche passed his first four years. The idyll was shattered when Pastor Nietzsche became ill and died at the age of 36. It may be that this was the decisive event of Nietzsche's life: we have record of no other so likely to have been the cause of his inability in later years ever to settle down in his own or anyone else's home. Nothing strikes one so forcibly when trying to see his life as a whole as the dichotomy between the utterly settled, domestic and localized existence of his immediate and more remote forebears and his own chronic footlooseness. The son of an intensely nationalistic and rooted family, he became a rootless cosmopolitan. The ill-health which plagued him in these later years can hardly be held to account for it, as it sometimes has been; on the contrary, a sick man would be more likely to avoid travel and domestic uncertainty than a fit one. But Nietzsche avoided as if by instinct every commitment which might have fastened him to a particular place. He never married and never became a father himself, and he eluded involvement with those institutions which provide most men, even the most brilliant, with a stable background to their lives: is it fanciful to see in the sudden and, as it must have seemed to him, catastrophic collapse of his earliest home an explanation of this fact?

He was passionately attached to his father, and the shock of losing him was profound. *Aus meinem Leben* provides us with the picture he retained of him, and with a record of the feelings that accompanied the son's anxious witness of his illness and death. Pastor Nietzsche, we read, was 'the perfect picture of a country parson'.

> Gifted with spirit and a warm heart [*Geist und Gemüt*], adorned with all the virtues of a Christian, he lived a peaceful, simple and happy life and was loved and admired by all who knew him. His good manners and cheerful disposition were an embellishment to the many social gatherings to which he was invited . . . He occupied his leisure hours with good reading and with music, and he achieved notable skill as a pianist, especially in the execution of free variations (i.e. improvisation; this was also true of Nietzsche himself).

An equally laudatory description is given us in *Mein Lebenslauf,* another autobiographical sketch, written during 1861:

> I still retain in my soul a vivid image of him: a tall, slim figure with delicate features and of a kind and pleasing demeanour. Liked and welcomed every-where, as much for his witty conversation as for his kindly sympathy, honoured and loved by the peasants as a parson whose words and deeds were alike benefi-cial, the most fond husband and loving father, he was the perfect model of a country parson.

Nietzsche's most famous recollection of his father, written in 1888, has been scoffed at as an obvious idealization:

> . . . he was delicate, lovable and morbid, like a being destined to pay this world only a passing visit—a gracious reminder of life rather than life itself. (EH–I 1)

This seems, however, to be less the idealized picture of an in fact forgotten father than a portrait of a sick and dying man: Pastor Nietzsche as he was for the last nine months of his life and as he was remembered most vividly by his 44-year-old son. The effect of those last months is best conveyed in the language of *Aus meinem Leben:*

> Up to then we had experienced only joy and happiness, our life had flowed smoothly by like a bright summer's day; but now black clouds towered up, lightning flashed and bolts from heaven came crashing down. In September 1848 my beloved father suddenly became mentally ill [*gemütskrank*]. Both we and he hoped for a speedy recovery. Whenever there came a day on which he seemed better he asked us to let him preach again and resume his confirmation lessons; for his active spirit could not bear to be idle. Several doctors tried to discover the nature of the illness, but in vain. Then we brought to Röcken the famous doctor Opolcer, who was then in Leipzig. This admirable man knew at once where to look for the seat of the illness. To the horror of all of us he diagnosed a softening of the brain; although the case was not hopeless it was certainly very grave. My dear father had to endure terrible pain, but the com-plaint refused to improve, but grew worse from day to day. He lay on his sickbed until July 1849; then the day of his release approached. On the 26th July he sank into a deep slumber and only now and then did he awake again . . . Died the 27th July 1849. When I awoke that morning I heard weeping and sobbing all around me. My dear mother entered in tears and wailed: 'Oh God! My dear Ludwig is dead!' Although I was still very young and inexperienced I had an idea of what death was: the thought that I was forever parted from my beloved father seized hold on me and I wept bitterly. The days that followed were filled with tears and with preparations for the funeral. Oh God! I had become a

fatherless orphan, my dear mother had become a widow!—On the 2nd August the earthly remains of my dear father were entrusted to the bosom of the earth . . . The ceremony began at one o'clock, accompanied by the tolling of the bells. Oh, I shall always have the hollow clangour of those bells in my ears, I shall never forget the gloomy melody of the hymn 'Jesu meine Zuversicht'.

These events occurred when the boy was 4 and were recorded when he was 14; the feeling of deprivation and the sense that the world had collapsed seem to have increased rather than diminished during the intervening ten years.[1]

The nature of Pastor Nietzsche's illness and its cause have been hotly debated in the Nietzsche literature since Nietzsche himself became insane; there is indeed no more powerful witness to the shock his works from *Human, All Too Human* onwards produced in readers of the 1880s and 1890s than the evident desire many of them had to prove the author mad. That this view is untenable I hope to show when we come to discuss what was probably the actual cause of Nietzsche's breakdown. On the immediate question of whether it is likely he inherited a mental weakness of any kind from his father, the answer must be a firm No. Evidence as to what precisely Pastor Nietzsche was suffering from when he died is scanty. All that can be said with definiteness is that he was subject to very minor epileptic attacks from time to time which he did not recognize as such and which were not considered sufficiently serious to warrant treatment or surveillance; about nine months before his death he fell victim to some nervous or brain affliction which proved fatal. Franziska maintained much later (in a statement to the clinic at Basel) that he had died from 'softening of the brain caused by a fall from a flight of steps' but was never in any sense 'mad'. The term *gemütskrank*, which Nietzsche used at the age of 14 to describe the condition into which his father declined, means mentally disordered or melancholy; it is a very imprecise term and need not (strictly speaking, should not) imply insanity in the clinical sense; certainly Nietzsche himself was never *gemütskrank* but *geisteskrank*, not mentally disordered but insane. Moreover, it cannot be considered likely that the 4-year-old

---

[1]The quotation from *Aus meinem Leben* is an extract only: the funeral is recorded in considerable detail, with the names of the officiating clergy. Nietzsche seems to have remembered the scene with great exactitude. In *Mein Lebenslauf* the death of his father is again described, this time with a commemorative verse:

> 'Ach sie haben
> Einen guten Mann begraben,
> Und mir war er mehr!'

All this thirteen years after the death of a father he had known only in infancy!

boy would have been allowed much contact with his father while the latter was 'mentally disordered', or that if he had he could have gained much more than an instinctive sense that something was not well.

Elizabeth's notorious unreliability and dishonesty in matters of biography make it impossible to quote her evidence in support of any contention where a difference of opinion is involved. In her biographies of her brother she does everything possible to fend off the suspicion that their father had been deranged, but she does it in such a way as to make that suspicion begin to seem well founded: she falsifies, for instance, the passage in *Aus meinem Leben* in which Nietzsche had written that 'my beloved father suddenly became *gemütskrank';* when she quoted it in the first volume of her biography of 1895 she made it read: 'my beloved father suddenly became seriously ill as the result of a fall'. This example is typical of Elizabeth's method of working. The honest and most sensible course would have been to have quoted Nietzsche's words and then denied they were true, bringing forward their mother's state-ment as expressing the truth of the matter and attributing Nietzsche's error to his youthful inability to understand what had happened to their father. Not only did she not do this but, having misquoted Nietzsche's manuscript, she failed to destroy it, leaving it in the Archive to be published in its correct form later.

The evidence that Pastor Nietzsche was ever 'insane' at all must be called at the best inconclusive; but there is no evidence whatever that he handed on this problematical insanity to his son. It is a pure supposition: knowing that Nietzsche had suffered a mental collapse and was insane beyond question, and learning that his father had died from 'softening of the brain', certain persons formed the convenient but baseless conclusion that the two events were con-nected. The obvious inference to be drawn if Nietzsche had in fact inherited a streak of insanity from his father was indeed drawn by Rohde who, writing to Overbeck on the 4th August 1889 (i.e. eight months after Nietzsche had become insane), charitably suggests that Elizabeth too must have 'the seeds of insanity' in her and adds: 'There was always something not quite right about her.' (Rohde knew that Pastor Nietzsche was supposed to have suffered from some kind of mental disorder.) Happily, his fears for Elizabeth's sanity proved unfounded: however much one may disapprove of her behaviour, dislike her opinions or question her judgment, it is impossible to attribute any of them to insanity.

But even if it be granted that the collapse of the last months of 1888 must have thrown its shadow before it, there is still no justification for thinking any of Nietzsche's works tainted. The development of his thought is quite consis-tent from *Human, All Too Human* onwards and gains rather than loses in cogency as he draws closer to the end. It was the unfamiliarity of his ideas, and not any want of rationality in their presentation, that alienated readers of his own time, and the fact that he became insane made it all the easier for these ideas to be discounted as the product of an unbalanced mind.

To return to the family at the Röcken parsonage: the blow of the father's death was followed in the first days of 1850 by a second tragedy. The infant Joseph suddenly died: according to his mother from 'cramps while teething'. It is just possible that the mildly epileptic condition in his father had reasserted itself.

Pastor Nietzsche's successor was due to arrive in the April of that year, and the family were therefore required to move from the parsonage. Grandmother Nietzsche had close ties with the town of Naumburg on the Saale, and thither the family repaired to begin a new phase of its existence. Naumburg was then still a walled town: its five gates were shut at ten in the evening and not reopened until five the following morning. In its own way, Naumburg was as quiet and conservative as Röcken, leading a life that had not changed in any essential for a century or more. It was here that Nietzsche lived from his sixth to his fourteenth year. Apart from him, the family was now composed entirely of women, and we can here briefly and conveniently trace its fortunes during those Naumburg years.

In the summer of 1855 Aunt Augusta died, and in April 1856 Grandmother Erdmuthe followed her. As a consequence of legacies from the grandmother, it was now possible for Franziska to set up a home of her own, and in the summer of 1856 she moved with her two children to the house of a friend and then to her own establishment. She was still only 30, and although she never remarried it seems to have been from lack of inclination rather than of opportunity, and we gain a false impression of Nietzsche's home surroundings at this time if we think of him as living with a 'widowed mother', with all the suggestion of gloom and over-possessiveness this term carries; it was only now, in fact, that, freed from the domination of the older women, she properly regained the elasticity and cheerfulness of temperament that had been her most notable feature as a girl. In the summer of 1858 she made a third move, to No. 18 Weingarten, where she lived the remainder of her life. It was from this house that Nietzsche departed when he left his mother for the first time to attend the Pforta boarding school, and it was to this house that he returned, thirty-one years later, to be cared for by her until she died.

Soon after his arrival in Naumburg he was entered at the local boys' school; he was nearly 6 and he could already read and write, having been taught by his mother. Here he made his earliest friends: two Naumburg boys named Wilhelm Pinder and Gustav Krug. Pinder's grandmother was a friend of

Grandmother Nietzsche's and one of the leading personalities of the town; his father, who was a town councillor, was a lover of literature, and it was at his house that Nietzsche first heard of Goethe: Councillor Pinder read Goethe's *Novelle* to the three boys. Krug was a cousin of Pinder's and his father, a noted amateur musician, was host to visiting musicians who came to play at Naumburg: Nietzsche's natural bent for music was powerfully encouraged by what he heard on these occasions.

Nietzsche has been accused, by those who seem determined to deny him every human quality, of being incapable of friendship. This is surely untrue. He had one lifelong friend in Overbeck, and if his intense friendship with Rohde withered away when the two men's paths diverged, it lasted as long as most intense friendships are likely to. No one, moreover, has written in praise of friendship more powerfully and beautifully than Nietzsche. Nevertheless, it must be said that what he sought in a friend was very often no more than a confirmation or echo of himself, or an audience for his discourses. It is rare to find him becoming attached to another because of the other's purely human qualities (Overbeck is the principal exception). He was in this respect, as well as in many others, so like Wagner that Ernest Newman's description of what Wagner expected from a friend applies exactly to Nietzsche too:

> He needed a receptacle for the volcanic outpouring of his ideas, and encouragement in the realisation of them; and the true friend, from his point of view, was one who gave himself up most completely to the role of listener and helper. In a sense he was, like all men who tower above their fellows, too big for ordinary friendship: there can be no genuine friendship between the central mountain and the surrounding hills—only a looking up to in the one case and a looking down upon in the other. 'A deplorable law governing genius', says Romain Rolland very truly, 'seems to decree that, with the superior mind, a strong dose of mediocrity in the other is required to satisfy the needs of friendship. A genius will form only a passing friendship with his peers.'[1]

This is not quite the same thing as saying that a man of genius is not capable of friendship *at all*, and Rolland's dictum should not be taken to imply that all such a man wants is worship. Nietzsche's closest associate, after his break with Wagner, was Peter Gast, a man of greatly inferior intellect (as Gast recognized very clearly), but full of admiration for Nietzsche. Gast wrote a beautifully clear hand; Nietzsche's handwriting was never very good and became worse as his eyesight deteriorated until it ended as an all but illegible scrawl which Gast alone was able to decipher; it is difficult to see how Nietzsche could ever have

[1] Ernest Newman: *The Life of Richard Wagner*, vol. I (London 1933), p. 89.

got his manuscripts into a condition fit for the printer without Gast's help. Posterity owes a debt to the truly immense labours Gast undertook as copyist that it has never really recognized. Moreover, Gast was always prepared to drop whatever he might be doing to come to Nietzsche's assistance whenever he was needed. In face of this, Nietzsche would indeed have been the monster of ingratitude he is sometimes painted as being if he had accepted Gast's devotion without feeling some sense of obligation towards him. But this in fact he did feel. Gast was by profession a composer, and Nietzsche is well known to have done all he could to further his friend's career, securing or attempting to secure performances of his music whenever he could and praising Gast's mediocre talent as that of 'another Mozart'. Nietzsche's critics have naturally ridiculed the extravagance of his eulogy of Gast's compositions, claiming to see in it nothing but a revelation of how absurd were his pretensions as an aesthetic judge. It is these same gentlemen, as a rule, who also accuse him of being incapable of friendship.

His boyhood friendship with Pinder and Krug was in some ways a model of what such a friendship could be. That Nietzsche was the dominant partner was inevitable (the friendship would not have arisen if he had not been); but this was surely because he was the most able of the three. Although he was no child prodigy, his intellectual and artistic ability was evident from the first, and it was no matter for surprise when he was awarded a free place at the famous Pforta school. In any event, the arrangement must have suited the other two, since the friendship not only lasted for the years of boyhood but endured the separation entailed when Nietzsche left Naumburg for Pforta, and then bore its finest fruit in the miniature literary society 'Germania' which the three friends formed as an aid to their artistic development and which they carried on for three years. Finally, it was Krug who introduced Nietzsche to the works of Wagner. The friends ceased to see and help one another only when Nietzsche left Pforta for Bonn and Leipzig, and his childhood days really were at an end.

The school years at Naumburg passed uneventfully enough. In the spring of 1851 Nietzsche and his two friends were transferred from the town school to a private preparatory school, where they stayed until the autumn of 1854 and where Nietzsche obtained his first grounding in Latin and Greek. Then they went on to the higher school, the *Domgymnasium;* after four years here, Nietzsche was awarded a free place at Pforta. He left the *Gymnasium* at the end of the summer term of 1858 and started at Pforta on the 5th October. He experienced little difficulty with school work. He was a studious boy but not a bookworm; as we might expect from his later character, he avoided the rough and tumble of the streets, and his short-sightedness, which had already declared itself,[1] hindered his participation in school sports, but he was always keen on the kind of outdoor activity he felt he could be good at. He learned to swim at an early age, and always remained a swimmer of more than average ability; he also became an excellent skater, and he indulged in the long country hikes that Germans of all ages seem so addicted to. He was strongly built and physically not a weakling: the stamina which enabled the man to endure year after year of ill-health was already present in the boy.

The weak spot in his constitution was his eyes. As soon as he went to school he was compelled to wear glasses, and he had to continue wearing them for the rest of his life; although he never became blind, the possibility that his eyesight would deteriorate virtually to the point of blindness was always present. The amount of reading and writing he did as a boy undoubtedly had a harmful effect and contributed to the headaches with which he began to be plagued and from which he was never again wholly free: during the summer of 1856 he was released from school for a period because of eye-trouble and persistent headaches.

Although Pforta was only an hour's walk from Naumburg, Nietzsche's removal thither marked the end of one epoch in his life and the beginning of another. His existence up to the age of 14 had been a secluded one: clasped to the bosom of a loving mother, at first in a tiny country village and then in a larger but hardly less quiet country town, he knew little of the realities of the greater world, and the Spartan discipline of Pforta stood in the sharpest possible contrast to the cozy domestic ease in which he had hitherto reclined. But before we follow him to Pforta, let us take a look at what he had been doing as a nascent artist and philosopher during these earliest years.

3

Other philosophers have written poetry and other poets have philosophized, but only in Plato have intellectual and artistic ability been combined at so high a level as they were in Nietzsche. Yet this double gift has injured his reputation as a philosopher, so that it may still be necessary to insist that he *was* a philosopher and not a poet and aphorist with a few fixed ideas. His memorability has worked against him: short passages stay in the mind but divorced from their context and for that reason sometimes nearly meaningless or capable of being seriously misunderstood. His temperament was that of an artist and for that reason his philosophical writings are impure, in the sense that

[1]Elizabeth was also short-sighted: this was one thing both children *did* inherit from their father.

they mingle reason and sensibility, logic and rhetoric, and sometimes *Dichtung und Wahrheit,* in a way that baffles the orderly mind which seeks to discover 'what Nietzsche means'. If the philosopher too long failed to be the subject of regular study at our universities, it was the artist who was to blame; for, though the philosopher provided the substance, it was the artist who dictated the form, which therefore often asserts the claims of art to the prejudice of those of logical clarity, and creates what the student anxious to 'do' Nietzsche (and possibly to have done with him) thinks needless difficulty.

But these disadvantages notwithstanding, the artist in Nietzsche was the saving of him. Because he was an artist as well as a thinker, he avoided the vices of German philosophy, while because he was in touch with what is valuable and profound in German philosophy he avoided also the slipshod thinking of the philosophist or wise-cracking aphorist. To enumerate the opposite defects of these two classes of thinker is to indicate the narrowness of the ridge upon which he stood.

The defects of German philosophy are those of professionalism: a closed atmosphere, books instead of life, inability to communicate discoveries to the world at large, contempt for good style, inbreeding, lack of general culture, gruesome earnestness. The defects of the cultured *philosophe* are those of amateurism: too many interests, superficiality, the cultivation of good style as an end in itself, the sacrifice of truth to wit, lack of intellectual honesty, philosophizing but no philosophy, inconsistency. Nietzsche achieves a balance between these two types of mind and two styles of expression: he is profound but not obscure; he aims at good style but reconciles it with good thinking; he is serious but not earnest; he is a sensitive critic of the arts and of culture but not an aesthete; he is an aphorist and epigrammist, but his aphorisms and epigrams derive from a consistent philosophy; he is the wittiest of philosophers, but he rarely succumbs to the temptation to sacrifice truth to a witty phrase; he has many interests but never loses sight of his main interests. He achieves, especially in his later works, a conciseness and limpidity notoriously rare in German writing: no modern thinker of a like profundity has had at his command so flexible an instrument of expression.

He was precocious intellectually but not precociously original, and he was 34 before his earliest work of consequence, *Human, All Too Human,* appeared. The earliest work of all—the poems and other writings of his Naumburg years up to 1858—is, indeed, strikingly unindividual: subject-matter and treatment are conventional, and there is a notable absence of the kind of spontaneity revealed by many a far less talented child in his first attempts. In *Aus meinem Leben* of 1858 he divided his poetical production to that date into three periods: the earliest was devoted to the description of natural scenes and dramatic events in ungoverned and often unrhymed verse ('Storm at Sea', 'Rescue', 'Shipwreck', 'Tempest'); then he sought to bring form and measure to the chaos, but succeeded in producing only dullness ('Andromeda', 'The Argonauts', 'Dryope'); finally he made a conscious effort to unite the formal qualities of the second period with the passion of the first ('Whither?', 'The Lark', 'The Nightingale's Lament', 'Hector's Farewell', 'Barbarossa'). In 1857 he wrote a poem on the siege of Sebastopol: with Pinder and Krug he fought the Crimean War in his back-garden, being for some reason passionately pro-Russian. He lists forty-six poems composed during the years 1855 to 1858, and says specifically that they are only a selection; he probably wrote about a hundred. The sign that he was a born writer, however, is not to be found in them, but in a remark in *Aus meinem Leben,* where, describing his earliest efforts at verse, he says: 'In any event, it was always my design to write a little book and then read it myself'—a childish expression of the narcissism of the true artist, who works because he wants to admire what he has done. Other youthful enterprises included two short plays on classical subjects written in collaboration with Pinder and, during 1856, the beginning of a novel to be called *Death and Destruction.* The most convincing piece of work was the already-quoted *Aus meinem Leben:* written in simple, direct prose, saying what it intends to say and no more, it is a creditable performance for a boy not yet 14.

The value of these juvenilia for a study of Nietzsche is that they provide the student with a starting-point: they demonstrate more clearly than any second-hand report how pious he was as a boy. One would scarcely expect him to harbour serious doubts as yet, still less to formulate objections; but the intensity of his religious feeling is startling:

I have already experienced so much—joy and sorrow, cheerful things and sad things—but in everything God has safely led me as a father leads his weak little child . . . I have firmly resolved within me to dedicate myself forever to His service. May the dear Lord give me strength and power to carry out my intention and protect me on my life's way. Like a child I trust in His grace: He will preserve us all, that no misfortune may befall us. But His holy will be done! All He gives I will joyfully accept: happiness and unhappiness, poverty and wealth, and boldly look even death in the face, which shall one day unite us all in eternal joy and bliss. Yes, dear Lord, let Thy face shine upon us forever! Amen! (*Aus meinem Leben*).

2

The Schoolboy

Youth is disagreeable: for in youth it is either not possible or not sensible
to be productive, in whatever sense. (MA 539)

1

Pforta was a hard school and a strict one, but it was what Nietzsche required at
the age of 14. Like those of most public schools of its time, its regulations read
as if they were designed for a prison for persistent offenders, but it is probably
a mistake to think them actually harmful to a boy who has to learn somehow
that ease and happiness are not the same thing, and may as well learn it from
people who have his welfare at heart. He has left us an account of a typical day
in Pforta school life.[1] Pupils were woken at 4 a.m. and had to be ready for
action by 5; classes started at 6 and continued in one form or another until
noon. They resumed at 1:15 p.m. and went on until ten to 4. Further classes
were held in the evening, and bedtime was 9 p.m. Behaviour at mealtimes was
strictly regulated, and there was little more than an hour during the day when
the student was left to his own devices. This routine was followed for five days
a week. Sunday was free, and there was one other day on which the boarders
could lie in bed an hour longer and then spend their time in revision of the
week's work. And there were also, of course, the long school holidays in which
to recover. At first Nietzsche disliked this life intensely. He suffered from
homesickness: in February 1859, after he had been at Pforta four months, he
was prostrated by an overwhelming desire to get away from it and go back
home, and he suffered a similar attack on returning from the summer holidays
of the same year. He confided his troubles to his tutor, Buddensieg, who
helped him to recover,[2] after which he became something of a model scholar,

[1] *Pforta Diary* for the 9th August 1859.
[2] The *Pforta Diary* for the 6th August carries a list of antidotes to homesickness provided by
Buddensieg.

18

chiefly because he excelled in the subjects the school placed most emphasis on.

The real interest of Pforta lay in Greek and Latin, and to a lesser degree in the German classics. The school was fundamentally, as Richard Blunck says, a world of books: the students breathed the air not of modern Europe but of ancient Greece and Rome and of the Germany of Goethe and Schiller, and it is entirely in character as an ex-pupil of Pforta that Nietzsche should have become a professor of classical philology, since that is what the curriculum of Pforta seems best designed to produce. Mathematics and the sciences took a decided second place, and mathematics was Nietzsche's worst subject: if he had not established so high a reputation as a classical scholar he would have failed the school-leaving examination on account of his poor showing in the mathematics paper. (The examiners are supposed to have been on the point of failing him on this account when one of them exclaimed: 'But gentlemen, are we really going to fail the best pupil Pforta has ever had?') But he attained to no exceptional brilliance in his other non-classical studies. He studied Hebrew in connection with his intention to take up theology, but he was never able to master the grammar, and he was in general a bad student of modern languages: he read Shakespeare and Byron in German translation, he never learned to master Italian even when living in Italy, and he could read French only with the help of a dictionary.

His studies did not use up all his intellectual energy, and as an outlet for his developing talents he proposed to his Naumburg friends Pinder and Krug that they should form a literary and musical society to be called 'Germania', under the auspices of which they would hear or read one another's productions and debate them. The society was formed with appropriate solemnity on the 25th July 1860, and for the following three years the friends met fairly regularly to read aloud what they had written or play what they had composed. Nietzsche's first work for 'Germania' was musical: pieces for a Christmas oratorio; he followed it with poems and essays, and in April 1862 with *Fate and History*, his earliest essay in philosophy.

In March 1861 Krug addressed the society on 'Some Scenes from *Tristan und Isolde*'. 'Germania' subscribed to the *Neue Zeitschrift für Musik*, which was then propagandizing hard for Wagner and the 'new music', and had bought a copy of Bülow's piano arrangement of the *Tristan* score, which had appeared in 1859. Krug was already a keen Wagnerian, and he sought to interest Nietzsche: he played various pieces from the opera, and Nietzsche, who was a fine pianist by this time, would join him at the keyboard and try to sight-read the unfamiliar and very difficult score, both youths making the best they could of the vocal parts. These sessions took place at the Nietzsche home, and Elizabeth records how fearsome the sounds were that came from the drawing-room while they were in progress. Krug also spoke to the society on the *Faust Overture* and the *Rheingold*. This was Nietzsche's introduction to Wagner, and it left him for the moment baffled—although he must have realized that his and Krug's rendition of *Tristan* could hardly have done full justice to the work. His favourite composer throughout the Pforta years was Schumann, whose restrained romanticism he found more to his taste than the unrestrained abandon (as he then saw it) of Wagner and Liszt, and whose example he followed in his own attempts at composition.

This literary and musical work was, of course, decidedly extra-curricular, but his school work too was bearing fruit: to 1861 belong the essays on Hölderlin and Byron and his studies of the Ermanarich saga and Norse mythology in general, which continued until October 1863. It was through the last that he made the acquaintance of Carl von Gersdorff, with whom he remained on friendly terms for many years. (Gersdorff was a day pupil with the professor of German studies, who showed him Nietzsche's Ermanarich essay, expressing great pleasure in it; as a consequence Gersdorff made a point of meeting Nietzsche.) He was also gaining an insight into the principles of scholarly criticism. Hitherto he had read the Scriptures with the uncritical eye of a believer; now he was learning to bring to them a more intelligent and therefore more sceptical appreciation: he was coming to see that there was no justification for reading the Bible in a slovenly and ignorant way while bringing all the resources of scholarship and historical criticism to bear upon the texts handed down from Greece and Rome. At Easter 1861 he was confirmed together with Paul Deussen, who was also a pupil at Pforta and who retained his connection with Nietzsche until the latter's death. During the weeks preceding the confirmation both he and Deussen dwelt in a kind of religious ecstasy which faded soon after the ceremony was over and never returned: Nietzsche's days of innocence were numbered, and within a year he felt able to declare religion 'the product of the people's childhood'.

But this was not the only change that was taking place within him. The upsetting period of puberty was now upon him, and the model pupil began to exhibit signs of waywardness. Its literary manifestation is the prose fragment *Euphorion*, written in the summer holidays of 1862. It was preserved by one Granier, a fellow-pupil to whom he sent it on the 20th July from Gorenzen, where he was staying: the fragment is a partly cynical, partly sentimental piece of youthful despair. In the letter that accompanied the manuscript Nietzsche wrote: 'I chucked away the plan for my repulsive story in disgust after I had written the first chapter. I am sending you the manuscript of this freak to use for—whatever you like.'[1] In the early months of 1863 he began behaving badly as well as writing badly. He became deeply attached to a rather unruly lad named Guido Meyer, who was usually in some sort of trouble with the school authorities. Soon afterwards Meyer was sacked; Nietzsche, in a letter to his mother and sister, called the day of Meyer's departure, the 1st March, 'the saddest day I have experienced at Pforta'. He got into the habit of sitting up late talking and drinking with the aforementioned Granier, among others, and was sometimes a trifle unwell the next morning and not feeling very much like Greek grammar. The climax came on the 14th April, a Sunday: he and another student named Richter went down to the nearby town of Kösen and drank four pints of beer each at the railway station; on their way back to school they had the ill-luck to encounter a teacher, who was scandalized to see that Nietzsche was drunk and Richter even more obviously so. Appropriate punishment was subsequently administered, and Nietzsche ceased to be a prefect for a time, a demotion that seems to have shaken him. In a letter to his mother of the following Tuesday he promises to try to pull himself together. 'I haven't any excuse,' he writes, 'except that I don't know how much [drink] I can take and we were a bit excited that afternoon.' And from then on he does seem to have pulled himself together; at any rate, the Pforta punishment book has nothing further to tell us about him.

He continues, however, to figure in the sickness register. The headaches which had started when he first went to school were getting worse. He had a particularly bad attack in mid-January 1861 and again in February, and he was allowed home for two weeks; but the headaches still persisted, and he wrote in his diary: 'I must learn to get used to it.' There are twenty entries in the sickness register between March 1859 and May 1864 recording his having suffered from rheumatism, catarrh, colds and head congestion, in addition to headaches, while he was at Pforta, the spells of sickness lasting on an average a week.

He left Pforta on the 4th September 1864. His *Valediktionsarbeit* was *De Theognide Megarensi* (On Theognis of Megara), written in Latin and his first original study in philology. A farewell evening was held on the 7th, and afterwards he wrote the finest of his early poems, 'Dem unbekannten Gott' (To the Unknown God). The following month he entered the University of Bonn as a student of philology and theology.

It is worth remarking, in connection with Nietzsche's drinking while at Pforta, that drunkenness was by no means uncommon at the public schools of

[1] Quoted in Blunck: op. cit., p. 87.

that time. Pforta enjoyed in Prussia a status similar to that of Rugby in England, and the amount of hard drinking that went on at Rugby is famous.

2

To pass in review the literary work of the Pforta years is to see the style, the ideas and the emotions of the mature Nietzsche beginning to appear. To begin with, his main interest was still poetry, but his urge to express subjective feelings in verse now had to contend with a desire for learning. 'At present I am in the grip of an unusual urge towards knowledge, towards general culture [*Bildung*]', he wrote in August 1859; 'it was Humboldt who aroused this in me. If only it may be as permanent as my dedication to poetry!' His dedication to poetry, however, was now beginning to be rewarded: he had developed a strongly rhythmic and euphonious style of verse in which he was able to express something of his true feelings. In his earliest poem of real quality, 'Ohne Heimat' (Homeless), written on the 10th August 1859, he sounds for the first time a refrain that was to appear again and again in his later writings: he is without a home but, for that reason, he is free:

> Flüchtge Rosse tragen
> Mich ohn Furcht und Zagen
> Durch die weite Fern.
> Und wer mich sieht, der kennt mich,
> Und wer mich kennt, der nennt mich:
> Den heimatslosen Herrn . . .

> Niemand darf es wagen,
> Mich danach zu fragen,
> Wo mein Heimat sei:
> Ich bin wohl nie gebunden
> An Raum und flüchtge Stunden,
> Bin wie der Aar so frei! . . .

(Fleet horses bear me, without fear or dismay, through distant places. And whoever sees me knows me, and whoever knows me calls me: the homeless man. No one dares to ask me where my home is: perhaps I have never been fettered to space and the flying hours, am as free as an eagle.)[1]

---

[1] Objectively, of course, he had a home at Naumburg; but, as I have tried to show above, his subjective feeling of homelessness had its origin in the death of his father.

A similar thought is expressed in a more concrete way in *Capri and Heligoland*, a fragmentary story written about the same time: 'We are pilgrims in this world—we are citizens of the world.' Already he is thinking of himself as a *Weltbürger*, at least now and then, rather than as a Prussian, and his development into the 'good European' of later years would no doubt have matured sooner if it had not been retarded by his association with Wagner. His fundamental antipathy towards narrow patriotism is best seen in the essay on Hölderlin, written on the 19th October 1861. Now almost worshipped as a being from a higher sphere, Hölderlin was at that time hardly known, and what reputation he had was based largely on his attacks on the Germany of his day. Nietzsche defends the poet and tries to justify his assault on German philistinism and 'barbarity', maintaining that this does not amount to 'attacking Germany'. Nietzsche himself later went much farther than Hölderlin in this direction, and *his* criticism of German philistinism and barbarism does broaden out into a root and branch condemnation of the entire state and people. (But then Hölderlin lived in the days of Goethe and Schiller, Nietzsche in the days of Wagner and the *Reich*.) The similarities between the two have often been noted, and are striking enough: both were vastly influenced by the Hellenic world, both reacted violently against the Germany of their time, and both died after a long period of insanity; Nietzsche calls the prose of *Hyperion* 'really music' and the same has been said of the prose of *Zarathustra*. The tutor who read this essay approved it, but wrote underneath: 'But I must give the author the friendly advice to attach himself to a healthier, clearer and *more German* poet.'[1]

The essay on Byron (written in December 1861) is less interesting, if only because Byron's reputation needed deflating rather than augmenting, and Nietzsche is here only reiterating the then current view of him. What he saw in Byron was essentially what his contemporaries and compatriots saw: Karl Moor come to life. Schiller's hero-villain was still the archetypal romantic rebel to the young Germans of the 1860s—Nietzsche's enthusiasm for Schiller at that time was based almost wholly on an enthusiasm for *The Robbers*—and Byron was the man who had done what Schiller had only dreamed of doing. Admiration for 'the hero as outlaw' is implicit in Nietzsche's essay; it is really admiration for the man with the courage to follow his instincts, and since this is very different from what he later meant by 'superman' it would be a mistake to overestimate Byron's influence on that concep-

---

[1]Quoted in Blunck: op. cit., p. 60; italics in the original. For more on this Hölderlin essay, see the Postscript.

tion. (Nietzsche refers to Byron's Manfred as an '*Übermensch* who controls spirits', but the word means no more than a man of great passion and strength, or perhaps 'almost a demi-god'; the specific significance he later gave it cannot be read into it here.)

His advocacy of Byron was in fact only an aspect of his growing restlessness under the influence of maturing sexuality; the connection is established very clearly by the *Euphorion* fragment written in the summer of 1862.[1] This story, which Nietzsche was right to call a freak, is a hotch-potch of 'satanic' absurdity:

A flood of soft, relaxing harmonies sweeps through my soul, [Euphorion informs us.] I know not why I feel so sad; I should like to weep and then die . . . The red of morning glows in the sky, a very spent firework that bores me. My eyes burn much more brightly, I fear they may burn holes in the sky. I feel I have burst out of my cocoon, I know myself through and through and all I desire is to find the head of my *Doppelgänger*, so I may dissect his brain . . . [The fragment ends:] Over the way lives a nun whom I occasionally visit in order to relish her moral behaviour. I know her very well, from head to toe, better than I know myself. She used to be a nun, slim and frail—I was a doctor . . . She lives together with her brother; they are married . . . I have made him thin and lean—as lean as a corpse. He will die soon—much to my delight—for I intend to dissect him. But first I will write the story of my life, because, apart from being interesting, it is also instructive in how to make young people old quickly . . . for in that I am a master. . . . —Here Euphorion leaned back and groaned, for he was suffering from spinal disease . . .

The rebellious mood of which this is a product lasted well into 1863. One of the poems of that year, 'Vor dem Kruzifix', depicts a drunkard throwing a bottle of schnapps at a figure of Christ on the Cross. This gesture is of course pseudo-Byronic, but it also expresses something more profound and lasting in Nietzsche than his passing phase of Byronic revolt. In April 1862 he had written in a letter to Pinder and Krug: 'Christianity is essentially a matter for the heart . . . To acquire bliss through faith is to demonstrate nothing more than the ancient truth that only the heart, not knowledge, can make us happy.' At about the same time he had written for 'Germania' an essay called *On the Childhood of the Peoples* in which he maintained that although religion was at first a sign of the creativity of peoples, in its late form its main effect was to rob 'this world' of all divinity in favour of the 'next world'.

---

[1]Euphorion, the child of Faust and Helen in the second part of Goethe's *Faust*, was well known to represent Byron, whose work was held to combine the Gothic and the Hellenic in a new and marvellous synthesis; Nietzsche's Euphorion is Nietzsche posing as Byron.

That God became man, [he wrote,] shows only that man is not to seek his bliss in eternity, but to found his heaven on earth; the delusion of a supra-terrestrial world has placed the spirit of man in a false relation to the terrestrial: it was the product of the people's childhood.

He had ceased to be a believing Christian, and with the waning of his faith in Christianity had come doubts concerning the validity of religion as such. His most solid attempt to set down his doubts was the essay *Fate and History*, written in March 1862 and delivered before 'Germania' in April:

If we could regard the teachings of Christianity and the history of the church with a free, impartial eye, we should have to arrive at many conclusions which conflict with commonly-held ideas. But as we are, fastened to the yoke of custom and prejudice from our earliest days, hindered in the development of our intellect [*Geist*] by the impress of our childhood, . . . we believe ourselves compelled to think we have committed almost a crime if we take up a free standpoint from which to pass a judgment on religion and Christianity that is above partisanship and corresponds to the needs of our time. Such an attempt [*Versuch*] is the work, not of a few weeks, but of a lifetime. To dare to launch out on the sea of doubt without compass or steersman is death and destruction for undeveloped heads; most are struck down by storms, very few discover new countries. From the midst of this immeasurable ocean of ideas one will often long to be back on firm land.

He recommends history and science as 'the only firm foundation upon which we can build the tower of our speculations', and it is noteworthy that his disillusionment with Christianity and religion has not led him to some other dogmatism or orthodoxy, but rather to a condition of permanent doubt. Already he calls philosophical inquiry a *Versuch*—an attempt or experiment— and employs the imagery of a stormy sea to describe the state of unconviction in which the true inquirer lives, foreshadowing the style of *Zarathustra*:

Have you never seen a sail faring over the sea, rounded and swelling and shuddering before the impetuosity of the wind? Like a sail, shuddering before the impetuosity of the spirit, my wisdom fares over the sea. (Z II 8)

To you, the bold venturers and adventurers [*Suchern, Versuchern*] and whoever has embarked with cunning sails upon dreadful seas . . . (Z III 2)

The sea is stormy: everything is at sea. Well then! Come on, you old seaman-hearts! What of fatherland! Our helm wants to fare *away*, out to where our *children's land* is! Out, away, more stormy than the sea, storms our great longing. (Z III 12 28)

By 1862 at the latest he had exchanged religious certainty for its opposite, and soon he was recommending the condition of uncertainty, of continually changing views and moods, as desirable in itself:

> Strife[1] is the perpetual food of the soul, and it knows well enough how to extract the sweetness from it. The soul destroys and at the same time brings forth new things; it is a furious fighter, yet it gently draws its opponent to its side in an inner alliance. And the most wonderful thing is that it never concerns itself with outward forms: names, persons, places, fine words, flourishes, all are of subordinate value: it treasures what lies within . . . I think now of much that I have loved; the names and the persons changed, and I do not say they always grew deeper and more beautiful in their nature; but this is surely true, that each of these moods meant for me a progress and that it is unendurable for the spirit [*Geist*] to have to step again on a step it has passed over; it wants to advance to greater heights and greater depths. (*On Moods*)

It would be possible to present Nietzsche's philosophy of power as an exegesis of the phrase 'Strife is the perpetual food of the soul', and the imagery of the step is one that he often employed in later years, as for example in the poem 'Meine Härte' (My Kind of Hardness):

> Ich muss weg über hundert Stufen,
> Ich muss empor und hör euch rufen:
> 'Hart bist du! Sind wir denn von Stein?'—
> Ich muss weg über hundert Stufen,
> Und niemand möchte Stufe sein.

(I have to pass over a hundred steps, I have to go up, and I hear you cry: 'How hard you are! Do you think we're made of stone?' I have to pass over a hundred steps, and no one wants to be a step. FW *Vorspiel* 26)

or in the late aphorism:

> For me they were steps, I have climbed up upon them—therefore I had to pass over them. But they thought I wanted to settle down on them. (G I 42)

To this extent, then, Nietzsche is already himself, and the interest of the work of the Pforta years lies in this foretaste of the mature man. The ideas he

---

[1] *Kampf.* Nietzsche employs the words *Kampf, Krieg, Streit* without much discrimination to denote a state of active and aggressive struggle as opposed to one of peace and repose. 'Strife' seems the best translation of these terms as Nietzsche uses them. That it does not mean armed conflict between nations is self-evident.

expresses are, of course, not original, but this is not important; in a sense there is no such thing as originality in the world of thought, but only a new way of seeing and presenting what has been thought before: a new synthesis of formerly disparate elements, a new emphasis, a startling light suddenly thrown into some half-forgotten corner. The will to power is, in a way, a commonplace idea whose significance Nietzsche was simply the first to appreciate; and what is important about his early work is not that he was beginning by repeating unoriginal observations, but that he had already taken the road he was to continue along.

Purely as a poet, his style was maturing all through the Pforta years, so that when he left Pforta he was able to express his uncertainty about the future and his sense of having deserted the God of his fathers for good in so relatively accomplished a poem as 'Dem unbekannten Gott':

> Noch einmal, eh ich weiterziehe
> und meine Blicke vorwärts sende,
> heb ich vereinsamt meine Hände
> zu dir empor, zu dem ich fliehe,
> dem ich in tiefster Herzenstiefe
> Altäre feierlich geweiht,
> dass allezeit
> mich deine Stimme wieder riefe . . .

(Once more, before I travel on and look along the way I am going, I raise my hands in solitude to you, my refuge, to whom I have solemnly dedicated altars in the deepest depths of my heart, that your voice may always call to me.)

To uncertainty about the future was added dissatisfaction with the past, with what he was and what he had done. In a short story, *A New Year's Eve Dream*, written in 1864, the author curses the Old Year for having been so barren; the Old Year rebukes him for his impatience and tells him: 'The fruit will fall when it is ripe, not before.'

27

3

The Student

Everything he is now doing is worthy and quite in order, yet he has a bad conscience about it. For the extraordinary is his task. (FW 186)

1

In retrospect, Nietzsche thought of his ten months at Bonn as time wasted. What they in fact represent is the period in his life in which he tried to live like any other young man and found he couldn't do it. The desire to be 'different' is common—and superficial; the man who actually is different very often doesn't want to be, because he has a premonition how much unhappiness his singularity is going to cost him. In the long run he cannot help himself; he must face the isolation and disappointment which life has in store for him as best he can; but at first he may resist his fate, or seek to deny it altogether, by involving himself with spurious enthusiasm in the pursuits which those around him appear to find normal. This is what Nietzsche tried to do at Bonn, and that is why he afterwards thought he had been squandering his time.

Initially he certainly experienced a sense of freedom at his liberation from Pforta, and he gave it rein on a holiday trip on the Rhein which he took with Deussen, who was also moving to Bonn, and a youth named Schnabel; the three indulged in a moderate amount of horse-play and wine-drinking, and Nietzsche enjoyed a brief flirtation with Deussen's sister. (Deussen's home was in the Rheinland.) Nietzsche and Deussen were enrolled at the university together on the 16th October 1864.

Bonn had an excellent reputation in the field of philology because of the presence there of Otto Jahn and Friedrich Ritschl, who were not only philologists of the front rank but men of wide culture and teachers capable of inspiring great devotion in their pupils. Jahn is best remembered for his biography of Mozart, and both would probably have risen to positions of eminence in any field they might have chosen. Nietzsche was at first attached to Jahn rather than to Ritschl, but when, as a result of a quarrel they were unable to settle, the two men left Bonn, it was Ritschl he followed to Leipzig,[1] and it is with Ritschl's that his name will always be associated. Their meeting, as described by Deussen,[2] could hardly have been more inconsequential. Nietzsche and Deussen had the same letter of introduction, and they went along with it to Ritschl's house. Ritschl tore it open and exclaimed: 'Ah, my old friend Niese!'—the Pforta teacher who had written the letter—'What's he doing now? Is he well? So your name's Deussen. Very well, come back and see me very soon.' The interview seemed to be at an end; but Nietzsche, who was standing by, remarked with a strangled cough that his name was in the letter too. 'Ah, so it is,' said Ritschl. 'There's two names, Deussen and Nietzsche. Good. Good. Very well, gentlemen, come back and see me very soon.' This was Ritschl's introduction to the youth who was to become by far his most famous pupil.

Soon after arriving at the university, Nietzsche joined the *Burschenschaft* 'Frankonia'. These 'students' unions' were formed in 1815 to unite students at all German universities in a movement that aimed at a liberal and united Germany, but by the 1860s their political ardour had cooled almost to freezing point, and they were hardly more than social clubs with ritualistic embellishments. Nietzsche did his best to fit in: he made something of a hit as a satirist, and his abilities as an improviser on the piano stood him in good stead. But what chiefly characterized the *Burschenschaften*, their *'Biergemütlichkeit'*—boozing—he could never bring himself to enjoy. His brief period of (mild) debauch was over, and his constitution was not in the ordinary way up to prolonged bouts of beer-swilling; he much preferred cream cakes, of which he could eat any number. Among the more foolish of the students' practices was the ritual of duelling, and since he was now a member of 'Frankonia' Nietzsche too began to feel in need of a duelling scar, the students' mark of manhood. (Illogically, no one could be considered a *good* swordsman until he had a scar to show.) Deussen[3] has told us how he obtained it. One evening he had been walking and talking affably with a member of another fraternity when he suddenly suggested they should fight a duel and provide one another

---

[1] It is not quite accurate to say that Nietzsche moved to Leipzig *because* Ritschl had gone there. Had he not been dissatisfied with his life at Bonn he would not have left it, even though Ritschl had departed; and what made him choose Leipzig rather than some other university was partly that Gersdorff was going there too. But Ritschl's presence at Leipzig was probably the deciding factor.

[2] Paul Deussen: *Erinnerungen an Friedrich Nietzsche* (Leipzig 1901), p. 20.

[3] Ibid., p. 22.

with scars. The combat, arranged according to the time-honoured rules and fought in the presence of accredited witnesses, lasted three minutes, at the end of which time Nietzsche was struck across the nose and blood was drawn; the judges declared this to be sufficient expiation. The resultant scar was minuscule, and Deussen's narrative seems to suggest, by its silence on the matter, that Nietzsche himself failed to get in a blow against his opponent.

It is to Deussen too that we owe our knowledge of an incident in February 1865 which has achieved some notoriety and is of importance in any consideration of Nietzsche's later insanity. Nietzsche told him, he says,[1] that he had gone alone on a trip to Cologne; a cab driver drove him around to see the sights and finally he asked to be taken to a good restaurant. Instead, he was taken to a brothel. 'I suddenly saw myself surrounded by half-a-dozen apparitions in tinsel and gauze, who looked at me expectantly,' Nietzsche said. 'I stood for a moment speechless. Then I made instinctively for a piano in the room as to the only living thing in that company and struck several chords. They broke the spell and I hurried away.' Deussen's view was that this incident was unique in Nietzsche's life, and that the words *mulieram nunquam attigit* could be applied to him. It is no longer possible to agree with this, since we have evidence now which was not available to Deussen when he wrote. It is virtually certain that the disease to which Nietzsche fell victim was a general paralysis of the insane; this means that he must almost certainly have contracted syphilis, and most students of his life are agreed that he did contract it, probably during his youth. Crane Brinton[2] says: 'The fact that Nietzsche did have syphilis may be regarded as proved (as certainly as anything of the kind can be proved)'; Walter Kaufmann[3] says more cautiously: 'All we can say is— and all sober and unsensational medical treatments of the subject seem agreed on this—that Nietzsche very probably contracted syphilis.' Richard Blunck[4] reproduces evidence which makes it impossible to doubt that Nietzsche was treated for a syphilitic infection by two Leipzig doctors during 1867, although he may not have been informed of the nature of his illness. How he contracted it remains strictly a matter for speculation, although the problem is surely not a very difficult one: a young man in Nietzsche's situation could hardly have come into contact with the disease anywhere but in a brothel. H. W. Brann[5] suggests that the poem 'Die Wüste wächst' inserted into the fourth part of

[1]Ibid., p. 24.
[2]Brinton: *Nietzsche*, p. 15.
[3]Kaufmann: *Nietzsche*, p. 49.
[4]Blunck: op. cit., p. 160 f.
[5]Brann: *Nietzsche und die Frauen*, p. 138.

Zarathustra is a reminiscence of a visit to a brothel, basing his suggestion on some echoes in the poem of the words used by Nietzsche to describe to Deussen his experience of February 1865; Thomas Mann[1] supposes that, having been taken to one against his will, he later returned voluntarily. In all events, the evidence there is disposes of any necessity to believe that Nietzsche inherited insanity from his father and was therefore 'mad all along'. For his fate was far from uncommon. Syphilis was incurable, and for that reason a patient would often not be informed he had contracted it: the consequence was a life punctuated by increasingly severe attacks of a 'mysterious' disease which often ended in madness and premature death. It has been suggested that Nietzsche might have contracted syphilis while working as a nursing orderly in the Franco-Prussian War, but the evidence adduced by Blunck that he was treated for the disease as early as 1867 makes it impossible that he could have contracted it as late as 1870 and unlikely that he came into contact with it in any other manner than that just suggested.

While he was at Bonn Nietzsche decided to abandon the study of theology. We have seen that his belief in the truth of Christianity and the validity of religion in general was virtually extinct before he left Pforta: at that time he had no firm idea what he was going to do with his life, but he must have realized that the profession of his father and both his grandfathers was not going to be his. He would probably never have embarked on the serious study of theology at all had his mother not been eager he should do so, but his attitude towards the subject hardened during his first Bonn months, and by Easter 1865 he had resolved to give it up. It was possibly the knowledge that his decision would upset his mother, and the fear that she might be able to dissuade him from carrying it out, that put him into the truculent mood in which he went home on Easter vacation. He permitted himself to make wounding remarks concerning the church and those who belonged to it and claimed to be superior now to such a primitive superstition as Christianity; he refused to go to church on Easter Day—knowing of course that Protestants are supposed to attend communion on this day if on no other—and finally informed his mother, without very much tact, that he was finished with theology. The upshot of all this was a domestic scene, with tears and recriminations; but the trouble was shortlived: Frau Nietzsche soon saw that, since God directs all our actions, he must have directed this action of Fritz's, and she resigned herself to accepting His will. But Elizabeth was angered by her brother's behaviour and shaken by his apostasy. She was a devout believer and had assumed he was; and after he went

---

[1]Mann: 'Nietzsches Philosophie' in *Neue Studien*. (For full details of these works, see the Bibliography.)

back to Bonn she took counsel with one of her uncles in an effort to find
counter-arguments to those he had employed to justify his attitude. She wrote
him an earnest letter defending the Christian faith, and his reply, of the 11th
June 1865, has become one of the best-known documents of his biography:

> Concerning your basic principle, that truth is always to be found on the side of
> the more difficult, [he wrote,] I agree in part. However, it is difficult to believe
> that 2×2 does not equal 4; is it therefore true? On the other hand, is it really so
> difficult simply to accept as true everything we have been taught, and which has
> gradually taken firm root in us and is thought true by the circle of our relations
> and by many good people, and which moreover really does comfort and elevate
> men? Is that more difficult than to venture on new paths, in conflict with
> custom, in the insecurity that attends independence, experiencing many waver-
> ings of courage and even of conscience, often disconsolate, but always with the
> true, the beautiful and the good as our goal? Is it the most important thing to
> arrive at that particular view of God, world and reconciliation that makes us feel
> most comfortable? Is not the true inquirer totally indifferent to what the result
> of his inquiries may be? For, when we inquire, are we seeking for rest, peace,
> happiness? No, only for truth, even though it be in the highest degree ugly and
> repellent. Still one final question: if we had believed from our youth onwards
> that all salvation issued from someone other than Jesus, from Mahomet for
> instance, is it not certain that we should have experienced the same blessings? It
> is the faith that makes blessed, and not the objective reality that stands behind
> the faith . . . Every true faith is infallible, it accomplishes what the person
> holding the faith hopes to find in it, but it does not offer the slightest support for
> a proof of objective truth. Here the ways of men divide: if you wish to strive for
> peace of soul and happiness, then believe; if you wish to be a disciple of truth,
> then inquire.

From this point of view he was never to waver, but on the contrary to
emphasize it again and again: the object of philosophical inquiry is truth; there
is no preordained correspondence between truth and happiness, between what
is true and what is pleasing; the genuine inquirer must be indifferent to 'peace
of soul and happiness', or at least he must not seek them, for if these are his
objectives he must go aside from the path that leads to those truths that are
ugly and repellent.

In the midst of his effort to become more lighthearted and superficial, and
possibly as a direct reaction to it, Nietzsche was growing more serious and
profound. He was already a 'freethinker', but in contrast to his predecessors
he was coming to realize that 'freedom' meant not only throwing off a burden
but taking on a heavier one in its place. He would soon feel little but contempt
for the 'liberal-minded' unbeliever who thinks he is free to dispense with the

divine architect but still keep the building, who has done away with the Lawgiver but still demands the protection of the Law he gave. He would soon see that if God ceased to exist as a reality for mankind life as such was deprived of significance and mankind might ultimately collapse under the weight of its own senselessness. Already by 1865 he had realized the seriousness of the situation: he and Deussen had bought copies of David Strauss's *Life of Jesus*, a prominent contribution to the happy demythologizing of religion then in progress; when Deussen said that he felt bound to agree with what Strauss had written, Nietzsche replied: 'That can have serious consequences; if you give up Christ you will have to give up God as well.'[1]

As far as creative activity went during these Bonn months, his chief interest was music: he composed and played a great deal, and in June 1865 he took part in a three-day festival in Cologne, singing as one of a 600-strong choir under Ferdinand Hiller.

He left Bonn on the 17th August of that year to transfer to Leipzig. After he had gone, he sent a letter of resignation to 'Frankonia' (dated the 20th October) which reveals how much at odds he had been with his environment:

> In resigning I am not ceasing to value the ideals of the *Burschenschaften*, [he wrote.] Only I will confess that the form in which they appear at present does not give me much pleasure. This may be in part my fault. I found it difficult to endure a year in the 'Frankonia'. But I thought myself duty bound to become a member; now I no longer feel any close ties with it. Therefore I am saying farewell. May 'Frankonia' soon pass through the stage of development in which it at present finds itself.

As a reward for this equivocal expression of goodwill, 'Frankonia' erased Nietzsche's name from its records.

2

The Leipzig years—1865 to 1869—marked the end of Nietzsche's youth. What is significant in them can best be studied under four heads: his progress as a student of philology, his discovery of Schopenhauer and Lange, his friendship with Erwin Rohde and the beginning of his association with Wagner.

Ritschl gave his inaugural lecture at Leipzig on the 25th October 1865 to a crowded hall; Nietzsche was present, and Ritschl, who was in a very lively

---

[1]Deussen: op. cit., p. 20.

mood, welcomed him and several other ex–Bonn students with jocular remarks from the platform. Nietzsche was a member of Ritschl's philology class from the first, and with three others was a founding member of the Leipzig Philological Society, formed in December at Ritschl's suggestion and under his tutelage. Nietzsche's first lecture to the society, given on the 18th January 1866, was on 'The Last Redaction of the Theognidea', a revision of his essay on Theognis. The following month, after having again revised the lecture, he took the manuscript to Ritschl and asked him for his comment. On the 24th, Ritschl called Nietzsche to his study and asked him what he intended to do with the work.

> I told him the first thing that came into my head, [Nietzsche writes,] that having served as the basis of a lecture to our society it had already served its purpose. Then he asked me my age, how long I had been studying, etc., and when I had told him, he declared he had never seen anything from a student in his third semester to compare with it for strictness of method or assurance in collation. He urged me strenuously to work up the lecture into a brochure . . . After this scene my self-confidence rocketed . . . For a time I went around with my head in a whirl; it was the period in which I was born as a philologist.[1]

The interview was a decisive event. Ritschl's regard for his ability as a philologist grew greater as time went on, and Nietzsche became in a sense his protégé. Ritschl was convinced he was phenomenally gifted in his subject and persuaded others he was, to the point of successfully recommending him for the vacant professorship at Basel University when he was only 24 and then securing for him his doctorate at Leipzig without an examination or any other formality. Nietzsche had adopted classical philology as his subject, I believe, only because Latin and Greek were 'pushed' at Pforta; he had not planned to devote his life to a university career; he had had no plans at all, but, like so many young men with no definite ambition, had become a 'student' because that was the easy and obvious thing to do. The interview of February 1866 changed all this, and by the summer of that year he was set upon the course that was to take him to Basel.

In November of the same year the university (i.e. Ritschl) set Diogenes Laertius as the subject for the philological prize essay; as expected, the prize went to Nietzsche. The essay on Theognis was published in 1867 under the title *Zur Geschichte der Theognideischen Spruchsammlung* in the *Rheinisches Museum für Philologie.* It was Nietzsche's first publication. The Laertius essay appeared in four parts in 1868 and 1869; other philological studies were

---

[1] *Rückblick auf meine zwei Leipziger Jahre,* written in August 1867.

published during these years in the *Rheinisches Museum* and the *Litterarisches Centralblatt*.

His studies were interrupted in 1867–68 by a year's military service. The German War of 1866 had flashed past too quickly to involve non-military men[1] but twelve months' so-called voluntary service was obligatory for Prussian youths, and Nietzsche was conscripted on the 9th October 1867; he served as a private in the mounted section of a field artillery regiment stationed at Naumburg. He did not exactly enjoy his military year, which was in any case cut short by a serious riding accident in March 1868, which kept him in bed for a month and necessitated his spending the rest of his service as a convalescent. He was in hospital when, on the 1st April, he was promoted to lance-corporal [*Gefreiter*]. 'I wish they'd made me a dischargee [*Befreiter*] instead,' he wrote. He got his discharge on the 15th October.

On his return to Leipzig he began to give thought to those areas of knowledge in which he was weak, especially science. He was still very young— 24—and he felt his life was becoming too narrow. He had already planned to quit university life altogether for a year or so and go to Paris with Rohde to sample 'the divine can-can and the yellow poison absinthe'. That this was a serious plan is proved by the number of times it is referred to in his and Rohde's letters to one another. His brilliance in his subject notwithstanding, he never exaggerated the importance of philology, but on the contrary was given to deprecating it as the crabbed study of dead books, so it is not surprising to find him thinking of giving it up, at least for a time, in favour of other studies or of another kind of life. But he had left it too late: in the early months of 1869 came the irresistible offer which was to tie him to philology and the life of a university for the next ten years.

His ambiguous attitude towards his subject comes out well in the letter to Rohde of the 16th January 1869 in which he tells him of his probable appointment—he announces it as a blow which he half welcomes and half regrets:

> We are certainly fate's fools: last week I had the idea of writing to you and suggesting we should study chemistry together and throw philology where it belongs, among the antique bric-à-brac. Now the devil 'Fate' lures me with a professorship of philology.

What Nietzsche's relation to Schopenhauer actually amounted to will be discussed later, but it cannot be denied that his discovery of Schopenhauer's

[1] Fought between Prussia on one side and Austria and Bavaria on the other, it began on the 14th June and ended in Prussian victory on the 22nd August.

chief book, *The World as Will and Idea,* was a major event in his intellectual life. It happened at the end of October or beginning of November 1865, shortly after he had arrived in Leipzig. He was still full of the disgruntled, unsatisfied feeling he had brought with him from Bonn.

> I lived then in a state of helpless indecision, alone with certain painful experiences and disappointments, without fundamental principles [*Grundsätze*], without hope and without a single pleasant memory . . . Now imagine how the reading of Schopenhauer's chief work must affect a man in such a condition. One day I found this book in . . . [a] second-hand bookshop, picked it up as something quite unknown to me and turned the pages. I do not know what demon whispered to me 'Take this book home with you'. It was contrary to my usual practice of hesitating over the purchase of books. Once at home, I threw myself onto the sofa with the newly-won treasure and began to let that energetic and gloomy genius operate upon me . . . Here I saw a mirror in which I beheld the world, life and my own nature in a terrifying grandeur . . . here I saw sickness and health, exile and refuge, Hell and Heaven.[1]

It will be most convenient to confine discussion of Schopenhauer's philosophy and Nietzsche's reaction to it to a separate section;[2] its strictly biographical effect is briefly told: he became a Schopenhaueran and did his best to acquaint his friends with the philosopher's outlook. Rohde and Gersdorff soon became 'Schopenhauerans' too, although it is not quite clear whether they did so independently or under Nietzsche's influence. Nietzsche certainly did introduce Deussen to Schopenhauer's work, and Deussen was in later years Schopenhauer's true continuator in Germany. A common admiration for Schopenhauer was what cemented the friendship between Nietzsche and Wagner and was perhaps the final reason for Nietzsche's domination by the older man; in any event, it is unlikely he would have grown so close to him had he been indifferent or opposed to Schopenhauer.

During these years Nietzsche felt himself entirely at one with the great pessimist; but the operative word is 'felt'; it was all very largely a matter of feeling: what Schopenhauer had to say chimed with what Nietzsche wanted to hear. A strong hint that this was so is his great enthusiasm at the same time for Friedrich Albert Lange's *History of Materialism,* which he read during the summer of 1866. In a letter to Gersdorff of the 16th February 1868—i.e. eighteen months or so after getting to know Lange's book—he recommends it in the warmest possible terms: it 'gives infinitely more than the title promises' and is 'a veritable store that one can look into and read again and again'. He

---

[1] *Rückblick auf meine zwei Leipziger Jahre.*
[2] See Chapter 5, where Nietzsche's debt to F. A. Lange will also be discussed.

refers to the 'materialist movement of our times, the natural sciences with their Darwinian theories . . . ethical materialism, Manchester-theory' which he finds outlined in the book. He planned to visit Lange but never got round to it, and when a new edition of the *History of Materialism* appeared in 1887 he bought a copy and read it through again. The point to note is that Lange's views are not simply different from Schopenhauer's but opposed to and incompatible with them: if Lange is right, Schopenhauer is wrong, and vice versa. Nietzsche was able to admire both at the same time because Schopenhauer's appeal was mainly emotional, while Lange's was entirely intellectual; or, to put it another way, Schopenhauer proposed a complete attitude towards life which could be accepted or rejected only by the complete man, while Lange merely discussed philosophy.

The Leipzig years also saw the appearance in Nietzsche's writings of certain ideas of which he was later to make use. Two are especially notable. He made a study of Homer and Hesiod and their legendary 'contest', and from it he received the first intimations of how important the concept of the agon or competition was in the development of Greek culture—an insight which came to be of great significance when he was assembling examples of the acquisition of power by indirect means. The first part of the Diogenes essay, published in 1868, carried at its head a motto from Pindar: 'Become him who you are!' Nietzsche adopted this motto as his own; it is quoted as one of the 'granite sentences' that close the third book of *The Gay Science:*

What does your conscience say? 'You should become him who you are.' (FW 270)

and he entitled his autobiography (1888): *Ecce Homo. How One Becomes What One Is.*

Nietzsche and Erwin Rohde were almost exact contemporaries. Rohde was born on the 9th October 1845, the son of a Hamburg doctor; he came to Leipzig at about the same time as Nietzsche, and they met when Rohde joined the Philological Society. Nietzsche described him in a letter to Gersdorff of September 1866 as 'a very clever but obstinate and self-willed fellow' (a pot-and-kettle remark if there ever was one). The friendship between the two grew firm in the Easter semester of 1867, and they were to take a long holiday trip together the following August. As time went on their tastes developed in concert, and they were soon united in a love of Greek antiquity, an enthusiasm for Schopenhauer and a devotion to Wagner; Nietzsche says they were also one in abhorring the 'mannerisms and vanities' of philology. Their friendship endured for a decade undiminished; it foundered on Rohde's inability to comprehend Nietzsche's development after about 1880, and by 1886, when they met for the last time, they were virtual strangers to one another. The following year Nietzsche tried to resume the relationship, but Rohde declined. From his letters to other people who also knew Nietzsche we can watch Rohde gradually losing patience with what he took to be Nietzsche's increasing perverseness in the conduct of his life and waywardness in his manner of thinking. 'What Nietzsche needs,' he exploded after reading *Beyond Good and Evil,* 'is to get a proper job!'[1] The remark is revealing and understandable. He himself had gone on to make a name in the study both of them seemed most fitted to pursue, he had married and had a family, he had settled down. Nietzsche, on the other hand, had retired, so it seemed, into a mountain fastness, whence from time to time he threw out half-comprehensible books for which he made the most grandiose claims imaginable; he had no family, no job, no ties, and no responsibilities; in his books he boasted of his isolation, in his letters he bemoaned it; for the life he had formerly led, and which his friends were still leading, he now had nothing but derision, and contempt for all that fills most men's lives seemed to hover over everything he wrote. If we add to all this Nietzsche's increasing egoism, we shall have no difficulty in accounting for Rohde's defection: he simply became exasperated with his former friend's behaviour.

In 1866, when the two became acquainted, Rohde was a rather withdrawn youth who rarely expressed his feelings openly; he confesses as much in the letter he wrote to Nietzsche at Christmas 1868, which helps us to gauge the depth of feeling involved in their relationship:

> I owe the best hours of my life to you alone; I wish you could see into my heart and know how grateful I am for all you have given me; you opened to me the blessed land of purest friendship into which I had formerly gazed, with a heart thirsty for love, as a poor child gazes into a rich garden. I, who have always been lonely, now feel myself united with the best of men; and it will be hard for you to grasp how that has changed my inner life.

Nietzsche's letters to him are full of protestations of friendship and of plans for a future the two were to share. The friends supposed during these years that their future careers would in any case follow parallel paths, but they discussed particular enterprises they might undertake together, the most dearly-loved of which was the visit to Paris already mentioned; Nietzsche's letter to Rohde of the 16th January 1869 in which he tells of his probable appointment to Basel is touching in its anxiety to convince him that he cannot

---

[1] See Chapter 12.

very well refuse the appointment, even though this cherished pl
doubt fall through because of it.

In August 1867 Nietzsche and Rohde went on a holiday trip together to
Bohemian Forest; while in that area, Nietzsche wrote, they heard a 'concert of
Zukunftsmusik' directed by Liszt. The term 'music of the future' was a journalistic perversion of the title of one of Wagner's main theoretical writings,
Das Kunstwerk der Zukunft (The Art-Work of the Future), in which he had
outlined his ideas on the collaboration of the arts of music, drama, painting
and mime in a future 'total artwork'; journalists of the time maintained—
some dishonestly but most through ignorance—that Wagner was defending
his horrible music by asserting it would sound fine a couple of centuries hence.
Zukunftsmusik was therefore a term of derision, and Nietzsche's use of it
shows that as late as the summer of 1867 he was still unimpressed by Wagner.
But he was still trying: later the same year he played the piano arrangement of
the *Valkyrie* with, he says, 'very mixed feelings', and he must have done more
experimenting between then and the 28th October 1868, the day on which he
announced his conversion to Wagner after hearing a performance of the
Tristan and *Meistersinger* preludes.

> I find it impossible to keep a critically cool head where this music is concerned,
> [he wrote to Rohde in excitement on the same day.] I am quivering in every fibre,
> every nerve, and I have never experienced such a lasting feeling of ecstasy as I did
> when listening to the last-named overture [i.e. the *Meistersinger* prelude].

He was hooked, but he might have struggled loose again before too long
had he not met the Master in person a bare eleven days after this ecstatic
experience. Wagner was at this time passing through one of the livelier of the
many domestic crises that make Ernest Newman's biography of him such
entertaining reading and give it its great length, and he had virtually fled into
hiding in Leipzig, where he was staying with his sister Ottilie and her husband, Hermann Brockhaus (a descendant of Schopenhauer's publisher). His
hideaway would certainly have remained no secret if the papers had got wind
of his presence in Leipzig, so he was preserving a strict incognito, and only
close friends of the family were permitted to see him. One such close friend
was Frau Ritschl, who was present one evening when Wagner played Walter's
Prize Song from the *Meistersinger* on the piano; she remarked that she already
knew the music through a student of her husband's who was an ardent
Wagnerian. Richard expressed his pleasure and said he would like to meet the
young man if that were possible. As a consequence, when Nietzsche returned
to his lodgings on the afternoon of the 6th November he found waiting for

him a note from a fellow student, Ernst Windisch: 'If you would like to meet Richard Wagner, come to the Café Théâtre at 3.45.' Windisch had been entrusted with delivering an invitation to the Brockhaus residence, the recipient being sworn to secrecy.

To the fact that Rohde was at home ill we owe Nietzsche's long letter of the 9th from which our knowledge of the meeting derives. Nietzsche and Windisch went along on the afternoon of the 7th, but Wagner had gone out 'with an enormous hat on' (presumably as a disguise), and they received an invitation for the following evening, a Sunday. Thinking there would be a large gathering, Nietzsche visited his tailor, who, as it happened, had promised to have an evening suit for him that very day. The suit was not quite ready, and he was promised it in three-quarters of an hour; when he went back it was still not ready, and it was at last presented to him at half-past six. With it came a bill, which the tailor's assistant demanded should be met before he would part with the suit. Nietzsche hadn't enough money on him—or in his possession, very likely—and tried to put the suit on (he had taken his own off to try the new one for size); a struggle ensued in which the tailor proved the victor; he disappeared, taking the suit with him, and Nietzsche stormed out into the pouring rain, fearful that by now he would be late for his appointment and hoping his old clothes would do. As it turned out, there was no large gathering: just the Brockhaus family, Nietzsche and Windisch, and Wagner. Nietzsche was introduced, and there followed the kind of evening so familiar to students of Wagner's biography, during which Wagner, surrounded by a small group of admirers, holds the floor:

> Before and after dinner Wagner played [the piano] and included all the important sections of the *Meistersinger*, imitating all the vocal parts and growing very exuberant. For he is a wonderfully lively and animated man who speaks very fast, is very witty and makes a gathering of this private sort very cheerful. In between times, I had a longish talk with him about Schopenhauer; and you can imagine what joy it was for me to hear him speak of him with a quite indescribable warmth, saying how much he owed to him and how he was the only philosopher who understood the nature of music . . . Afterwards he read a portion of the autobiography he is now writing, an extremely amusing scene from his Leipzig student days, which I still cannot think about without laughing . . . At the end of the evening, as we two were about to leave, he pressed my hand very warmly and cordially invited me to visit him to play music and talk philosophy.

To the fascination of the music was now added the fascination of the man: from the former Nietzsche did in time break free but from the latter never again. His 'revolt against Wagner' of later years—which was really a return to himself—was not a sundering of the bands that tied him to the beloved tyrant but a resolve to go his own way despite them. Wagner was 31 years older than Nietzsche—old enough, that is, to be his father, the significance of which fact has not escaped the psychologists—and incapable of seeing the world through any eyes but his own. A 'friend' of Wagner's was his servant, or he ceased to be a friend and became, in Wagner's estimation, an enemy—Wagner divided mankind into friends and enemies. Viewed in retrospect, and with the operas and the Bayreuth theatre and festival as its outcome, his life is a magnificent one and he a towering individual, pre-eminent even in the century of individuals; but if we try to see him as his contemporaries did, it is not surprising that some he tried to use turned from him, and sometimes cursed him for the hold he still had upon them. Foremost among these was Nietzsche—of all the men Wagner ever met the most like him in genius and ambition and the highest above him in intellect; and the Sunday evening scene with music from the *Meistersinger* turned out to be the opening of a tragedy which was to end with the stage thunder of *The Wagner Case* and the maledictions of *Nietzsche contra Wagner*.

3

At the beginning of 1869 the chair of classical philology at Basel University fell vacant, and Ritschl was asked to suggest a possible candidate for it. The post also involved teaching Greek language at the associated High School. Ritschl suggested Nietzsche. On the 10th January he told him that the question of offering him the Basel chair was under discussion. On the 13th February Nietzsche was appointed, and on the 23rd March he was awarded his doctorate by Leipzig without examination, on the basis of the work he had published in the *Rheinisches Museum*. Basel desired him to consider becoming a Swiss national, in case his duties as a Prussian citizen should involve his being called to military service at any future time; this also involved his applying to the Prussian authorities for release from his military obligations: Nietzsche made the two necessary applications. He was at home in Naumburg from the end of March until, on the 12th April, he left for Basel. On the 17th he ceased to be a citizen of Prussia; he never subsequently fulfilled the qualifications required for Swiss citizenship, however, and was thus for the remainder of his life formally stateless. He arrived in Basel early in the morning of the 19th.

This, in brief, constitutes the events of the first quarter of 1869 and closes

41

the door on Nietzsche's youth. At 24 he had gone as far as he could in his career of philologist; in the ordinary way it would have been many years before he could have hoped for a chair at a university—now he was suddenly transported to one without effort. To his sister and mother it seemed an incredible piece of good fortune, but he himself was far from certain that it was the best thing for him. 'One should not,' he wrote later, 'become a university professor at 24'—an opinion with which most people will surely agree. One cannot help feeling that Ritschl had allowed his enthusiasm to run away with his better judgment: what Nietzsche needed at this time was not more responsibility but less, not a narrowing of his field but an enlargement of it. Above all, he needed more *experience*—for the good of his psyche and of his intellect. He had been at school since he was 6—eighteen years—and now he was to stay at school ten years more; when he left Basel in 1879 he was 34, and he had never been away from the atmosphere of the classroom for more than a few months at a time since he had enrolled in the boys' school at Naumburg. His aim as a philosopher was to break through the formulae of thought and vocabulary of the schools to grasp reality, or as he put it, *Dinge*—'things'. 'We must not allow books to come between us and things,' he wrote, but for the first thirty-four years of his life he was immersed in books, and for much of that time in the most bookish of disciplines, philology, in which the only 'things' *are* books. It was the origin of the one real weakness in his composition: his lack of knowledge of how 'ordinary' men and women actually live.

Not the least of the inducements held out to him to accept the Basel post was the salary that went with it. The Nietzsche family were in a strict sense poor: the mother's main support was her widow's pension, and the son's education would have been impossible without state aid. The salary of a university professor was one which he was hardly placed to refuse.

Financial considerations, pride in having 'got on' so far so fast, the absence of any obvious alternative, these were what made it, in the last resort, impossible for him to refuse to go to Basel. But he went there in a frame of mind that must have disturbed Ritschl had he suspected it. On the eve of setting out for his new life, he expresses something less like dissatisfaction with philology than outright contempt for it:

> The time is up, the last evening at home has arrived, [he wrote to Gersdorff on the 11th April]: tomorrow morning I must go out into the wide, wide world, into a new unfamiliar profession, into a difficult and oppressive atmosphere of duty and work. Once again I am saying a farewell: the golden age of free, untrammelled activity . . . is irretrievably past: now there reigns the stern goddess Daily-Duties . . . I now have to become a Philistine myself! . . . You cannot

accept offices and dignities without paying a price—the only question is whether the bonds are to be of iron or of thread. And I still have the courage left to break the bonds now and then. [The influence of Schopenhauer upon him has, he says, been too profound for him ever to slip into being nothing but a 'professional man'.] To permeate my science with this new blood [Schopenhaueran philosophy], to transmit to my listeners that Schopenhaueran seriousness that is stamped upon the brow of the high-minded man—this is my desire, my boldest hope; I want to be something more than a taskmaster to efficient philologists.

The tone of this letter—in its entirety it sounds even more high-flown—is perhaps the outcome of a compromise Nietzsche felt he ought not to be making. In his heart he was already through with philology; under Schopenhauer's influence he was moving towards something more satisfying and fulfilling to his peculiar nature than a professorial chair, something which could hardly yet be called a philosophy but was ashamed to call itself anything less.[1] He was very ambitious; as yet he did not know in which direction to realize his ambitions, but he suspected it was not to be in the direction of philology. Hence his not altogether honest decision to become 'more' than a mere trainer of future philologists. After all, it was to be trained in philology that his hearers would presumably be attending his lectures—and not to have palmed off on them the philosophy of Schopenhauer instead. Fortunately for him, he failed to live up to this programme: once he began teaching he found, perhaps to his surprise, that he was a good teacher and that he enjoyed being one.

[1] In the last months at Leipzig, when his mind was turning in various unphilological directions, he had had the idea of taking his doctorate in philosophy, and had even decided upon the subject for his thesis: On the Concept of the Organic since Kant. But the project belongs to those which he had left too late.

II

1869–1879

How little reason and how greatly chance rules over men is shown by the almost invariable disparity between their so-called professions and their evident unsuitability for them: the fortunate cases are exceptions . . . , and even these are not brought about by reason. A man *chooses* a profession when he is not yet capable of choice: he does not know the various professions, he does not know himself. (*Wir Philologen*)

4

The Professor

He who possesses greatness deals harshly with his virtues and interests of the second rank. (FW 266)

Basel was a completely German town, and it had a narrow escape from incorporation into the *Reich*. When Nietzsche joined it the university there was already 400 years old; it was a small one, but its reputation extended far beyond the borders of Switzerland, and the fact that it engaged him at all at so young an age showed it was willing to experiment.

Upon his arrival he took up temporary lodgings while he looked for a permanent residence. He found it after two months at No. 45 Schützgraben, near the Spalentor, where he engaged a large room. When Franz Overbeck came to Basel he lived in the same house, and almost every evening for five years he and Nietzsche had their meal together in Overbeck's room.

The task Nietzsche had taken on was not a particularly light one. He tells Ritschl in a letter of the 10th May 1869 that he has enough to do 'not to get bored':

Each morning of the week I give my lectures at 7 o'clock, [he writes.] On Mondays I hold a seminar, . . . on Tuesdays and Fridays I have to teach at the High School twice, on Wednesdays and Thursdays once: up to the present I enjoy this . . . I have seven pupils for my lectures, which they say I should be content with here.

The subjects of his lectures during these first years reflect his real interests. His inaugural lecture on *Homer and Classical Philology*, delivered on the 28th May and privately printed later in the year, made it clear that he considered philology the handmaid of art. During 1869 he lectured on the *Choephorae* of Aeschylus and the Greek lyric poets (also, at the request of his pupils but with

47

some distaste, on Latin grammar); in 1870 on Sophocles' *Oedipus Rex* and on Hesiod; in 1871 on the Platonic dialogues, 'an introduction to the study of philology' and Latin epigraphy. The emphasis is on the Greeks, and especially on poetry and drama. In his public lectures, when he was able to give way to his predilections without restraint, he spoke on *The Greek Music-Drama* (18th January 1870) and *Socrates and Tragedy* (1st February 1870). Later in the year he wrote *The Dionysian Principle*, but he seems not to have delivered it. The lecture on Socrates was privately printed in 1871, and all three are preparatory studies for *The Birth of Tragedy*. The longest of the lectures of these early years is *On the Future of our Educational Institutions*, which he delivered on the 16th January, the 6th and 27th February and the 5th and 23rd March 1872; it has frequently been reprinted since his death, but he did not think it sufficiently important or representative of his thought to seek publication of it himself. (This is true of all his lectures and writings of these years except *The Birth of Tragedy* and the four completed *Untimely Meditations*.)

When he began at Basel he found he had a talent for teaching and for arousing the interest of his students. Carl Bernoulli says[1] that in the early years of the twentieth century he had talked with former pupils of Nietzsche's—then, of course, grown men. 'When they are asked about him,' says Bernoulli, 'they seem to be united in the impression they had sat at the feet not so much of a pedagogue as of a living ephor from antique Greece, who had leapt across time to come among them and tell them of Homer, Sophocles, Plato and their gods. As if he spoke from his own knowledge of things quite self-evident and still completely valid—that was the impression he made upon them.' He was quite content for them to read Greek authors in German translation, so long as they read as much as possible: he was less interested in cramming Greek grammar and language (he took an advanced knowledge of that for granted) than in making his pupils familiar with the world of antique Greece. He would sometimes leave the curricular path to expatiate on something not strictly relevant—for example, he would suddenly ask: 'Now tell me, what is a philosopher?' and when the inadequate answer had been given, deliver an impromptu lecture on the subject. One incident in class has become famous. He suggested the students might like to read the description of the shield of Achilles in the *Iliad* during the summer vacation; at the beginning of the following semester he asked one of them if he had in fact read it. The student (his name has not been recorded) said he had, although this wasn't true. 'Good, then describe the shield of Achilles for us,' said Nietzsche. An

[1]Carl Albrecht Bernoulli: *Friedrich Nietzsche und Franz Overbeck. Eine Freundschaft* (Jena 1908), vol. 1, p. 67.

embarrassed silence followed, which he allowed to continue for ten minutes—
the time he thought a description of Achilles' shield should have taken—
pacing up and down and appearing to be listening attentively. Then he said:
'Very well, X has described Achilles' shield for us, let us get on.'

His appearance during the ten years he was in Basel excited comment
because of his excessive attention to dress, amounting almost to dandyism.
According to Bernoulli he was, apart from an old state counsellor from Baden,
the only man in Basel to wear a grey topper. He was a little under middle
height, stockily built, and his youth was to some extent obscured by the
moustache which was already a fine adornment to his upper lip. (A photo of
him in 1867 shows the moustache already *in situ;* another taken while he was in
Basel reveals a considerable increase in size and thickness, and it is well on the
way to the characteristic 'Nietzsche moustache' of the 1880s, best seen in the
well-known photo of 1882, in which it seems to cover the entire mouth. In a
photo taken with his mother about 1890 the moustache exceeds all reasonable
bounds, arching out over the mouth and extending as far as the chin.) Ludwig
von Scheffler, one of his students, has described Nietzsche's appearance when
he first called on him in 1875:[1]

I had not expected that the professor would come storming into the room . . .
like Burckhardt. I also knew well enough that a challenging tone in a writer does
not always echo his behaviour as a private man. But I was nonetheless surprised
by the modesty, even humility, of Nietzsche's demeanour when he came in. In
addition, he was of small rather than middle stature . . . And the iridescent
glasses and deep moustache gave his face that impression of intellectuality
which often makes even short men somewhat imposing. Yet his whole personality expressed nothing less than indifference to whatever external impression
he might be making.

This last observation seems not to square with Nietzsche's care in dressing,
which Scheffler also notes; but by 1875 dressing well was probably a habit
rather than a conscious effort. Scheffler also says what we hear from other
witnesses too: 'He who has never heard his voice only half-knows Nietzsche'.

He went to Basel prepared to dislike the people with whom he would have
to mix. To Ritschl he wrote (the 10th May 1869): 'Of the people of Basel
and their aristocratic Philistinism much might be written and even more
spoken.—This is the place to cure you of republicanism.' But once settled in
he enjoyed the company of the higher bourgeoisie well enough, Philistines or

[1] Quoted ibid., vol. 1, p. 252.

not, and was a popular young man with the rather closed and self-satisfied society of the little town.

When he was appointed to Basel, the university had asked him to take out Swiss citizenship to avoid being removed from his post by military obligations as a citizen of Prussia; but although he attempted to comply with this request, he had no hesitation in thwarting its object as soon as he felt impelled to do so, which happened in August 1870 after the outbreak of the Franco-Prussian War. He applied on the 8th to be released to 'make himself useful as a soldier or nursing orderly', and on the 11th he was granted leave 'for medical services' with the Prussian forces. From mid-August he worked as a nursing orderly at Erlangen, Wörth, Sulz-bei-Weissenburg, Hagenau-Bischweiler, Luneville and Nancy. On the 7th September, back at Erlangen, he collapsed with dysentery and diphtheria after having tended casualties for three days and nights continuously. He went into a military hospital himself, from where he was removed to his home at Naumburg to convalesce. By the end of October he was back at Basel.

The discontent with academic life which had filled him when he took up his professorship had been submerged under the flood of new impressions that accompanied his first year at the university; now, perhaps under the influence of the war and certainly under the influence of Wagner, it came to the surface again. That university teaching was a 'yoke' had all along been a commonplace of his correspondence with Rohde, with whom he had never ceased to keep in close touch since leaving Leipzig, and late in 1870 he suggested they remove themselves from academic life by founding a kind of secular monastery. The suggestion, in a letter of the 15th December, is vague in its details, but references to Wagner make it clear that the idea was an offshoot of his Wagner-enthusiasm. 'One day we shall throw off this yoke,' he says; '*for myself* I am quite decided on that.' His suggestion, he adds, is not an eccentricity but an 'imperative necessity [*Not*]'. He and Rohde will write books, but how they will live is not discussed. He says that he has just finished reading Rohde's latest letter to him and he feels, like him, that 'it would be a disgrace if we could not one day emerge from this passionate yearning [*sehnsüchtigen Schmachten*] by means of a forceful deed [*kräftige Tat*]'. This language is Wagnerian: the phrases quoted in German all belong to Wagner's characteristic vocabulary, and the entire project suggests the re-awakening of his ambition to be something 'great' under the impact of Wagner's achievements in independence. In 1876, as we shall see, Nietzsche did achieve for a brief period something very like his secular monastery.

Meanwhile, he was anxious that his separation from Rohde should end, and he urged him to find some way of coming to Basel. A means of bringing this about seemed to present itself in January 1871, when the chair of philosophy at the university fell vacant. Nietzsche applied for it, and suggested Rohde as his replacement in the chair of philology. In his enthusiasm for securing Rohde's appointment he overrated his chances of being found acceptable for the philosophical post. He lacked formal training in philosophy, and his well-known partiality for Schopenhauer—to say nothing of his championing of Wagner— did not help matters: he failed to secure the appointment, and Rohde did not come to Basel, then or at any later time.

The friendship between the two had grown no cooler; on the contrary, distance seemed to lend enchantment, and for some years yet Nietzsche was to feel that Rohde was his brother-in-arms against the Philistine world. But there were other friends of his youth with whom he still kept in contact: Pinder and Krug, from the Naumburg days, and Deussen, from Bonn and Leipzig. Towards Deussen he tended to adopt a rather fatherly, even schoolmasterish, attitude, and the small number of letters we have from him to Deussen reveal him in an unattractive light: without saying so in as many words, he succeeds in giving the impression he is dissatisfied with Deussen's progress and that the latter ought to be thinking more seriously about the course his life was to pursue. Since Deussen's later achievement in no way falls short of that of any of Nietzsche's acquaintances of his student days, we cannot think very highly of Nietzsche's judgment concerning him. His need to dominate others intellectually emerges very clearly here, and even more clearly in the comic outcome of his long friendship with Heinrich Romundt, who had been a fellow-student at Leipzig and was now a private tutor in Basel, lodging at No. 45 Schützgraben. In the letter suggesting the foundation of a secular monastery he names Romundt as a possible third member, which implies a very high opinion of his qualities. One day, some time later than the point we have reached, Romundt announced his intention of becoming a Roman Catholic. Nietzsche's perturbation was immense, but through the quasi- (or rather pseudo-) philosophical objections shines as clear as day the wounded *amour-propre* of the consummate egoist: Romundt had been under his almost-daily influence for the best part of a decade, and yet that influence had amounted to so little that he was proposing to do something that must have seemed to Nietzsche impossible for a thinking man. To have been born a Catholic was one thing; but to decide to become one after having listened to Nietzsche for ten years—no, that he could neither understand nor forgive.

The need to impress his opinions upon his contemporaries and to call them his friends only if they agreed with him was present in his nature beyond question; yet at the same time he was capable of forming a warm attachment with older men over whom he held no intellectual sway. The most important was, of course, Wagner, but at Basel he met two others for whom he retained a strong affection for the rest of his life. The elder was Jakob Burckhardt, the historian. Burckhardt was born in Basel in 1818; his most famous work, *The Culture of the Renaissance in Italy,* appeared in 1860, when he was 42, and when Nietzsche got to know him in 1869 he was totally set in his ways. He was present at Nietzsche's inaugural lecture, and Nietzsche would very much have liked to have formed a regular friendship with him. But Burckhardt drew back from any close acquaintanceship: the evidence of those best placed to see how Nietzsche and Burckhardt behaved towards one another—Jakob Mähly, Overbeck and Peter Gast, who knew both men at Basel—has made it clear that Burckhardt did not desire any intimate relationship with Nietzsche and treated him with no more than politeness.[1] The influence of the one upon the other is a matter for debate, but was in any case slight. Martin discusses them as examples of 'contrasting human and philosophical types',[2] and the contrasts are indeed far more striking than the similarities, which derive mainly from a common source in Schopenhauer. Burckhardt's particular study was the history of culture (as opposed to political history); his deeply pessimistic nature made Schopenhauer's philosophy attractive to him, and his scorn of Hegel's philosophy of history as 'our old familiar friend progress' in disguise won Nietzsche's approval. Burckhardt's general attitude towards historical study is the same as Nietzsche's, but even here we cannot properly speak of his having influenced the younger man, since it derives from Schopenhauer's, which Nietzsche would already have known. Nietzsche sought to interest Burckhardt in his writings, and Burckhardt responded very favourably to *Human, All Too Human,* saying it reminded him of the work of the great French moralists; he also found much to praise in the immediately succeeding works: what he admired was their coolness and independence, in contrast to the enthusiasm and involvement of *The Birth of Tragedy* and the *Meditations.* (It was precisely this change which alienated Rohde.) In later years, he ignored Nietzsche, while Nietzsche continued to admire him. Erich Heller calls Burckhardt's failure to respond to Nietzsche's entreaties for a word of encouragement 'all but inhuman coldness' and compares it with Goethe's similar coldness towards those he thought might upset the subtle balance he had achieved.[3] But the balance Burckhardt had achieved was far more precarious than Goethe's, and to read Burckhardt is to receive the impression he is fighting to stave off a thorough-going melancholia. Burckhardt's philosophic

[1] See Alfred von Martin: *Nietzsche und Burckhardt* (Munich 1941, 1947), pp. 173 ff., where the evidence is assembled and discussed.
[2] Ibid., p. 7.
[3] Erich Heller: 'Burckhardt and Nietzsche' in *The Disinherited Mind* (London 1952).

pessimism appears to have derived from an early loss of faith in the Christian religion combined with a temperamental bias towards introspection; Schopenhauer himself, who never had any faith to lose and had a strongly sensual side to his nature, was far less of a natural pessimist than Burckhardt. In any event, by the time Nietzsche was propounding the means by which Burckhardt might have been able to overcome his philosophical hopelessness, Burckhardt was too old to change his character or his mind, and it was possibly the sense that this was so that made him keep the younger man at arm's length.

A few months after Nietzsche had settled in Basel, Franz Overbeck arrived from Jena to take up the chair of 'critical theology'. Overbeck, who was born in 1837 and was thus seven years Nietzsche's senior, became the one permanent friend Nietzsche had whose friendship was founded on a purely personal, instinctive basis. Although he became for a while a keen Wagnerian under Nietzsche's influence, he was for most of his life quite at variance with Nietzsche in his opinions, and his background was as different from Nietzsche's as it could have been. His father was a German businessman naturalized British; his mother was French. He was born in St. Petersburg and was already 11 before he came to live in Germany; he spoke English, French and Russian at home, and learned German when he had to go to school in Dresden. Overbeck had a talent for making friends. After his death in 1905 he was attacked by Elizabeth Nietzsche for his failure to collaborate with the Nietzsche Archive during his last years; by way of reply, a former colleague at Basel wrote a testimonial to Overbeck's qualities as a man and as a scholar and sent it to as many of Overbeck's friends as he could call to mind: it was published over more than a score of signatures, many of them famous in the academic world, from nearly a dozen universities. But his closest friend for most of his life was Nietzsche, whom he met when he took up lodgings at No. 45 Schützgraben. His account of his friendship is an unqualified expression of thanks for the experience.[1] 'Our friendship was without any shadows,' he writes. At the same time, he is not sparing in his criticism, which he had certainly voiced while Nietzsche was still able to understand it; but in this instance criticism did not constitute a 'shadow'. As the years passed, Overbeck moved away from Nietzsche philosophically, and with Nietzsche's last works he was quite unable to agree; at the same time, however, he moved closer as a friend, so that in the last years he and his wife were, apart from Gast, Nietzsche's only real intimates.[2]

[1]Printed in Bernoulli: op. cit., vols. 1 and 2.
[2]Ida Overbeck's recollections of Nietzsche are extraordinarily vivid and sympathetic; from them we obtain a rare glimpse of how he seemed when relaxed in the company of people whose intellect and opinions he respected and with whom he could hold genuine conversation. They are printed in

Finally, of all the people who knew him it was Overbeck who rushed to Turin when it appeared Nietzsche had become mad and might be doing Heaven knew what. There seems to have been not one serious quarrel or difference between them during the whole of their association—and this, in Nietzsche's story, is unique. The conclusion to draw is that Overbeck, who cuts a rather colourless figure beside the hero of the Nietzsche biographies, was in fact a master in handling men—or at least in handling Nietzsche—who knew instinctively when to give way and when not to, when to speak and when to keep silent, in order to preserve a friendship whose continuance he desired.

An odd coincidence is that Overbeck met Wagner under circumstances very similar to those under which Nietzsche met him. When he was a student at Leipzig he had been a friend of the Brockhaus family and had been present at social gatherings at their house when Wagner was present. Wagner had not impressed him much: he wrote to his parents that Wagner had 'quelque chose de phraseur et de pathetique' when expounding his ideas.[1] During the 1870s, under Nietzsche's influence, his opinion changed, and by 1875, when he visited Bayreuth during rehearsals for the festival, he was a member of the *Patronatverein* and an ardent propagandist for the Wagnerian cause.[2]

It was in 1871 that Nietzsche first became really ill. We have seen how he probably contracted syphilis while in Bonn or Leipzig, and that from his earliest years he was subject to headaches, probably through his faulty eyesight. Until 1870, however, he had suffered no serious consequences; in that year his constitution was weakened by the attack of dysentery and diphtheria which put an end to his war service, and almost as soon as he returned to Basel he began to suffer from regularly-recurring periods of exhaustion; these grew so serious that he was compelled to ask for leave of absence. It was granted him on the 15th February 1871 'until the end of the winter semester, for the purpose of restoring his health'. He left almost at once in the company of his sister for Lugano, where they stayed until the beginning of April and where, instead of resting, he worked hard on *The Birth of Tragedy*. As a probable consequence, he was still unwell in the summer, which he spent with Elizabeth and Gersdorff in the Bernese Oberland. In October he went to Naumburg and visited Leipzig, where he spent some pleasant days with Gersdorff and Rohde

---

Bernoulli: op. cit., vol. 1, pp. 234–51.
[1] Quoted in Bernoulli: op. cit., vol. 1, p. 61.
[2] The *Patronatverein* (Society of Patrons) was a national organization formed by Wagner and his chief supporters to help finance the Bayreuth Festival of 1876. Much is made in the Wagner literature of this show of support, but the aim of the *Verein*—to cover the cost of the festival—was not achieved, and its real significance is that it adds to Wagner's already mighty achievements yet another: the formation of the first organized fan club.

and was introduced to Wagner's publisher, Fritzsch, who was to bring out *The Birth of Tragedy*. He returned to Basel at the end of the year. For all that he appeared cured, it had been an ominous interlude; although he could hardly have appreciated it, his constitution had been permanently undermined: henceforward he was never properly well again, and any attempt to under-stand his behaviour from 1871 onwards must constantly take into account the fact that, in addition to whatever else he might be doing, he was engaged upon a day-to-day battle with ill-health. The enemy which appeared most often was migraine: it would attack overnight and sometimes persist for three days, during which he would be incapable of eating or, if he ate, of retaining what he had eaten. Such an attack would leave him exhausted and an easy victim for other ailments. Yet his resistance was tremendous: again and again he seemed to be done for, and again and again he recovered; until at last he summed up his experience in the well-known epigram: 'What does not kill me makes me stronger' (G I 8). It may be a doubtful dictum in general, but in his own case it appears to fit the facts.

5

Wagner, Schopenhauer, Darwin and the Greeks

For me they were steps, I have climbed up upon them—therefore I had to pass over them. But they thought I wanted to settle down on them. (G I 42)

1

As soon after coming to Basel as he conveniently could, Nietzsche visited Wagner at Tribschen. Wagner was at work when he paid his first call on the 15th May (1869), but invited Nietzsche to come back for lunch; Nietzsche was unable to do this, so Wagner suggested he return two days later, on Whit Monday. The meeting was so successful that he was again invited, this time to attend Wagner's birthday celebrations on the 22nd. Nietzsche's teaching duties made this impossible, and he was next at Tribschen for the weekend of the 5th to the 7th June. From then onwards he was a regular visitor, staying with the Wagner family twenty-three times between May 1869 and April 1872, when Wagner departed for Bayreuth. He was a guest for Christmas 1869 and again in 1870; on that occasion he formed part of the tiny audience which heard the first performance of the *Siegfried Idyll*, Wagner's Christmas and birthday present to Cosima. (Her birthday fell on the 24th December.) Before the year 1869 was over he had been accepted—one might almost say adopted—as a member of the household, with a room of his own which he might use any time he chose to; often he had charge of the Wagner children, who treated him like an elder brother.

The importance in Nietzsche's life of his relationship with Wagner can hardly be exaggerated. The experience was an awakening: his eyes were opened to the possibilities of greatness that still existed in human nature. He learned the meaning of genius and strength of will, expressions he had used

56

without any very lively sense of their real significance. In course of time he learned other things from Wagner, and not always those things Wagner would most willingly have taught him: that even the most sincere man is still very much an actor, that pettiness and greatness can co-exist in the same soul, that love and hate are not mutually exclusive but opposite aspects of the same emotion. By observing Wagner he became a psychologist, having before him one of the most versatile and open natures ever to appear on earth, and the decisive insight from which the theory of the will to power grew came when he recognized that Wagner's tremendous art-works were essentially a product of his equally tremendous need to dominate other people.

Tribschen was (and is) a large, square house in German Switzerland over-looking Lake Lucerne. Wagner moved there from Munich in April 1866, and was joined a month later by Cosima, wife of Hans von Bülow, and her three daughters, one of them Wagner's also. (He and Cosima were married in August 1870. Nietzsche was asked to be a witness, but he was then serving with the Prussian forces in France.) During his six years' residence there, Wagner completed the *Meistersinger* and *Siegfried* and composed *Götterdämmerung;* he was thus at the very height of his powers when Nietzsche became an intimate of Tribschen.

We have seen that Nietzsche was an enthusiastic Wagnerian before he left Leipzig, and we may hazard a guess that the proximity of Lucerne to Basel—they are about fifty miles apart—assisted his decision to accept the Basel post. In any event, he wasted little time before he sought Wagner out. It is true Wagner had invited him to call, but this could have been no more than a piece of conventional politeness: there was no great likelihood he would even re-member the Leipzig student. But, as it turned out, Nietzsche had made an impression; Wagner did remember him, and the more he got to know him the better he liked him. Nietzsche was overwhelmed, and his devotion to Wagner soon left all restraint behind. His letters of this period witness to the bound-lessness of his infatuation. In his earliest letter to Wagner (of the 22nd May 1869) he signed himself 'your most faithful and devoted follower and ad-mirer', and before long he was addressing Wagner as *Meister*. His letters to his friends were full to overflowing with praise for Wagner's genius and joy at his own good fortune. To Gersdorff he wrote rapturously (the 4th August):

> I have found a man who reveals to me as no other the image of what Schopen-
> hauer calls 'the genius' and who is quite possessed by that wonderfully intense
> philosophy [i.e. Schopenhauer's]. He is none other than Richard Wagner, about
> whom you should believe none of the judgments to be found in the press, the
> writings of musical scholars, etc. *No one* knows him and is capable of judging

him because all the world stands on a different footing from him and is not at home in his atmosphere. There dwell in him such uncompromising idealism, such deep and affecting humanity, such exalted seriousness of purpose [*Lebensernst*], that when I am near him I feel as if I am near the divine.

This excited and not quite coherent language characterizes a dozen similar outpourings. His own career began to take second place in his estimation to the importance of furthering Wagner's plans: he proposed in 1870 to take a two-year vacation from Basel to work for the Bayreuth undertaking, and in 1872 he had the idea of abandoning his professorship altogether so as to make himself available to Wagner. If these sacrifices were not in fact demanded of him it was because they would have served no useful purpose.

But although he was willing to surrender his time and energy to the service of the older man, his devotion to 'Wagnerism' was always ambiguous. It is true he began to evidence a predilection for Wagnerian turns of phrase, amounting to a decline in his ability to use the German language properly, and urged his friends to study certain of Wagner's prose writings, even recommending the fearfully absurd *State and Religion,* which Wagner had written for the edification of his patron King Ludwig of Bavaria and which Nietzsche calls 'profound' and adds: 'Never has a king been addressed in a more dignified and philosophical manner.'[1] But with the fundamentals of Wagner's 'philosophy' he never agreed. Wagner's pose as philosopher and seer had no justification: his brain was intensely alive, but his reasoning powers were of the slightest; he pontificated on matters he was utterly ignorant of; and he had the habit of decking out his writings with half-understood terminology from Feuerbach and Schopenhauer, giving them a spurious air of profundity. That Nietzsche admired some of them must be accounted a demonstration of love's proverbial blindness. (He attains the sublime in unconscious irony when, in a letter of April 1873, he tells Wagner he has in hand a polemic against 'the famous writer' David Strauss, in which he intends to expose stylistic shortcomings 'of the most detestable sort' in the wretched man's prose. Wagner's own prose style is one of the most 'detestable' in all German literature in its opacity and labyrinthine contortions.) It was in Wagner's writings on aesthetics, and especially in the five works of 1849–51, that Nietzsche found ideas he could use. A brief account of their main arguments will show what he gained from them.[2]

[1]Letter to Gersdorff of the 4th August 1869.
[2]Quotations are taken from W. A. Ellis's translation of Wagner's *Prose Works* (8 vols., London 1892–99) and cited by page number. *Opera and Drama* constitutes vol. 2; the remainder are included in vol. 1.

The series from *Art and Revolution* to *A Communication to my Friends* forms a group and belongs to the period between *Lohengrin* and the *Rheingold* when Wagner composed hardly anything for five and a half years while he thought out anew the problem of the relation between music, words and dramatic action in opera. The five essays possess a logical and emotional consistency that gives them, as a whole, a very moving quality: *Art and Revolution* begins with a vision of the theatre of antique Greece as the centre and supreme expression of a people's cultural life; *A Communication* ends with the announcement of Wagner's intention, at 'some future time', of providing Germany with a model for the restoration of the theatre to this exalted status.

Art and Revolution (July 1849) enunciates one of the two main clauses of Wagner's aesthetic: that the individual arts were once component parts of a single art-work, the tragedy of ancient Athens. Drama, he says, is the 'highest conceivable form of art' (p. 33) because, in its true perfection, it is a union of all the arts. Only once has it achieved this perfection: in the tragic drama of Athens; this supreme art-form disappeared when it disintegrated into its individual components. At last 'every impulse of Art stood still before Philosophy . . . To *Philosophy* and not to Art, belong the two thousand years which, since the decadence of Grecian Tragedy, have passed to our own day' (p. 35). During the Christian era the delight in beauty, which the church has pressed into its service, has been not an expression of the people's culture but a profound contradiction of the entire Christian world-outlook: admiration for beauty is pagan (p. 40). *The Art-Work of the Future* opens with the assertion: 'As Man stands to Nature, so stands Art to Man' (p. 69). Nature, says Wagner, works from necessity, man from caprice or egoism, and therefore he goes astray. 'But Error is the mother of Knowledge; and the history of the birth of Knowledge out of Error is the history of the human race' (p. 70). In art, this egoism of the individual is reflected in the egoism of the individual arts in isolation; but the truly necessary art is the art produced by nature. Nature produces art not through the individual but through the mass of men together, and this is the second main clause of Wagner's aesthetic: the true artist is the 'folk'. The 'folk', indeed, was responsible for every human invention, from speech to the state; but its highest invention was the drama, the total art-work, in which the whole man expresses himself with all his powers. The 'folk' still exists, but has been submerged in a welter of individuals; it must be re-awakened to a consciousness of its 'mission of redemption', which is to restore to art 'the instinctive laws of Nature' (p. 81). The art-work of the future will be a co-operative product, in which the architect, painter, mime, poet and musician will desert their egoistic individuality to collaborate with one another towards a single end; but, in a mystic way not made clear, the true creator of the art-work will be the 'folk'. In *Art and Climate* (February 1850) Wagner answers the criticism that the weather in northern climes will not permit a 'rapt intoxication of the sense of beauty'. The following work, *Opera and Drama* (January 1851), reveals as nothing else he wrote the limitations and perfect self-centredness, as well as the almost limitless fertility of Wagner's amazing mind: through nearly 400 pages of tortuous prose he struggles to sustain a thesis whose objective falsity is almost palpable but whose strength lies in its truth when applied to Wagner himself. He begins with the claim that 'the error in the art-genre of Opera consists herein: that a Means of expression (Music) has been made the end, while the End of expression (the Drama) has been made a means' (p. 17) and goes on to show that opera and drama hitherto have been maimed art-forms and that the forthcoming *Nibelung's Ring* was not only in general but in all its details the only valid form of dramatic work. *A Communication to my Friends* (August 1851) sets out to explain apparent contradictions between his operas and his theories, and ends with the announcement of the project which was to take up much of Nietzsche's time and energy while he was attached to Wagner: 'I propose to produce my myth [the *Ring*] *in three complete dramas,* preceded by a lengthy *Prelude . . .* for their performance, I shall abide by the following plan:—At a specially-appointed Festival, I propose, some future time, to produce these three Dramas with their Prelude, *in the course of three days and a fore-evening*' (p. 391). This festival will constitute a model for the folk-art-work of the future; how it is to be brought about he leaves to the future and to the thoughts of his friends.

The most generalized effect upon Nietzsche of these art-theories of Wagner's was to turn him towards drama. Hitherto he had had no special interest in drama and seen no special value in it; later he was to deprecate it; but during his Wagnerian period he saw it through Wagner's eyes. His evaluation of Athenian tragedy was precisely Wagner's, and his theory as to why it declined is perfectly well expressed in Wagner's words: 'To *Philosophy* and not to Art, belong the two thousand years which, since the decadence of Grecian Tragedy, have passed to our own day.' That art is essentially non-Christian, a view Nietzsche retained for the rest of his life, is also clearly announced in *Art and Revolution.* The duality inherent in Schopenhauer's philosophy, which Nietzsche transferred to his own, also appears in Wagner's aesthetic, and the dualism of *The Birth of Tragedy* probably derives as much from Wagner as from Schopenhauer. Wagner accepted the dichotomy of Man and Nature, Art and Man, with his usual blithe indifference to difficulties, and under his influence Nietzsche too tried to solve problems by means of two self-sufficient principles: Apollo and Dionysus of *The Birth of Tragedy* correspond not only to intellect and will, taken from Schopenhauer, but even more closely to art and nature, taken from Wagner. Man goes wrong, says Wagner, because his intellect leads him from nature, but 'Error is the mother of Knowledge, and the history of the birth of Knowledge out of Error is the history of the human race'. Wagner never asks himself how it can happen that continual error leads finally to knowledge, and there is no better symbol in Nietzsche's writings of his break away from Wagner's influence than the section which opens *Human, All Too Human* in which he calls this very point into question:

> Almost all philosophical problems still pose the same question as they did two thousand years ago: how can something originate in its opposite, for example rationality in irrationality, the sentient in the dead, logic in unlogic, disinterested contemplation in covetous willing, living for others in egoism, truth in error? Metaphysical philosophy has hitherto surmounted this difficulty by denying that the one originates in the other and assuming for the more highly-valued thing a miraculous source in the very kernel and being of the 'thing-in-itself'. Historical philosophy, on the other hand, which can no longer be separated from natural science, the youngest of all philosophical methods, has discovered in individual cases . . . that there are no opposites . . . and that a mistake in reasoning lies at the bottom of this antithesis: in this interpretation there exists, strictly speaking, neither an unegoistic action nor completely disinterested contemplation; both are only sublimations, in which the basic element seems almost to have dispersed and reveals itself only under the most painstaking observation. (MA 1)

This passage is a watershed in Nietzsche's philosophy: on one side is the dualism he inherited from Wagner and Schopenhauer; on the other, the monism he evolved himself.

For a time he accepted, at least in part, Wagner's theory of the *Gesamtkunstwerk*—the total art-work—but he never accepted Wagner's mystique of the 'folk'. Wagner's glowing picture of the people as genius had no effect on him even in the first flush of enthusiasm in 1869, and in his lecture on *Homer and Classical Philology* he goes out of his way to pour scorn on the idea of poetry's being produced by the mass of the people: 'The masses have never experienced more flattering treatment than in thus having the laurel of genius set upon their empty heads,' he says; the 'contrast between popular poetry and individual poetry does not exist at all'. In *The Art-Work of the Future* Wagner had devoted a few lines to Homer:

Neither was the true *Folk-epic* by any means a mere recited poem: the songs of Homer, such as we now possess them, have issued from critical siftings and compilings of a time in which the genuine Epos had long since ceased to live . . . before these epic songs became the object of . . . literary care, they had flourished mid the Folk, eked out by voice and gesture, as a bodily enacted Art-work.

The *Iliad* was, in fact, a communal music-drama, but the music has been lost and all we have left is a 'mere' poem. Nietzsche appears to be directly contradicting this when he says of Homer that 'we gain nothing with our theory of the poetising soul of the people, . . . we are always referred back to the poetical individual'.

Agreement or difference over theory was, however, of secondary importance: what mattered most was the personal relationship. Nietzsche's own summing-up is well known: 'I offer all my other human relationships cheap; but at no price would I relinquish from my life the Tribschen days, those days of mutual confidences, of cheerfulness, of sublime incidents—of *profound* moments. I do not know what others may have experienced with Wagner: over *our* sky no cloud ever passed' (EH II 5). It has been said that the facts fail to support this idealized account, and since *Ecce Homo* is usually dismissed as the last wild words of a mind on the brink of dissolution the references in it to Wagner are discounted. But *Ecce Homo* is quite lucid on the subject of Wagner, and what it tells us is what Nietzsche took with him from his Tribschen years: what, sixteen years later, he remembered of his life with Wagner. He tells us: 'over *our* sky no cloud ever passed.' We are not obliged to take it literally and when we catch the rumble of thunder declare his memory to have been at fault. What he is recalling is a total situation, and when he says that he was happier in Wagner's company than he ever was in anyone else's we have no choice but to believe him. It is a commonplace of commentary that Wagner became for him a 'father figure', and there were indeed special reasons why he was peculiarly fitted to assume the role Pastor Nietzsche had vacated twenty years before. He was just the age Pastor Nietzsche would have been had he lived, both men having been born in 1813; he was born in Leipzig and his voice retained strong traces of the Saxon dialect, which he would sometimes exaggerate for comic effect; and it is also a fact that he looked like Pastor Nietzsche.[1] But although Nietzsche may have understood that Wagner had taken on

---

[1]Richard Blunck: op. cit., contains a photo of Pastor Nietzsche. The resemblance to Wagner, while far from exact, is sufficiently close to be quite striking and certainly close enough for his son to have noted it. Blunck records that Wagner and Nietzsche were distantly related: their mothers had a common ancestor in one Caspar Spörel or Spörl, who lived from 1530 to about 1600 and was Bürgermeister of Saalburg (p. 20).

a paternal role in his life, he nowhere attempts to account for Wagner's hold over him in this way. What he does say is this:

> Constituted as I am, a stranger in my deepest instincts to everything German, so that the mere presence of a German hinders my digestion, my first contact with Wagner was also the first time in my life I ever drew a deep breath: I felt, I reverenced him as a being from *outside* [*als Ausland*], as the opposite, the incarnate protest against all 'German virtues' . . . Wagner was a revolutionary—he fled from the Germans . . . The German is good-natured— Wagner was by no means good-natured . . . [He employs the same terminology when he tries to account for the ending of the friendship:] What was it I never forgave Wagner? That he condescended to the Germans—that he became *reichsdeutsch*. (EH II 5)

In his later years he employed the name 'German' as an ideogram for the type of man his countrymen represented for him: the middle-class man, the contented conformist in thought and morals, the *ungeistiger Mensch;* and in this sense Wagner was decidedly 'un-German'. It was his character seen in relation to their common environment, his strange and rebellious conduct, that fired Nietzsche's imagination. Wagner's contemporaries recognized well enough to what species of man he belonged: that of the out-and-out Bohemian. From *Tannhäuser* onwards his operas reveal an unmixed contempt for normal standards of behaviour, and there is no Wagnerian hero who does not flout them. (Even in the genial *Meistersinger* the representatives of middle-class respectability are held to ridicule.) So far as his own behaviour was concerned, he fashioned his morals with the indifference to public opinion of a Goethe or a Rimbaud. The Bohemianism of his temperament found visible expression in outlandish dress: when Nietzsche was first received at Tribschen on Whit Monday morning 1869, Wagner was wearing his Dutch painter's costume— black velvet jacket, knee-breeches, silk stockings, buckled shoes, Rembrandt beret and a bright blue cravat. The exaggerated splendour of his apartments— the satin walls, the profusion of art-objects, the perfume—was as far-famed as were his operas and a subject of derision for the Philistine world. His egoism was popularly regarded as having crossed the frontiers of sanity, and to many well-meaning persons he was quite simply mad: the Bayreuth undertaking was thought of as the project of a megalomaniac for whom the existing opera houses were not good enough. To his intimates too Wagner seemed no less abnormal than he did to the world at large; they knew how abnormally demanding he was, how much he wanted from his friends; but his genius was so apparent to them that many felt they were serving their own best interests in serving him. This was the 'incarnate protest' against all things 'German' that first fascinated and then captivated Nietzsche, and whose fascination he never denied even when he had decided Wagner was decadent.

A word about Cosima. During the period we are dealing with she was devoted to Wagner to the exclusion of everyone else, and although she was, so far as we know, invariably kind to Nietzsche, she was also inclined to patronize him, and she didn't hesitate to comment adversely on his work when it failed to rise to the heights she and Wagner had come to expect—that is, when it reflected opinions other than Wagner's or, even worse, when it had nothing to do with Wagner at all. She gave him little commissions to perform for the cause[1] and invited him to Tribschen because his presence seemed beneficial to *Wagner*. All this notwithstanding, she made a deep impression on Nietzsche. He wrote his *Five Prefaces to Five Unwritten Books* as a present for her, in his daydreams of later years she plays Ariadne to his own Dionysus (Wagner is Theseus), and among the letters he sent out after his mental collapse was one addressed to her which read simply: 'Ariadne, I love you. Dionysus.' Later, while at the Jena clinic, he is recorded as having said: 'My wife Cosima Wagner brought me here.'

2

Nietzsche's attachment to Wagner was strengthened by their mutual attachment to Schopenhauer, and it is significant that when he broke away from Wagner around 1876 he broke away from Schopenhauer too; for, his reputation as a 'disciple' notwithstanding, his final philosophy is opposed to Schopenhauer's at every point. What appealed to Nietzsche most, in fact, was the personality of the man, to which his own bears quite a close resemblance.

At the beginning of his life of Schopenhauer, Professor W. Wallace, writing in 1890, makes some pertinent remarks about the differences between philosophy in Germany and in England up to that time:

> With a few striking exceptions, it may be said that in England . . . the fountain head of the philosophical stream has not been in the Universities and the professional element has been entirely secondary. In Germany, on the contrary, the treasures of learned wisdom have been entrusted to the keeping of a chosen official order, the teachers in the Universities . . . While German philosophy has used a technical dialect of its own, English philosophy has been written in

---

[1] Wagner himself entrusted Nietzsche with the task of arranging the printing of his autobiography, *Mein Leben*, by a Basel printer and taking charge of the proofs, a sign of how close Nietzsche had grown to him.

the ordinary language of literature . . . Schopenhauer reminds us more of England than Germany . . . For the work of a systematic teacher he was without the requisite preparation of methodical training, and still more wanting in the regular, precise and almost prosaic faculty which metes out wisdom in palpable bulks for consumption by audiences drawn not primarily by philosophical passion, but by the pressure of academic ordinances. But if he was unsuited to be a teacher of that systematic logic and ethics in which he had never been a thorough learner, he was by his very dilettantism, by his literary faculty, by his interest in problems as they strike the natural mind, qualified to stimulate, to guide, perhaps even to fascinate, those who like himself were led by temperament, by situation, by inward troubles, to ask the why and the wherefore of all this unintelligible world.[1]

Nietzsche's name could be substituted for Schopenhauer's in this passage without detracting from its truth. Like Schopenhauer, he was a true philosopher working outside the discipline within which German philosophers usually work; and like him he found that his path to recognition was, perhaps for that very reason, a hard one.

The World as Will and Idea appeared at the end of 1818 (dated 1819 on the title page), published by the Leipzig firm of Brockhaus. When, in 1834, Schopenhauer asked how many copies were still left he was told that very few were—the greater part of the edition having been sold as waste paper. The work had, in fact, aroused no interest whatever. Schopenhauer was 30 when his great book appeared; when he was 56, in 1844, he persuaded Brockhaus to bring out a second edition, but recognition and success still eluded him until, in 1851, he published *Parerga und Paralipomena* (a deliberately pedantic title meaning 'Chips and Scraps'), a miscellany of essays which is far more easily approachable than his chief work and which revealed to a large body of readers the presence in their midst of a writer and thinker of the front rank. Its success stimulated interest in *The World as Will and Idea,* and in 1856 the philosophical faculty at Leipzig offered a prize for a statement and criticism of his philosophy. From then until his death in 1860 he was famous, but not nearly as famous as he would have liked to have been, and he died an embittered and disappointed man.

The kind of influence and acceptance he longed for came only after he was dead. We have seen that his chief book was unknown to Nietzsche until 1866, when he first read it, but it had long before captivated Richard Wagner, and with Wagner's rise to world fame in the 1860s and 1870s Schopenhauer became more widely known through Wagner's advocacy; in addition, younger

[1] W. Wallace: *Life of Arthur Schopenhauer* (London 1890), pp. 11 ff.

men like Nietzsche had fallen under his spell, and by the mid-1870s his name had acquired the sort of notoriety in Germany that Shaw's had in the first years of the twentieth century in England. But it was a lonely eminence upon which he stood: neither Wagner nor Nietzsche, his most famous 'disciples', deserves that name, and his true successor, so far as he had a successor at all, was Paul Deussen. We have to distinguish when speaking of Schopenhauer between three different aspects of his work: his philosophy, his philosophizing, and his effect as a popularizer of the philosophy of the East. His philosophy is not a system but 'a single thought', as he himself says in the preface to the first edition of *The World as Will and Idea*, incapable of development but only of increasing elaboration, and Schopenhauer himself followed it to its last conclusions, leaving nothing for any 'disciple' to do except agree; the 'influence' of this single thought has long since run its course, and if there were no more to him than this, he would by now be only a name in the history of philosophy. But there was more: both his main work and the *Parerga* are full of genuine wisdom and original thinking, set down in the most attractive literary style any German philosopher to that time had had at his command. It was this Schopenhauer who became famous and who is still read—but who could no more have a 'successor' than could, say, Emerson or Carlyle, whom he also resembles in the earnestness of his tone and the independence of his mind. The one respect in which he could prove to be the starting-point of further development was in his aspect as a popularizer in the West of the concepts of Indian philosophy, and it is here that Deussen's work can be called a fruitful continuation of Schopenhauer's. Nietzsche took from Schopenhauer what he could use and left the rest behind; Wagner was overwhelmed by *The World as Will and Idea*, in much the same way as Nietzsche was, but, being incapable of criticizing it, he simply surrendered to it, in so far as he understood it, to the detriment of his understanding of himself; Deussen, by contrast, learned Sanskrit, studied Indian philosophy at the source, and devoted his talents to translating and expounding it in the West, his inspiration being the conviction that Schopenhauer had shown the great value of this hitherto little-known world of thought and that the wisdom to be derived from it was identical with that to be derived from Schopenhauer's own philosophy.

In his first enthusiasm, Nietzsche accepted Schopenhauer *tout court* and 'denied the will' as vehemently as Wagner thought he was doing. (It is a valid criticism of Schopenhauer's philosophy that its ultimate exhortation to 'deny the will' is a practical impossibility, and that neither Nietzsche nor Wagner came within a thousand miles of the ascetic sainthood demanded by the moralist in whom both undoubtedly believed with great sincerity. Schopenhauer himself was notoriously a good-liver, a fact which Nietzsche did not forget when he came to write the fourth part of *Zarathustra*, in which Schopenhauer appears.) But this was a passing phase that left little mark on his own philosophy: what he retained was the picture of a philosopher who stopped at nothing in his search for truth, who was not afraid of 'hard truths', and, uniquely among German philosophers, could really write—for it must not be forgotten that a part of Schopenhauer's influence, perhaps its largest part, was due not to what he said but to the way he said it. The fine style is, indeed, the clue to the mystery of how so strange and hopeless a doctrine as Schopenhauer's could have achieved domination over the minds of so many young men, conflicting as it does with what most young men have always thought worthwhile. Schopenhauer appealed to them directly as an artist, and he offered 'the world, life, . . . Hell and Heaven' explained, accounted for, mastered in a single flash of inspiration. When he broke away from Christianity and religion, Nietzsche spoke of setting sail upon a sea of doubt, from the midst of which one would often long for firm land again: Schopenhauer was firm land upon which he temporarily came to rest.

Although he later laughed at the gross inconsistency between Schopenhauer's doctrine and the way in which the philosopher actually lived, Nietzsche never really lost his respect for the 'sage of Frankfort', from whom he had received his first intimation of how a philosopher might work entirely alone and yet in the end prove victorious. But for Schopenhauer's philosophy he did at last lose all respect, considering it not only totally mistaken but a grave symptom of the decadence of Western man. It is true he received the concept of the primacy of the will from Schopenhauer, but the will to power is so different from Schopenhauer's will that the two principles have virtually nothing in common except the word 'will', and if Nietzsche had been more careful with his terminology he might have employed some other expression.

Schopenhauer's philosophy takes its beginning from Kant, whose only true successor he thought himself to be, and it derives from two of Kant's main conclusions: that the world of objective reality is a world of 'appearance', and that practical reason is primary, theoretical reason secondary, in the life of man. Kant's world as noumenon and phenomenon, as thing-in-itself and appearance, becomes Schopenhauer's world as will and idea; Kant's theoretical reason is identified with intellect and his practical reason with will, and will is primary, intellect secondary.

In his thesis *On the Fourfold Root of the Principle of Sufficient Reason* (1813) Schopenhauer had named four types of knowledge: logical, ethical, scientific and mathematical. In none of them, he said, do we move beyond establishing relations between ideas. Now, in *The World as Will and Idea*, he speaks of another kind of knowledge that relates not ideas to ideas but ideas to an immediate reality: knowledge of oneself. The 'single thought' that constitutes his philosophy is the proposition: 'My body and my will are one.' I am aware of myself objectively, in the same way as I am aware of other things, as an object extended in space and time, as 'phenomenon'; but I am also aware of myself subjectively, as living, feeling, suffering, desiring—or, in Schopenhauer's comprehensive term, as will. This is a form of perception radically different from intellectual perception. The intellect divides reality into fragments, and all it sees are 'appearances' or 'ideas', but the immediate awareness of self is not a perception of this kind: through knowing myself as will I feel the inner unity of life, outside space and time. Because it is in the nature of the intellect to fragmentize and isolate things, in ordinary life we look upon ourselves as individual, isolated objects. But all knowledge is relative, depending upon other knowledge, and the fragmentation of the world is not complete even on the intellectual level. There is a basic unity linking all things, and this basic unity is perceived by us through the mode of knowledge just described: we perceive an identity between our physical body and our immaterial will, and this principle of identity is the clue to the unity of all things, material and immaterial. Schopenhauer insists very strongly upon the absolute antithesis between intellect and will, and limits the attributes of will to an uncomplicated urge to live, attributing all other qualities, including consciousness, to the intellect. The reason he must do this becomes clear from the next stage of his argument: if we can understand that our bodies are the outward form of our will, and our will the inward form of our bodies, we must see that all other objects are the outward form of an inner will also. The will that we feel as our true being is also the true being of all things; and since time, space and separation are properties of the phenomenal world alone, the noumenal world of the will must be one and indivisible.

The world as Schopenhauer sees it is a duality: outwardly a world of events, of objects, of time, space, cause and effect, phenomena, 'idea'; inwardly a silent world, without time or space, cause or effect, the noumenal world, the thing-in-itself, one everywhere-present 'will'. The will is the primary force of life; it keeps the universe going; it literally 'makes the world go round', for Schopenhauer identifies it with physical forces such as gravity and with the instincts of the animal and the blind drives of the vegetable worlds. Intellect evolved as a 'tool' of the will and is therefore secondary to it; but those peculiarly-constituted individuals in whom the intellect develops can wrest it free from the will's dominion. Intellect fully liberated from will Schopenhauer calls 'genius'.

The crux of Schopenhauer's philosophy is the ethical judgment that the individual will is evil and must be denied. The reason this is so is as follows: The individual is, in a quite literal sense, embodied will: the oneness of the noumenal world is fragmented in the phenomenal world into a multitude of separate 'wills', each an incarnation of the primary force of life. The individual, as a piece of will, comes into existence intending to exist for as long as possible; he cannot do otherwise, for the will is essentially desire for life, will to live. As a consequence, the individual has to see all things and all other people in their relation to himself, and in the long run *use* all things and all other people as if they existed for his benefit. But since all things and all other people feel precisely the same way, the outcome is universal conflict. Conflict produces unhappiness, and wherever there is will there is suffering; the nature of the will is to strive, and this striving will always produce strife, and unhappiness will always predominate over happiness. The only good is the negative good of amelioration: happiness can never be a positive quality, only a decrease in suffering. Life is incurably miserable, and the response of him who has realized this is one of denial: he 'denies the will', renounces all striving, frees himself from the bonds of desire and becomes an ascetic and saint, waiting only for deliverance from life. Death—by which Schopenhauer means total extinction—is the only real good; before death, the good life is that of a type of genius, the saint, with whom 'only knowledge is left: will has vanished'. This is Schopenhauer's 'pessimism'—his conviction that life is *incurably* evil—and it distinguishes his philosophy from all others.

The most profound difference between Nietzsche's mature philosophy and Schopenhauer's is that Nietzsche's is not metaphysical but materialistic, and his will to power an induction from observed data not a metaphysical postulate like Schopenhauer's will to live. We have seen how Nietzsche was able to reconcile his enthusiasm for Schopenhauer with an admiration for F. A. Lange's *History of Materialism,* and when his enthusiasm cooled he was led to adopt a position so like Lange's that we are justified in seeing a direct influence at work. Lange was, like Schopenhauer, a follower of Kant, but with a decisive difference. According to Lange, ultimate reality is not only unknowable, as Kant maintained, but the very *idea* of it is a consequence of the way we think; that is, the concept of the thing-in-itself is part of the phenomenal world. Translated into Schopenhaueran terms, the will is nothing but one more idea. Because even the idea of ultimate reality must belong to the plane of appearance, says Lange, nothing meaningful can be said about it, and philosophers must concern themselves only with the material world—the world of phenomena, the only world we know. Although he occasionally forgets this, and writes about the will to power and the eternal recurrence as if

69

they were descriptions of ultimate reality, Nietzsche's true position is in no doubt: both are materialist conceptions as defined by Lange, and this is brought home very clearly by his general attitude towards the 'beyond', the 'real world' and the thing-in-itself: so far as we are concerned, he says again and again in different ways, these things do not exist. The most famous formulation of his 'this-sided' orientation is 'God is dead': it is intended to imply all that ever has been or ever could be subsumed in the name 'God', including all God-substitutes, other worlds, ultimate realities, things-in-themselves, noumenal planes and wills to live—the entire 'metaphysical need' of man and all its products.

There are two further important distinctions. The first is temperamental. The basis of Schopenhauer's world-outlook is that life is suffering, and this is a temperamental conclusion. It is not proved, and cannot be; Schopenhauer merely feels it to be true, and he exerts himself rhetorically in an effort to transmit this feeling to his readers. But if his readers do not feel that happiness is only the amelioration of suffering and persist in enjoying life on occasion, there is nothing further Schopenhauer can do: to be a 'Schopenhaueran' one must first be a pessimist. There was, it is true, a strong vein of pessimism running through Nietzsche's nature, and this is what attracted him to Schopenhauer at first; but it was not the decisive element, and in the long run pessimism about life as such was not possible for him. In a way, he transferred it from life to man, so that he was able to reconcile a fundamental optimism concerning the nature of life with pessimism concerning the mass of mankind. He did not deny that much of life was suffering, but he considered that suffering was the coin which purchased happiness and that to desire happiness without suffering was to ask the impossible. The second distinction is that Schopenhauer was unable to free his philosophy from a built-in dualism that makes some of its stages decidedly shaky, while Nietzsche, who took over this dualism into his early philosophy, was able to subsume it in a logically more satisfying monism. The dualistic tendency in Schopenhauer is present at the outset in the dichotomy of will and idea, and this is emphasized with even greater force by his insistence on the absolute antithesis between will and intellect. The corresponding duality in the early Nietzsche is between Dionysus and Apollo in *The Birth of Tragedy;* and Walter Kaufmann's question 'Whence comes Apollo?'[1] suggests itself as an objection to Schopenhauer: Whence comes the intellect? Schopenhauer answers that it developed from the will, as its tool, but nothing points more directly to the metaphysical character of his philosophy than his failure to explain at all convincingly *how* it

---

[1]Kaufmann: op. cit., p. 131.

developed, or why, if intellect arose from will, it is the will's absolute antithesis. (The answer to the latter objection is that it *has* to be if the will is to be one, equally present everywhere and in all things, since to allow the will any attributes other than will itself would mean allowing to insensate objects attributes they obviously do not possess; this is why even consciousness must be an attribute of intellect and not of will.) The full force of this duality is not felt until the end, that is, until the saint overcomes the will and 'only knowledge is left: will has vanished'. How this is possible, given all that has gone before, Schopenhauer never begins to make clear. What has gone wrong is that the initial duality has proved intractable. Intellect cannot overcome will unless it, too, has will, and will is the one thing denied it absolutely; conversely, if intellect *does* overcome will, it must itself be an aspect of will—its conscious aspect possibly. This solution is prohibited by Schopenhauer's insistence that the will is wholly evil, should be 'denied' (i.e. overcome) and, in the saint, *is* overcome. The final stages of his philosophy are, in fact, little more than a statement of what Schopenhauer himself desires the person who has read his philosophy shall feel impelled to do. The saint, he hopes, will desire to deny the will; what this desire can be if it is not itself will Schopenhauer cannot say. By making the will supreme metaphysically and then saying it is wholly evil, he has deprived 'good' of any will of its own. As a consequence, the will cannot be 'denied', evil cannot be overcome or even diminished, and the situation justifies even stronger pessimism than Schopenhauer's own famous brand.

Finally, the *fons et origo* of the errors that pervade Schopenhauer's philosophy is the way in which he makes free with ultimate reality. In *The World as Will and Idea* he speaks of the will, the ultimate reality of existence, in as familiar a way as some religious apologists speak of God. But I think it in the highest degree improbable that the nature of 'ultimate reality' will ever be apprehensible to finite minds, or that anything meaningful will ever be said about it. When Schopenhauer conceived that he had reached the inmost core of existence with one leap, he was guilty of a grave error of judgment regarding the distance involved. Nietzsche, who is generally accounted 'arrogant', was in this respect the soul of modesty: neither the will to power nor the eternal recurrence purports to describe ultimate reality, which is considered unknowable and is consequently ignored; and it is in this that the difference between him and Schopenhauer is most extreme.

Wagner's art-theories and Schopenhauer's philosophy occupied a deal of Nietzsche's time during his Leipzig and Basel years, but they contributed nothing to his mature philosophy. (The influence of Wagner's personality and Schopenhauer's example is a different matter.) Both are in the strict meaning of the word eccentric, whereas Nietzsche's thought is part of the mainstream of Western philosophy and is concerned with problems central to the 'predicament' of modern man. Wagner and Schopenhauer belong to the nineteenth century, Nietzsche is a precursor of the twentieth in the sense that he anticipates what is now part of the consciousness of every thinking person: Nietzsche's philosophy presupposes a crisis in human affairs of which there is no hint in Wagner or Schopenhauer. To discover the origin of that philosophy we must turn away from them and towards three other phenomena which occupied his mind during these years: the philosophy of Greece, the decline of Christian belief, and the problem posed by Darwin's theory of evolution by natural selection.

3

Every philosopher whose thought constitutes a major contribution to philosophy stands at first before a certain new situation which he feels no one but he is equipped to grasp and explain. The classic example is that of Kant, who was 'awakened from his dogmatic slumbers' by the realization that the general conclusions of British philosophy, and especially those of David Hume, had rendered the world inexplicable and destroyed the basis from which previous attempts to explain it had been made, yet could not simply be refuted: in ordinary language, the conclusions of British philosophy were true but unacceptable. Hume represented to Kant a danger which could not be circumvented; it had to be faced and a new world-picture produced which took it into account but was not nullified by it. Kant's philosophy was an answer to the challenge of British nihilism—and so was Nietzsche's. The adversary this time was Charles Darwin, in whose name the theory of evolution had become victorious. It is unnecessary to stress that Darwin did not invent that theory; but it *is* necessary to stress that before Darwin evolution was one of a number of theories concerning the genesis of the human race, while after Darwin it appeared to be the proved theory. The philosophical crisis produced by Darwin was essentially the crisis of evolution, which became a pressing 'problem' only after he had shown, by his hypothesis of natural selection, that there existed a mechanism through which it could actually have taken place. Nietzsche accepted the fundamental implication of Darwin's hypothesis, namely that mankind had evolved in a purely naturalistic way through chance and accident: there appeared to be purpose in evolution, but Darwin had shown that the higher animals and man could have evolved in just the way they did entirely by fortuitous variations in individuals. Natural selection was for

Nietzsche essentially evolution freed from every metaphysical implication: before Darwin's simple but fundamental discovery it had been difficult to deny that the world seemed to be following some course laid down by a directing agency; after it, the necessity for such a directing agency disappeared, and what seemed to be order could be explained as random change. 'The total nature of the world,' Nietzsche wrote in *Die fröhliche Wissenschaft*, 'is . . . to all eternity chaos' (FW 109), and this thought, basic to his philosophy, arose directly from his interpretation of Darwin.

Darwinism completed a view of reality that Nietzsche had been constructing in his mind during his youth. Firstly, he had lost his faith in revealed religion: the meaning of reality was now a mystery. He turned to Schopenhauer for an explanation, but at the same time he imbibed the antidote to Schopenhauer: F. A. Lange. The metaphysical world had not been revealed to man; had it been revealed to Schopenhauer? No, because it was unrevealable. Whatever came into the mind was an 'idea'; consequently the thing-in-itself was an idea, the will was an idea, the whole metaphysical world was an idea. This attitude Nietzsche accepted. The phenomenal world was the only world, people could not possibly 'get in touch' with a suprasensible reality. If the fact of evolution seemed to suggest the operation of an outside force upon the mundane world, Darwin had shown that here, too, the hypothesis of a directing agency was not needed to account for the observed phenomena.

The consequences were momentous. God, if he existed, was unknowable: he could be no more than an idea in the minds of men. Nothing that existed in the phenomenal world could have come from 'outside': if the universe were intelligible, it must be intelligible from within. Part of that intelligibility had been expounded by Darwin: the 'divine' attributes of man had in reality descended to him from the animals. Man was in touch with no 'beyond', and was no different from any other creature. But, as God had been the meaning of the universe, so man had been the meaning of the earth. Now God and man, as hitherto understood, no longer existed. The universe and the earth were without meaning. The sense that meaning had evaporated was what seemed to escape those who welcomed Darwin as a benefactor of mankind. Nietzsche considered that evolution presented a correct picture of the world, but that it was a disastrous picture. His philosophy was an attempt to produce a new world-picture which took Darwinism into account but was not nullified by it.

Nietzsche's knowledge of and sympathy with antique Greece was profound, and one of the best-known things about him is that he rejected Winckelmann's and Goethe's vision of the Greeks as a race of beautiful children and saw them as a cruel, savage and warlike people who created a uniquely valuable culture by governing and redirecting their impulses. He showed a special appreciation of the Hellenic world of the sixth century—formerly considered little more than a barbarous preliminary to the glories of the fifth—and it is probable that even if he had not been an original thinker himself he would still be remembered for his exposition of this era. His feeling for sixth-century Greece was so marked that we ought to consider whether it has any bearing on his philosophy. That it has becomes apparent, I think, when we understand in what way he thought his own time similar to that of the pre-Socratic philosophers.[1] The situation of his own time he characterized as 'nihilistic': values and meaning had ceased to make sense, and philosophy was faced with an unexplained universe in a way that had not been so since before Plato. Philosophy from Plato onwards had been founded upon suppositions that were no longer valid, and to find philosophers who had faced their problems without presuppositions one had to go back to Heraclitus, Pythagoras and Socrates.

Not only did Nietzsche discover the nature of his dilemma among the Greeks, he also discovered the key to its solution. Long before he had formulated the theory of the will to power he had discovered that the driving force behind the culture of Hellas had been contest, agon, the striving to surpass. Dissatisfied with the received picture of life in antiquity, he had employed his mastery of classical philology to make for himself a picture corresponding, he thought, more nearly to the truth. This, indeed, he considered the object of classical philology: 'The entire scientific and artistic movement' of philology, he said in *Homer and Classical Philology*, is 'bent . . . upon bridging over the gulf between the ideal antiquity—which is perhaps only the magnificent blossoming of the Teutonic longing for the south—and the real antiquity.' In the antique world as he saw it, the 'base' emotions were inextricably involved with the 'higher' emotions:

> When one speaks of *humanity*, [he wrote in 'Homer's Contest', one of the *Five Prefaces to Five Unwritten Books* of 1872,] there lies behind it the idea that humanity is that which *separates* and distinguishes mankind from nature. But in reality there is no such separation: the 'natural' qualities and those called specifically 'human' are inextricably entwined together. Man is in his highest and noblest powers entirely nature and bears in him nature's uncanny dual character.

[1]Nietzsche, however, refers not to the 'pre-Socratic' philosophers, but to the 'pre-Platonic'. In *Philosophy in the Tragic Age of the Greeks* he speaks of 'the republic of geniuses from Thales to Socrates' (section 2), and one misunderstands his admiration for the 'pre-Socratics' unless one realizes that he regarded Socrates himself as the last of them.

Those capacities which are dreadful and accounted inhuman are, indeed, perhaps the fruitful soil out of which alone all humanity in impulse, act and deed can grow. Thus the Greeks, the most humane people of antiquity, have in them a vein of cruelty, of a brutal delight in destruction.

The Greeks were cruel, savage and predatory; yet they had become the most humane people of antiquity, the inventors of philosophy, science and tragedy, the first and finest European nation. How had this Hellenic world come into being? In 'Homer's Contest' Nietzsche draws attention to the opening of Hesiod's *Works and Days*, a passage he calls 'one of the most noteworthy Hellenic thoughts and worthy to be impressed on the newcomer immediately at the gateway of Hellenic ethics':

> *Two* Eris-goddesses are on earth. If we are reasonable, we should like to praise the one Eris as much as to blame the other; for these two goddesses have quite different dispositions. For the one, the cruel one, promotes evil war and feud. No mortal likes her, but under the yoke of necessity we show honour to the burdensome Eris according to the decree of the Immortals. She, as the elder, gave birth to black night. Zeus, the high-ruler, however, set the other Eris upon the roots of the earth and among men as a much better one. She urges even the unskilled man to work; and if one who lacks goods sees another who is rich, he hastens to sow and to plant and to put his house in order, as the rich man has done; one neighbour competes with another who strives after prosperity. This Eris is beneficial to men. The potter also has a grudge against the potter, and the carpenter against the carpenter; the beggar envies the beggar and the singer the singer.

He comments on this passage:

> The whole of Greek antiquity thinks of spite and envy otherwise than we do, and judges as does Hesiod, who first designates as evil that Eris who leads men against one another to a war of extermination, and then praises another Eris as good who, as jealousy, spite, envy, rouses men to deeds, but not to deeds of war but to deeds of *contest*.

The Greek view, he says a little later in the same Preface, was that 'every natural gift must develop itself by contest'.

He had already declared that 'Strife is the perpetual food of the soul', and had thereby paraphrased the philosopher who said 'War is the father of all things'. Heraclitus, 'the dark' sage of Ephesus, the prophet of 'eternal becoming', embodied in his teaching, so Nietzsche thought, the profoundest insight into the nature of the Greek soul. In *Philosophy in the Tragic Age of the Greeks* he speaks of Heraclitus with great enthusiasm: Heraclitus conceived of actuality as a struggle between opposites, he says, and this conception,

> drawn from the purest fount of Hellenism, . . . is Hesiod's good Eris transfigured into the world-principle; it is the idea of a contest . . . translated out of the gymnasia and palaestra, out of the artistic agonistics, out of the struggle of the political parties and of the cities, into the most general principle, so that the machinery of the universe is regulated by it. [Moreover, Heraclitus taught] eternal and exclusive becoming, the total instability of all reality, which continually works and becomes and never is, [and this] is an awful and bewildering idea . . . It required an astonishing strength to translate this effect into its opposite, into the sublime, into happy astonishment. (Section 5)

As Nietzsche has presented it, this is very like his own final philosophy, and he was later to suggest that Heraclitus might have taught the eternal recurrence itself.

Fascinating though the earliest philosophers may be, we should beware—as Nietzsche did not beware—of imagining that we see them in anything but the vaguest outline. They seem gigantic—but perhaps this is an effect of the mist in which they are shrouded. Perhaps Heraclitus was a grumpy old eccentric, like Schopenhauer; Nietzsche, however, paints for himself an heroic picture of the ancient sage, 'the proud and lonely truth-finder',[1] and reproduces that picture whenever he wishes us to see the practice of philosophy as a hard and solitary calling. Nietzsche-as-Heraclitus, stark and alone against a backdrop of Alpine crags, is a figure liable to appear in any of Nietzsche's works from *Human, All Too Human* to *Ecce Homo*. The 'Wanderer' of the last section of *Human, All Too Human* (MA 638), of the prologue and epilogue to *The Wanderer and His Shadow*, and of section 380 of *The Gay Science*, is Nietzsche-Heraclitus; so, with a glance at Heraclitus' doctrine of fire, is the self-portrait contained in the poem called 'Ecce Homo':

> Ja! Ich weiss, woher ich stamme!
> Ungesättigt gleich der Flamme
> Glühe und verzehr ich mich.
> Licht wird alles, was ich fasse,
> Kohle alles, was ich lasse:
> Flamme bin ich sicherlich.

[1] Lecture 10 of *The Pre-Platonic Philosophers*.

(Yes, I know whence I have sprung! Insatiable as a flame I burn and consume myself! Whatever I seize hold on becomes light, whatever I leave, ashes: certainly I am a flame. FW *Vorspiel* 62)

The philosopher who conducts the very un-Socratic dialogue in the lectures of 1872 called *On the Future of our Educational Institutions* is at once a prevision of Nietzsche as a solitary, and a modern version of Heraclitus. This is how the philosopher describes his role:

> . . . do you wish to live a solitary life in hostile isolation from [the] multitude?
> . . . Do you suppose that you can reach in one leap what I finally had to win for myself only after long and determined struggle, in order even to be able to live like a philosopher? And do you not fear that solitude will revenge itself upon you? Just try living the life of a hermit of culture—one must possess overflowing wealth in order to live for the good of all on one's own resources! (Lecture 1)

Nietzsche's largest-scale portrait of himself in his Heraclitean posture is the figure of Zarathustra, a proud and lonely truth-finder prouder, lonelier and more enigmatic even than his model.

But there was another side to Nietzsche's persona: the patient investigator, the 'scientific' philosopher who examined small, individual questions and sought to understand reality in its details. It was this side of him which had expressed itself when he called philosophy an 'experiment' (*Versuch*), and which adopted experimentation as a philosophical method:

> Give me any kind of sceptical proposal to which I am permitted to reply: 'Let's try it!' [*Versuchen wir's!*] But I want to hear nothing more of any thing or any question which does not permit of experimentation. (FW 51)

This side of him he identified with Socrates. The locus classicus for the argument that Nietzsche admired Socrates and modelled himself upon him is chapter 13 of Kaufmann's book, and to this I must refer the reader. The Socratic tone—reasonable, logical, mildly sarcastic, mocking and self-mocking—is more frequent in Nietzsche than those who know only Zarathustra would suppose. Moreover, Socrates himself—a far more lively and realistic figure than the largely fictional Heraclitus—was a 'problem' for Nietzsche which occupied him all his days: the 'Problem of Socrates' (G II) was the problem of reason itself, and the recognition that reason, the faculty of ratiocination, was a questionable faculty was what made it possible for Nietzsche both to admire Socrates and to call him a 'decadent'. In the 'Essay in

Self-Criticism' prefaced to the 1886 edition of *The Birth of Tragedy* Nietzsche says that the 'task' of the book had been to 'take hold of . . . the *problem of inquiry itself* . . .' (GT Vorrede 2):

> . . . what, viewed as a symptom of life, is the meaning of all inquiry? What is the end—or worse, what is the beginning—of all inquiry? Is the spirit of inquiry perhaps no more than fear in the face of pessimism and flight from it? A subtle means of self-defence against—the *truth?* And, morally speaking, something like cowardice and falsehood? Amorally speaking, a piece of slyness? (GT *Vorrede* 1)

This question-mark set against philosophy as such was personified for Nietzsche in the figure of Socrates, the man who had become 'absurdly rational'. Socrates had had to fight the instincts of his age, and 'To *have* to fight against the instincts is the formula for *décadence:* as long as life is *ascending,* happiness and instinct are one' (G II 11). But all philosophers fight against the instincts of their age:

> What does a philosopher firstly and lastly require of himself? To overcome his age in himself . . . I am, as much as Wagner, a child of this age, that is, a *décadent:* only I grasped this, only I defended myself against it. (W *Vorwort*)

Nietzsche had had to 'overcome his age', and to fight against the instincts of a decadent age was to be no less a decadent. Philosophy was precisely the self-questioning of life, and as such it was a symptom of decadence. The healthy life is a joyful life, he says, and where pain and suffering predominate over joy, life is unhealthy, i.e. decadent. The joyful life needs no explaining—it is its own justification; only where suffering predominates is an 'explanation' felt called for, and where explanations (i.e. philosophies) are offered, one may infer a state of affairs in which life is found distressful.

Darwin and the Greeks, then, and not Wagner and Schopenhauer, were the starting-point of Nietzsche's philosophy; and the reason his early works represent a false start is that he sought to interpret the Darwinian problem and the evidence of ancient Greece in the light of Wagnerian aesthetics and Schopenhaueran metaphysics. Not until he had put both behind him did he enter into his own proper field.

4

The Wagnerian–Schopenhaueran outlook dominates Nietzsche's first book, *The Birth of Tragedy,* which begins as a study of Greek culture and ends as a polemic for Wagnerian opera. It is laid out in twenty-five sections; the change in direction occurs in section 16, and the latter part of the book has the air of having been tacked on to an already complete thesis. *The Birth of Tragedy out of the Spirit of Music* was published in January 1872. Two years previously Nietzsche had delivered at Basel his lectures on *The Greek Music-Drama* and *Socrates and Tragedy,* neither of which has anything to do with Wagner and his artistic aims. In July 1870 he paid a visit to Tribschen in the company of Rohde and while he was there read to the company his *Greek Music-Drama.* 'Wagner had "certain doubts" about the lecture,' writes Newman, 'which he expressed to the young professor "in clear and searching" terms.' These 'doubts' of Wagner's were sufficient at this time to set Nietzsche worrying over the direction his thoughts on Greek culture were taking, and he made a better impression with a sketch for a book to be called 'The Origin of the Tragic Idea', which he presented to Cosima for Christmas 1870. 'Cosima was delighted with the sketch, but characteristically notes in her diary that she was "particularly pleased that Richard's ideas can find an extension in this field". As usual, she could see little reason for the young professor's existence except in so far as his Greek scholarship might be put to Wagnerian uses.'[1]

Work on *The Birth of Tragedy* proper must have begun about the beginning of 1871. On the 15th February Nietzsche was granted leave of absence from the university on account of ill-health and went to Lugano in the company of Elizabeth, where, Elizabeth tells us, he worked unceasingly on the new book. What this book was to be like must have been determined in his mind by the end of February at the latest, for it is described in a Foreword written during that month. This Foreword, addressed to Wagner but later rejected in favour of the much shorter one which stands at the head of the publication of 1872, makes it clear that the book was intended to be not about Wagner but about Greek culture and its meaning for the Germany of the 1870s. Its title was to be 'Greek Cheerfulness', and no discussion of Wagnerian music-drama enters into it.

At the beginning of April Nietzsche left Lugano to go back to Basel, but en route he called at Tribschen, arriving on the 3rd and staying until the 8th. It is a valid supposition that 'Greek Cheerfulness' was completed, or almost completed, and that Nietzsche took it with him to read to the Wagners. What happened during this week we can only guess, but there seems no avoiding the conclusion that Wagner persuaded Nietzsche to alter his book. This he proceeded to do when he returned to Basel, and on the 26th he sent the manu-

---

[1]The quotations are from Newman: op. cit., vol. 4 (London 1947), p. 319: the quotes-within-quotes are from Cosima's diary.

script of the beginning of the work to Fritzsch, saying that its 'real object' was to throw light upon Wagner in his relation to Greek tragedy: the title was now 'Music and Tragedy'. During October he was in Leipzig with Rohde and Gersdorff, and it was then that he handed Fritzsch the completed manuscript of *The Birth of Tragedy out of the Spirit of Music.* The short 'Foreword to Richard Wagner' is dated 'the end of 1871'.

The weight of the book is now thrown on to the argument that Wagnerian music-drama is a rebirth of antique tragedy, and if we had no other evidence this alone would suffice to show how far Nietzsche had succumbed to Wagner's influence. There is no suggestion in his letters of this time that he had altered his work unwillingly or against his better judgment: Wagner had talked to him and he now saw things in a different light—that is what it amounts to. Whatever changes were taking place within him he kept, for the moment, to himself; so far as his public actions were concerned he was willing to do anything to aid Wagner's cause. As for Wagner himself, he was incapable of acting in any way other than he did. To say that he rushed into print on the slightest provocation would be to understate the case. He had grasped the fundamental axiom of the craft of publicist—get your name known—and he spread his name over the German press in a way unexampled until the age of modern advertising. It has been said that he did himself more harm than good by many of his publications; that he was his own worst enemy where arousing unpopularity was concerned; and that his way would have been less rough had he restrained his inclination for public controversy. I think this highly doubtful. Wagner never worried about unpopularity or about being in the wrong, and no one has ever been more careless of his 'good name'. He did not desire a good name, he desired power and fame; and because he really desired them he had them. Later generations have been under the illusion it was the Wagnerian *operas* which created the commotion which surrounded the name of Wagner during the latter half of his life, whereas the truth of the matter is that Wagner himself created both the operas *and* the commotion almost independently of one another: if he had been a cobbler he would have made himself the most talked-about cobbler in the history of boots. So we need not ask whether *The Birth of Tragedy* was likely to further Wagner's cause to account for his interest in it. Nietzsche's book would provide an organ of publicity: that sufficed.

The effect of the book on the public was what might have been anticipated: the convinced Wagnerians thought it wonderful, and the first edition was soon exhausted, but to members of Nietzsche's own profession it seemed little short of a jettisoning of scientific standards in favour of propaganda. This was the opinion of Ritschl, to whom Nietzsche sent an advance copy at the end of December 1871: he recorded in his diary for the 31st the comment '*geistreiche*

Schwiemelei', which may be paraphrased as 'intellectual debauch'. Nietzsche waited a month and then wrote to him on the 30th January expressing disappointment at not having received his observations. Ritschl replied on the 14th February. He was polite but he left his opinion in no doubt: he objected to the book on the ground it was not scholarly but dilettante, and that this might lead young students to undervalue exact knowledge. The charge is about the gravest that could have been brought against a professional philologist, and it is perfectly justified; but the tone in which it was delivered took much of the sting out of it, and when Nietzsche sent it on to Rohde he remarked that Ritschl had 'lost none of his friendly generosity towards me'.

The first public retort came on the 1st June, with the publication of Ulrich von Wilamowitz-Möllendorff's *Zukunftsphilologie!* Wilamowitz, a philologist who had been a pupil at Pforta at the same time as Nietzsche, considered *The Birth of Tragedy* an impudent perversion of philology for Wagnerian ends and accused its author of gross errors of fact and general incompetence. Wilamowitz's attack was countered in October by Rohde's *Afterphilologie*, described as an 'Open Letter from a Philologist to Richard Wagner'. Rohde accused Wilamowitz of 'boundless stupidity and boundless untruthfulness' and of failing to understand what Nietzsche was driving at. Nietzsche supplied his friend with material for *Afterphilologie*, and wrote him on the 25th October that he and Rohde's other associates had found the pamphlet 'Lessing-like'. But this was not the sum of what the stupid Wilamowitz had called down upon his untruthful head: in a November issue of the *Musikalisches Wochenblatt* appeared an 'Open Letter to Friedrich Nietzsche, Professor of Classical Philology at the University of Basel' indited by the *Meister* himself. Wagner no doubt meant well, but his defence of Nietzsche, rightly castigated by Newman as 'the bluster of an incorrigible amateur', must have done more harm than any attack.[1] At the beginning of 1873 Wilamowitz returned to the fray with *Zukunftsphilologie! Zweites Stück*, which is directed against Rohde rather than Nietzsche. The exchange had by then declined into farce: Wilamowitz's first contribution had set the tone with its abuse of Nietzsche and his book; Rohde had retorted in kind; Wagner, whose arsenal of contumelious epithets was inexhaustible, had called Wilamowitz a 'scuffling peasant'; now Wilamowitz was back again, doubly redoubling strokes upon the foe. In later years Rohde and Wilamowitz both laughed at this youthful episode, and none of the shots exchanged really hits home: Ritschl's friendly letter does far more harm.

---

[1] Ellis's translation of Wagner's 'Open Letter' can be found in vol. 5 of the *Prose Works*.

What it all meant to Nietzsche is revealed in a letter to Wagner of mid-November 1872:

> After all that has happened to me lately I really have no right to be depressed, since I truly live in a solar system of friendship, comforting encouragement and strengthening hope. Yet there is one point that is disturbing me very greatly at the moment: our winter semester has started and I have absolutely no students! Our philologists have failed to appear! . . . The fact is very easily explained—I have suddenly got such a bad name among my professional colleagues that our little university is suffering for it! . . . Up to the last half-year the number of philologists was continually increasing—now it's as if they'd all blown away!

During the winter semester 1872–73 he delivered only one lecture, and this was to two non-philologists. His advocacy of Wagner was perhaps partly to blame, but his really serious error had been to treat in a wholly unprofessional way a subject in which he was supposed to be a professional specialist. We can see now that he had had certain philosophical ideas floating vaguely before his mind's eye, and in his study of antique tragedy he had tried to pin them down; but his contemporaries could see only what was before them in black and white: a thoroughly unscholarly study of a problem for the solution of which all the scholarly apparatus available would hardly have been sufficient.

Nietzsche's early philosophy, apart from those writings he abandoned or considered too slight for publication, comprises *The Birth of Tragedy* and the four *Untimely Meditations*. The field of inquiry is 'culture', and the aim is to discover what kind of culture will best promote the development of 'philosophers, artists, and saints'.

What is of value in *The Birth of Tragedy* is what links it with Nietzsche's philosophy as a whole: the hypothesis that creation is a product of contest, and that the creative force is controlled and redirected passion. What vitiates it is its reliance upon the duality of will and idea, nature and man—here called Dionysus and Apollo—the metaphysical character of which Nietzsche seems not to be fully aware. The book opens with an erroneous comparison indicative of confusion:

> We shall have gained much for aesthetics once we . . . have arrived at a direct apprehension that the evolution of art depends upon the duality of the *Apollonian* and the *Dionysian*, in the same way as the generation of life . . . depends upon the duality of the sexes. (GT 1)

The duality of the sexes is not a duality in the sense Apollo and Dionysus turn out to be: Apollo and Dionysus are imagined as opposed drives, while male and female are opposite aspects of the same drive. Nietzsche is thinking of Apollo and Dionysus not as phenomena but as disembodied 'principles', and as such they can be described only in metaphor: *dream* and *intoxication* stand towards one another in much the same relation as the Apollonian and Dionysian:

> Apollo, as the god of all plastic powers, is at the same time the soothsaying god . . . Apollo may be described as the glorious divine image of the *principium individuationis*, from whose gestures and looks there speaks to us the whole delight and wisdom of 'illusion', together with its beauty. . . . Dionysian rapture [arises] either through the influence of those narcotic potions of which all primitive peoples and races speak in their hymns, or through the powerful . . . approach of spring . . . [Man] feels himself to be god, he himself steps along with the same ecstasy and elation as the gods he has seen in dreams. Man is no longer an artist, he has become a work of art: the artistic power of all nature . . . is made manifest in this delirium. (GT 1)

The artist 'imitates' dreams or drunkenness, or, in a unique instance, both at once:

> In relation to these immediate creative conditions of nature, every artist is an 'imitator', either as Apollonian dream-artist or Dionysian intoxicated-artist or finally—as, for example, in Greek tragedy—as dream and intoxicated artist in one. (GT 2)

Apollonian art is an art of masks: unable to endure the face of reality, the artist masks it with 'illusions'. The Olympian pantheon is included here:

> The same drive that materialized in Apollo generated the whole Olympian world . . . What was the tremendous need out of which sprang so illustrious a society of Olympian beings? . . . The Greek knew and felt the terrors and horrors of existence: in order to be able to live at all he had to set before it the glittering dream-image of the Olympians . . . Wherever we encounter the 'naive' in art, we have to recognize the most potent effect of Apollonian culture, which always has first to overturn an empire of Titans, and kill monsters and, by means of powerful and joyful illusions, triumph over a dreadful insight into the depths of reality and an intense susceptibility to suffering . . . The 'naivete' of Homer can be understood only as a perfect victory of Apollonian illusion. (GT 3)

The thought is Schopenhaueran, the intrepidity Wagnerian; what is specifically Nietzschean is the language of combat: 'overturn an empire of Titans and kill monsters and . . . triumph over . . . suffering'. What seems like repose, and in the most successful case actually is repose, is the outcome of a conflict and a victory: that is Nietzschean. But this outlook is still involved in a confusing dualism: Dionysus appears to be a name for the reality of which the Greeks find it too painful to bear the sight; but there can be only one 'reality', and Apollo, who overcomes it, must be part of it; yet he is set over against it. This is still the world as will and idea.

Nietzsche's theory of the rise and fall of tragedy is reduceable, in its essence, to a few brief quotations:

> Drama is an Apollonian materialisation of Dionysian insights and powers. (GT 8)

> It is an unimpeachable tradition that Greek tragedy in its oldest form depicted only the sufferings of Dionysus, and that for most of the time Dionysus was the only hero. But it may be claimed with equal certainty that, to the time of Euripides, Dionysus never ceased to be the tragic hero, but that all the famous figures of the Greek stage . . . are only masks of that original hero Dionysus. (GT 10)

The greatness of Aeschylus and Sophocles lies in their having embodied Dionysus in Apollonian form. Their work was wrecked by Euripides:

> Greek tragedy . . . died by suicide, in consequence of an insoluble conflict. [Euripides fought against Aeschylus and Sophocles] not with polemics, but as a dramatic poet who set up *his* conception of tragedy against the traditional conception. (GT 11)

> To eliminate from tragedy that original and all-powerful Dionysian element and to construct it anew on the basis of un-Dionysian art, custom and philosophy— this is the . . . purpose of Euripides . . . Euripides was in a certain sense only a mask: the divinity which spoke through him was neither Dionysus nor Apollo, but a quite new daemon named *Socrates*. This is the new antithesis: the Dionysian and the Socratic, and the art-work of Greek tragedy perished through their conflict. (GT 12)

> The 'supreme law' of 'aesthetic Socratism' is ' "What is to be called beautiful must also be rational", a parallel to the Socratic dictum "Knowledge alone makes virtuous".' (GT 12)

Dionysus is the explosive ungoverned force of creation; Apollo is the power that governs him; who, then, is Socrates? Here is how Nietzsche describes him:

Socrates must be designated the specific *non-mystic,* in whom the logical has become, through superfetation, as overdeveloped as has the instinctive in the mystic. (GT 13)

[Socrates is the] type of the *theoretical man* . . . he seems to us to be the first who was able not only to live under the guidance of . . . the scientific instinct but— which is much harder—to die by it; and that is why the picture of the *dying Socrates*—man freed from fear of death by knowledge and reason—is the emblem above the portal of science which reminds us of the mission of science: to make existence seem intelligible and thereby justified. [Socrates is] a turning-point . . . of so-called world-history. (GT 15)

What drives Socrates is neither Apollo nor Dionysus, but something new: logic. From here onwards, Socratic optimism is set against Dionysian pessimism, and philosophy usurps the place of art.

Nietzsche considered *The Birth of Tragedy* a work of philosophy, and he designated it his 'first book', that is, as something distinct from the considerable quantity of work he had produced in the fields of philology, classical studies and philosophical reflections. In this context, the fact that modern scholarship has confirmed his intuition of the birth of tragedy from Apollo's harnessing of Dionysus seems almost an irrelevance; one is bound to side with those critics of his own day who thought the book eccentric and unscholarly. In the 'Essay in Self-Criticism' Nietzsche virtually repudiated it—and yet many of its insights were perfectly valid and in advance of their time. There is a lesson in this fact. In philosophy there is no such thing as being right for the wrong reasons: the reasons *are* the philosophy, and if the conclusion does not follow from them, it matters little that there might be other reasons from which it would follow. Nietzsche tries to show how tragedy originated in the rites of Dionysus, and he fails: the duality Apollo–Dionysus is not viable, because the origin of Apollo is not accounted for. Later he will conceive of Dionysus as will to power, and Apollo as the sublimation of Dionysus (and he will therefore use the name Dionysus to designate the entire creative force, Dionysus-plus-Apollo), but he does not arrive at this conclusion in *The Birth of Tragedy.* While, therefore, it may be right to say, as Francis Cornford does, that the book was 'a work of profound imaginative insight, which left the scholarship of a generation toiling in the rear',[1] scholarship had first to 'toil' before such a judgment could be made about *The Birth of Tragedy.*

[1]Cornford: *From Religion to Philosophy* (1912), p. 111.

6

Basel and Bayreuth

Wagner was merely one of my illnesses. Not that I should wish to be
ungrateful to this illness . . . the philosopher is not free to dispense with
Wagner . . . I would understand what a philosopher meant who declared:
'Wagner *summarises* modernity. There is nothing for it, one must first be
a Wagnerian.' (W *Vorwort*)

1

In his summing-up of Nietzsche's mental history, Kurt Hildebrandt concludes that between 1873 and 1880 he 'passed through a period of neurosis,
the fundamental cause of which was a psychical conflict', and the climactic
point of which was reached in 1879.[1] The course of his inner life during the
earlier part of this period, which came to a muffled climax with his flight from
and return to Bayreuth in 1876, constitutes an almost perfect mechanism for
the production of neurosis: increasing tension between his desire for independence and the feeling of subservience to Wagner; conflict between the world of
'free-thought' into which he was moving and the Teutonic-mystic 'Bayreuth
idea'; emotional frustration coinciding with the marriage of his closest friends;
ever-present ill-health the existence of which provided a retreat and 'excuse'
for indecision. Nietzsche later characterized the 'decadent' as one who desires
what harms him; we should, in this case, speak of the 'neurotic', and a sign that
Nietzsche was becoming neurotic during the mid-1870s is that his emotional
inclination was all towards what he knew intellectually he should be giving up:
hence the dichotomy between his private opinions on Wagner and Bayreuth
and those expressed in his published works. He could see that the 'ideological'

[1]Hildebrandt: *Gesundheit und Krankheit in Nietzsches Leben und Werk* (Berlin 1926), p. 159.
Hildebrandt, who was head-physician of the Heilstätten Wittenau, Berlin, can find no 'insanity' in
Nietzsche's life and work until the last quarter of 1888.

86

side to Wagner, which had been subordinate while he was the lonely artist in his Tribschen retreat, had come more and more to the fore after he had gone to Bayreuth, and that with this ideology he would sooner or later have to break; but when he saw Wagner at work, heard his voice and his music, associated with his family and his collaborators, or listened to attacks upon him from men who were unworthy to fasten his shoes, his old love for the man and his mission reasserted itself with irresistible force. At such times the idea of deserting him seemed unthinkable; yet it continued to be thought. He confided his doubts to his notebooks, but this did not dispel them: his whole way of thinking was changing, or rather it was returning to something like what it had been before he had met Wagner. His letters to his friends were still full of enthusiasm for the cause, and this was not feigned: he desired to be a Wagnerian still. As the first festival drew nearer his psychic condition grew worse, and his retreats into illness more frequent. In the summer of 1875 he was apparently as keen as any of his friends to attend the orchestral rehearsals at Bayreuth; but although Overbeck, Rohde and Gersdorff were there, he was in Steinabad, a small Black Forest resort for stomach complaints. Taking into account all we know of him at this time, we cannot doubt that the stomach trouble which drove him to Steinabad and away from Bayreuth at just this moment was psycho-somatic in origin. His chronic indecision about Wagner, his inability to come down wholeheartedly for or against, manifested itself most clearly, as might be expected, at the time of the festival itself.

Nietzsche paid his last visit to Tribschen on the 25th April 1872 and stayed until the 27th; Wagner had left for Bayreuth on the 22nd, and Cosima was engaged in packing his books, letters and manuscripts. Nietzsche stayed on to help her. Wagner's departure for a place as (relatively) far away as Franconia marks the beginning of Nietzsche's long process of liberation: even if he had not been subconsciously turning away from Wagner, the increased distance between them would of itself have loosened the bonds.

The ceremony of laying the foundation stone of the Festival Theatre had been fixed for Wagner's birthday, the 22nd May. Nietzsche went to Bayreuth on the 18th, and on the 22nd he accompanied Wagner in his carriage to the theatre site on the hill outside the town. It was pouring with rain, and formalities were kept as brief as possible: Wagner smote the stone, followed by some of his collaborators and singers, and clambered back into the carriage looking, says Newman, 'deathly pale'. It was, in all conscience, a moving, perhaps even daunting, moment for him, and Nietzsche included in *Richard Wagner in Bayreuth* a description of him sitting silent and withdrawn as they drove back to the town. The remaining formalities took place in the old opera house, and Nietzsche was also present there in the evening when Wagner conducted Beethoven's Ninth Symphony. Rohde and Gersdorff were also in Bayreuth, and among other guests Nietzsche met was Malwida von Meysenbug, who was to be as good a friend to him as she had been to Wagner.

He next saw the Wagners in the following November. In the interim, Elizabeth paid the first of her long visits to Basel, arriving on the 1st June and staying until the end of September; she was now a slim and prim young lady of 26, still unmarried and still living for most of the year with their mother at Naumburg. On the 10th November Wagner and Cosima set out on a tour of German opera houses in search of singers for the *Ring*. They were in Strassburg from the 22nd to the 25th, and there Nietzsche joined them for a couple of days.[1] As a consequence of something said during this meeting he was expected at Bayreuth for Christmas and New Year. Either he failed to realize this or he deliberately stayed away: he spent Christmas in Naumburg, where he and Krug made music as of old. Gersdorff, who *had* been in Bayreuth at the end of 1872, visited Nietzsche in Basel the following January, but made no reference to Nietzsche's being in Wagner's bad books: this information reached him only in February, when he received a letter from Cosima thanking him for the Christmas present of the *Five Prefaces to Five Unwritten Books*. He refers to it in a noteworthy letter to Gersdorff of the 24th of that month. Since Gersdorff's departure, he says, he has been ill again, and the three-day Shrovetide Carnival at Basel had so worked on his nerves that he has been forced to 'flee' to Gersau, on Lake Lucerne. He has received letters from Wagner and Cosima which have revealed to him that Wagner had been very annoyed with him.

> God knows how often I give the *Meister* offence, [he writes;] each time it happens it takes me by surprise, and I cannot understand what has caused it . . . Tell me what you think about these repeated offences.[2] I cannot imagine how anyone could be more faithful to Wagner in all essentials or more deeply devoted than I am: if I *could* imagine it, I would be more so. But I have to preserve some freedom for myself in small, subsidiary matters, and in a sort of necessary 'sanitary' abstention from *frequent* personal association—but this is really only so as to be able to remain faithful to him in a higher sense . . . This time I had not imagined for a moment I had given such grave offence; and I am afraid that such experiences will make me even more uneasy than I am already.

[1]Not in Stuttgart, as Newman says (op. cit., vol. 4, p. 370); the Wagners stayed in Stuttgart only one day, the 21st, and then went on to Strassburg. See Otto Strobel: *Richard Wagner. Leben und Schaffen. Eine Zeittafel* (Bayreuth 1952), p. 106.
[2]This suggests there were many more occasions of 'offence' than have been left on record.

The inner resistance to Wagner is asserting itself more forcefully—but so, at the same time, is a refusal to admit its existence. Nietzsche resents Wagner's touchiness—but he blames himself for it; he needs to preserve his freedom—but only in order to serve the better. This was a condition that could not last: in the long run he would have to abandon all thought of independence or he would have to abandon Wagner.

Two events of 1873, however, served to tie him, for the moment, more closely than ever. He and Rohde were in Bayreuth from the 7th to the 12th April, and Wagner told them of the difficulties facing the Bayreuth plan: unless more money was forthcoming the entire undertaking was in danger of collapse. Nietzsche returned to Basel imbued with the Master's rage and chagrin, and at once began venting his spleen on the wretched German nation, which was standing by while its greatest son went down, in the first of the *Untimely Meditations—David Strauss, the Confessor and the Writer*. During the spring and summer the financial situation of Bayreuth deteriorated still further, and by August it was in such a way that a public appeal for funds was proposed; Wagner suggested that a manifesto to go with it should be written by Nietzsche. A meeting of the *Vereine* was due to be held at the end of October to discuss future plans, and the manifesto would be submitted to them for their consideration. Nietzsche drafted his manifesto, *Mahnruf an die Deutschen* (Exhortation to the Germans), in the third week of October and took it with him for the assembly to be held on the 31st. Wagner had had the idea that an inspection visit to the festival hill would encourage the delegates with a sight of the theatre going up, but he had failed to take into account the one thing in Bayreuth still outside his control: the weather was fine on the 30th and on the 1st November, but on the 31st the skies opened and the tour of inspection was held ankle-deep in mud, and the growing theatre was viewed through a curtain of teeming rain; Nietzsche was called upon to make another sacrifice in the Wagnerian cause, this time in the form of a new hat, which was ruined in the downpour. At the town hall delegates listened to the *Mahnruf* and applauded but rejected it; a more moderately-toned appeal by one Adolf Stern, of Dresden, was adopted a few days later, Nietzsche's being held in reserve. It was never issued; its tone is admonitory, accusatory almost, and it reads less like an appeal than a threat. Nietzsche appears to have forgotten that its object was to persuade people not initially sympathetic to give money. (Not that Herr Stern's effort succeeded in doing that: the appeal failed hopelessly.)

The summer months saw his life proceeding along its accustomed lines: Elizabeth came to Basel at the beginning of June and stayed with him until the 21st October; he spent a month's holiday from mid-July to mid-August at

Graubünden in the company of Gersdorff; at the beginning of October Rohde paid a visit. More important, his students were returning. During the summer semester of 1872 he had opened a series of lectures on *The Pre-Platonic Philosophers*, and the series was resumed during the summer of 1873; nine students attended, plus two non-student listeners. One of these was Gersdorff; the other, Paul Rée.

Rée was a pioneer of the psychological approach to problems of philosophy and as such exercised a profound influence on Nietzsche: when *Human, All Too Human* appeared in 1878 those of his friends who were dismayed by its tone and outlook blamed Rée, and Nietzsche himself called his new outlook 'Réealism'. Rée had arrived in his life, in fact, at just the moment at which he could function most effectively as a catalyst to Nietzsche's as yet obscure dissatisfaction with the world of thought in which he was involved. Rée was 23 in 1873 and intellectually even more precocious than Nietzsche. He had been a law-student but the Franco-Prussian War had interrupted his studies, and afterwards he had relinquished law in favour of philosophy. When he first met Nietzsche he was already full of the ideas which were to find their first tentative expression in 1875 in his short book *Psychologische Beobachtungen* (Psychological Observations), and a fuller exposition in 1877 in his major work *Der Ursprung der moralischen Empfindungen* (The Origin of the Moral Sensations). The latter was written during 1876–77 at Sorrento in company with Nietzsche, who was writing *Human, All Too Human*, and Nietzsche's copy of it carries the dedication in Rée's hand: 'To the father of this work, with most grateful thanks, from its mother'; nonetheless, the priority was undoubtedly Rée's, and it is only a false perspective that makes the title of his main work seem 'Nietzschean'—the truth being that similar titles in Nietzsche's works were suggested to him by the example of Rée (e.g. the second chapter of *Human, All Too Human:* 'Towards a History of the Moral Sensations'; and the fifth chapter of *Beyond Good and Evil:* 'Towards a Natural History of Morals'). Rée was an atheist who realized that the 'religious experience' was a reality and tried to account for it with the notion of 'subjectivism': belief in God was, he thought, a subjective phenomenon which could be accounted for independently of whether God had any objective existence. The religious experience was an 'interpretation', not a given fact, and the origin of this interpretation could be discovered through an examination of the general nature of human beings: that is, through *psychology.* Of particular importance for Nietzsche was Rée's investigation of morality: according to Rée, morality was custom and not 'nature', there was no specific moral sense, and good and evil were no more than conventions. What struck Nietzsche about him was what he called his 'coldness', by which he meant his independence and clarity, as a thinker: 'coldness' was precisely what Nietzsche himself lacked at this time. Rée's later philosophy does not concern us: his 'subjectivism' developed into an almost perfect solipsism which recalls Fichte at his most extreme and which, as Bertrand Russell says of Fichte, seems almost to involve a kind of insanity. Having arrived at the insight that the world was 'meaningless', his mind seems to have been paralysed by the idea: it was the end, as well as the beginning, of his philosophy. For Rée, the senselessness of existence was a source of despair; for Nietzsche, on the contrary, it became the ground of freedom. 'What would there be to create if gods—existed?' Zarathustra exclaims (Z II 2): to this state of mind Rée could never attain.

The year 1874 was decisive for the Nietzsche–Wagner relationship. Nietzsche's notebooks dated January of that year are full of critical comments on Wagner, as a man and as an artist, and the second *Meditation—On the Use and Disadvantage of History for Life*—which appeared in February, deals with considerations remote from Wagner's concerns.

In that same month the financial difficulties of Bayreuth were temporarily ended by the offer of a subsidy by King Ludwig, and after a few changes of plan the first festival was definitely fixed for the summer of 1876. In the meantime, Wagner pushed ahead with completing *Götterdämmerung*, and he was engaged on scoring the third act when Nietzsche paid what was to be his last private visit. It was a painful one, and his behaviour is the clearest evidence that his feelings towards Wagner were by this time decidedly ambivalent. During the spring and summer he had been writing the third *Meditation— Schopenhauer as Educator*—and his own work was coming to seem more important to him in and for itself, and not as a mere appendix to Wagner. He reveals as much in a letter to Gersdorff of the 4th July. Gersdorff, who was still heart and soul with Wagner, appears to have sensed a cooling on Nietzsche's part; Nietzsche denies it, but a few lines later he virtually admits it, inasmuch as he excuses it: even within the bounds of a short letter he cannot now maintain a consistent attitude:

How did you get the odd notion, dear friend, that I should be forced to visit Bayreuth by a threat? [he asks.] One would think I didn't want to go there of my own free will—and yet I joined the people at Bayreuth twice last year and twice the year before last—and all the way from *Basel* . . . We both know, of course, that Wagner's nature tends strongly towards *mistrust*—but I haven't been thinking it would be a good idea to stir up this mistrust even more. Finally— remember I have duties towards myself which are very hard to fulfil in my very defective state of health. Really, no one should force me to do anything.

A month later he went to Bayreuth and stayed with the Wagners at their new house, Wahnfried, until the 15th August. Why did he go? In the above-quoted letter he had advised Gersdorff against visiting Wahnfried on the ground that 'their house and their lives are in a state of confusion and it would not be a suitable time just now'. The Wagners had moved into Wahnfried on the 28th April; another month had passed, but Wagner was now busier than ever. The orchestration of the closing act of the *Ring* was the most colossal task of its kind even he had undertaken, and this alone should have ruled out any unnecessary interruption. (*Götterdämmerung,* and therewith the entire *Nibelung's Ring,* was completed on the 21st November.) In addition he had already begun rehearsing the earlier parts of the tetralogy, and he was occupied with this during the whole month of August. (The pianist Karl Klindworth was staying at Wahnfried to assist him.) Nietzsche's arrival was unexpected and not very welcome: he was, in fact, in the way, as he must have realized he would be. Was that, perhaps, precisely the reason for his visit: to annoy Wagner? If so, he succeeded.

On the 8th and 9th June Nietzsche had attended two concerts given in Basel by Brahms. Brahms' music held little appeal for him, but one of the objections to Wagner which appear in his notebooks at this time is that Wagner was unable to appreciate the qualities of the other great German composer of his day. It was no secret that Wagner disliked Brahms as a man and was unable to warm towards him as a composer, and contempt for Brahms was almost a dogma in the Wagnerian legion. It must therefore have been with malice aforethought that Nietzsche took with him to Wahnfried a piano score of Brahms's *Triumphlied* and left it on the piano in the music room. He played pieces from it, and when it was removed he put it back. It was a large, red-bound score, and every time Wagner came into the room there it was with the detested name printed across it. The upshot of all this was a scene, with Wagner red-faced and angry at what he took to be deliberate provocation on Nietzsche's part and Nietzsche (according to Elizabeth) icy calm and silent. Here we may allow Elizabeth to be telling the truth: Wagner's lack of self-control was famous, but the storm when it came was of such violence that it quickly blew itself out; Nietzsche, on the other hand, was far too inhibited to be capable of this kind of air-clearing thunderclap, and it is quite consistent with the nature of both men that Wagner should have shouted and stormed and Nietzsche remained silent. But this does not mean he remained indifferent: instead of reacting to a real or imagined offence with a forthright rejoinder, as Wagner did, he treasured it in his heart and carried it with him through the years; and we may feel sure that when he came to indite his anti-Wagner writings of 1888 the scene of August 1874 was still clearly in his mind.

His action regarding the Brahms score must be seen as a deliberate (and successful) attempt to provoke Wagner: it was a miniature rebellion. After he had left on the 15th in the company of Overbeck he did not see Wagner again until July 1876, almost two years later. In the interim the conflict within him grew sharper. His health grew worse, and on the 2nd January 1875 he wrote to Malwida von Meysenbug, from Naumburg, where he spent Christmas:

> Yesterday, the first day of the year, I looked into the future and trembled. Life is dreadful and hazardous—I envy anyone who is well and truly dead.

To Gersdorff he wrote in June that he had been so unwell—'headaches of the most violent kind lasting for several days and then returning after only a few days' interval, vomiting for hours at a time without my having eaten anything'—that his doctor had told him he must forget about going to Bayreuth for the rehearsals that summer. He asks Gersdorff to prepare the Wagners for the news that he will be absent: 'Wagner will be angry; I am angry at it too.' As already mentioned he went to Steinabad instead of to Bayreuth, and his letters from there to Rohde, Gersdorff and others should be read for an understanding of his spiritual condition at this time. They are *not* the letters of a serious invalid, and the activities recounted in them—early-morning bathing in water too cold for the other patients, two-hour walks before breakfast—suggest the writer was not so ill that sitting in a theatre would have been too much for him. As soon as he reached Steinabad, in fact, he began to feel much better, and he lapsed back into his former condition only after returning to Basel. There he was joined by Elizabeth, who had decided to settle in the town for a time and set up home for herself and her brother; Nietzsche found the resulting domesticity much to his liking.

Two other events of 1875 helped to disengage him from Wagner: the publication of Rée's *Psychological Observations* and the arrival in Basel of Peter Gast. (Gast's real name was Heinrich Köselitz; he adopted his pseudonym when he began to work seriously as a composer, and he is generally known by it.) In December of the previous year Gast had met Overbeck at the office of the Chemnitz publisher Ernst Schmeitzner, who was later to become Nietzsche's publisher, and had decided to go to Basel to study. His meeting with Nietzsche was the turning-point of his life. From being Nietzsche's student he became his 'disciple'; and although his devotion was not quite so extreme as is generally thought (or as Nietzsche himself perhaps believed), it was sufficiently intense to seem somewhat unhealthy, especially in view of the closeness of their ages—Gast was only seven years younger than his idol. As early as the summer of 1876 we find him acting as Nietzsche's amanuensis, and by 1879 he was, not to mince words, in love with him. For our knowledge of Gast's feelings during the years 1879 to 1881 we are indebted to a series of letters he wrote to an Austrian woman friend.[1] In the letter of the 12th September 1879 Gast says he has just learned that Nietzsche is on the point of death. The news has set him 'sobbing and weeping'. 'I have never loved a man as I do *him*,' he writes, 'not even my father . . . I feel as if my greatest duty lay in dying with him. I cannot describe this feeling.' For much of 1880 he was Nietzsche's sole support, and his kindness was abused in a way that only Nietzsche's desperately sick condition can excuse; time and again he lost patience with the demanding invalid, time and again he reproached himself for it: 'You know that I will do anything I can for Nietzsche,' he writes on the 15th March, 'for I cannot just look on and see so excellent a man left helpless and deserted.' By the following October Nietzsche's health had improved a little, and he seems to have been conscious he had acted badly towards Gast: he wrote to him that he reproached himself for having demanded so much of the latter's time. Gast repeats this to his Austrian friend, and adds: 'In the moral sphere I stand far below Nietzsche; I realise it from every word he writes: everything proceeds from a great soul' (letter of the 22nd October). His sense that Nietzsche was an exceptional man and that, all annoyances apart, he was really in need of help, always brought Gast back to his side, actually or metaphorically. In the Nietzsche cult of later years Gast functioned as the proto-apostle, the first of the few, and his activities in this role are certainly open to censure. Nor can it be denied that his understanding of Nietzsche's philosophy was minimal, or that he encouraged tendencies in Nietzsche which a wiser man would have tried to curb. Against this must be set the fact that he brought to Nietzsche a warmth of approval for which he looked in vain elsewhere. A creative writer needs criticism, but he also needs someone to believe in him and so reinforce his belief in himself. Gast believed in Nietzsche, and this, for the Nietzsche student, is his virtue.

At Christmas 1875, which he spent at Naumburg, Nietzsche sustained his first general collapse. A period of prostration followed, and although he gradually improved he was forced to abandon temporarily his work at Basel. In search of health he went to Lake Geneva with Gersdorff during March 1876, and in the early days of April to the city of Geneva. He was by then sufficiently recovered to enjoy playing the role of tourist and to propose marriage to Mathilde Trampedach.

[1]Printed in Erich Podach: *Gestalten um Nietzsche* (Weimar 1932), pp. 71 ff.

It is at odds with received opinion about Nietzsche, and yet it is true, that for much of his life he was on the look-out for a wife. Those passages in his letters in which he disclaims the idea of marriage are balanced by those in which he discusses its possibility and by the two proposals we know him to have made, both of which were produced so soon after meeting the lady in question that the thought of finding a wife must have been present in his mind *before* meeting her. The subject of marriage was very much in the air among Nietzsche's circle: Pinder and Krug were married in 1874, and he met their wives at Naumburg during the Christmas of that year; Overbeck became engaged in 1875 and was married in 1876; Rohde became engaged in 1876 and was married in 1877; Gersdorff also married in 1877. Since Nietzsche himself did not marry we must suppose that in the last resort there was something within him resisting it, but the evidence forbids us to assume he was opposed to marriage from the first or on principle. He certainly wanted to marry Lou Salomé in 1882, and he frequently discusses the possibility of a 'convenient' marriage in his letters to Elizabeth. Whether his desire to marry Mathilde Trampedach was truly serious is more doubtful. He had arrived in Geneva on the 6th April and made the acquaintance of the young conductor Hugo von Senger, who introduced him to Mathilde: she was not yet engaged to Senger but the two had an 'understanding'. She was 21 and exceptionally pretty and self-assured: she probably behaved towards Nietzsche in a more familiar and affectionate way than he was used to expect, and he no doubt misunderstood her. On the 11th they spent an intense evening together discussing poetry and the higher things of life, and back at his hotel he wrote her a brief proposal of marriage. He has to return to Basel the following morning, he says, but his letter will be brought to her by Senger: an unfortunate choice of messenger, but one which proves he could not have known of the relations between Senger and Mathilde. (He committed a similar blunder when he proposed to Lou Salomé through Paul Rée, who already had an arrangement with her himself. On this occasion, however, he repeated the proposal in person.) Mathilde wrote him in Basel turning him down. Later she married Senger. She had never thought of Nietzsche as a prospective husband, and so far as we know she never met him again. Her letter of refusal was a skilled piece of work, since it made Nietzsche feel he ought to apologize for having proposed at all. His reply, of the 15th April, is submissive:

> You have been generous enough to forgive me; I feel it from the gentle tone of your letter, which I really did not deserve . . . I have only one last wish: that if you ever read my name or see me again, you will not remember the fright I caused you. I ask you to believe in any case that I should like to make amends for my ill conduct.

One senses in these words a certain relief. Had he regretted his sudden proposal, and was he now glad it had not been accepted? It seems likely: love is not love which alters between the 11th of the month and the 15th.

The climax of this period of Nietzsche's life came with the first Bayreuth Festival. Bearing in mind what had gone before we can understand his behaviour without much difficulty. The festival proper was due to begin on the 13th August and to consist of three complete cycles of the *Ring*. Nietzsche arrived on the 23rd July, towards the end of the second cycle of rehearsals. He was a sick man and ought not to have gone: but this time he could not bring himself to stay away. The first act of *Götterdämmerung* was rehearsed on the evening of his arrival, and he attended but had to leave in the middle because of a headache. On the following day he was present at the rehearsal of the second act and on the 26th of the third act. A third rehearsal cycle began on the 29th: Nietzsche attended the *Rheingold* on that day and the *Valkyrie* on the 31st, but on the latter occasion his eyes were so bad he was unable to look at the stage, and the following morning he wrote Elizabeth he was leaving because he could endure no more. On the 2nd or 3rd August he went to the resort of Klingenbrunn in the Bohemian Forest, whence he wrote his sister, who was then in Bayreuth:

> I know quite definitely that I can *not* endure it there; we ought to have realised that beforehand! Remember how circumspectly I have had to live during recent years. I feel so wearied and exhausted by my short stay there I shall be hard put to it to recover.

He stayed at Klingenbrunn for ten days and spent much of his time writing, despite a persistent headache: the material formed part of *Human, All Too Human*. (According to a letter he wrote to Mathilde Maier two years later he sketched about a third of the whole book—i.e. of volume one in the final edition.) During these ten days he gradually recovered, and when Elizabeth asked him to return to Bayreuth he complied: he arrived back on the 12th August and witnessed the first public cycle of the *Ring* from the 13th to the 17th. (There was no performance on the 15th.) The second cycle was given between the 20th and the 23rd, but Nietzsche did not attend—he had given his tickets away—and on the 27th, the day the third and last cycle began, he returned to Basel. In view of his close connection with Wagner he could have been at the centre of things throughout the festival, but he chose instead to remain on the perimeter, apparently not enjoying himself in the least. He stayed at Malwida's house—he could, one imagines, have stayed at Wahnfried had he desired—and avoided Wagner as if he feared personal contact. Few noticed he had left, and they were glad to see the back of him: his moroseness and ill-humour had been sadly at odds with the prevailing mood of elation and satisfaction.

That, for Nietzsche, was 'Bayreuth'. His disappointment was acute, and he cursed his ill-health: in later years, however, he attributed his behaviour to a sudden enlightenment about the nature of the festival:

> Anyone who has any idea what visions had been flitting across my path even at that time can guess how I felt when I one day came to myself in Bayreuth. It was as if I had been dreaming . . . Where was I? I recognised nothing, I hardly recognised Wagner. In vain I scanned my memories. Tribschen—a distant isle of the blessed: not the shadow of a resemblance. The incomparable days of the foundation-stone laying, the little band of *initiates* who celebrated them and who did not lack fingers for delicate things: not the shadow of a resemblance. *What had happened?*—Wagner had been translated into German! The Wagnerian had become master of Wagner! . . . Truly, a hair-raising crowd! . . . Not a single abortion was missing, not even the anti-Semite.—Poor Wagner! To what a pass had he come!—Better for him to have gone among swine! But among Germans! (EH–MA 2)

And much more in the same vein. Like so much in *Ecce Homo* it is fearfully overdriven and exaggerated—but not for that reason untrue. The 'ideological' side to Wagner—the German nationalist and anti-Semite—which even in 1888 Nietzsche preferred to think had never been part of the man's essential make-up, had come to the fore and could no longer be ignored: 'Bayreuth' was not only Wagner the great artist, it was Wagner the Teutonic mystagogue as well. It is important to notice that the 'new' Nietzsche, the author of *Human, All Too Human,* already existed *before* the festival of 1876 had properly begun: the festival itself was the occasion, and not the cause, of Nietzsche's intellectual divorce from Wagner. (In this respect *Ecce Homo* is misleading.) The conflict within him had, metaphorically, torn him in half: emotionally he was with Wagner; intellectually he had repudiated him. The fourth *Meditation—Richard Wagner in Bayreuth*—which appeared in the second week of July 1876 but was mainly the work of 1875, is a final effort to heal the split, and in itself it is a success: Wagner has never been more sympathetically described. But within a month of its publication Nietzsche was at work on *Human, All Too Human,* which is quite definitely anti-Wagnerian and was recognized to be so by Wagner himself.

The key to an understanding of Nietzsche at this time which his contemporaries, and he himself, lacked is the concept of the psycho-somatic illness: it can hardly be doubted that his symptoms—stomach trouble, eye trouble, vomiting, chronic headaches—were of this kind, induced as a gross exacerbation of an existing weakness.

2

The four *Untimely Meditations* contain Nietzsche's thoughts on the nature of culture in the post-Darwinian world in general and in the *Reich* in particular. The tone is youthful, aggressive and uncompromising. The enemy is delineated in horrible detail in the opening *Meditation—David Strauss, the Confessor and the Writer:* he is the 'cultural Philistine', who hasn't the first idea of what culture really is but is ashamed to admit it. He is hard at work in the new *Reich:*

> Of all the evil consequences which have followed the recent war with France perhaps the worst is a widespread if not universal error . . . that German culture too was victorious in the struggle . . . This delusion . . . is capable of turning our victory into a complete defeat: *into the defeat if not the extirpation of the German spirit [Geist] for the benefit of the 'German Reich'.* (UI 1)

Nietzsche defines culture in a way that leaves the modern German denuded of it:

> Culture is, before all things, unity of artistic style in all the expressions of the life of a people. Much knowledge and learning, however, is neither an essential means to culture nor a sign of it, and if need be can get along very well with the opposite of culture, barbarism, which is lack of style or a chaotic jumble of all styles. But it is in this chaotic jumble of all styles that the German of our day dwells. (UI 1)

David Strauss's recent book *The Old Faith and the New* had been a huge success with the German public and was already considered a 'classic'; and this was proof that the 'cultural Philistine' was an imbecile in cultural matters.

The Old Faith and the New is a summary of Strauss's opinions: he disclaims all belief in revealed religion and pins his hopes upon a secular and rational culture, and the grounds of Nietzsche's objections are of importance for an understanding of his 'atheism' and of why he cannot be called a 'nineteenth-century rationalist'. Nineteenth-century rationalism was characterized by insight into the difficulty in accepting revealed religion, and obtuseness regarding the consequences of rejecting it. The characteristic tone of nineteenth-century rationalists is a manic cheerfulness: they are like prisoners set free. Strauss is a typical figure, and he sounds very old-fashioned today with his breezy self-confidence and bland approval of the way his world is going. Nietzsche's objection is not simply that he does not like this world, but that the moral and logical problems posed by the rationalist outlook have not been faced. In an aphorism of 1888 directed against George Eliot he formulates with the conciseness characteristic of his last years his basic argument against the conventional rationalist position:

> They have got rid of the Christian God, and now feel obliged to cling all the more firmly to Christian morality: that is *English* consistency . . . With us it is different. When one gives up Christian belief, one thereby deprives oneself of the *right* to Christian morality . . . Christianity is a system, a consistently thought out and *complete* view of things. If one breaks out of it a fundamental idea, the belief in God, one thereby breaks the whole thing to pieces . . . Christian morality is a command; its origin is transcendental . . . it possesses truth only if God is truth—it stands or falls with the belief in God.—If the English really do think they know, of their own accord, 'intuitively', what is good and evil . . . that itself is merely the *consequence* of the ascendency of Christian evaluation. (G IX 5)

Nietzsche really did give up belief in God, and his contempt for Strauss is rooted in the fact that Strauss only pretended to give it up, even if it was to himself that he pretended. Strauss does not suffer from the 'death of God' because he does not really believe in it; he can renounce Christianity and welcome Darwin as a benefactor of mankind without distress of spirit because he does not know what he is doing:

> He announces with admirable frankness that he is no longer a Christian, but he has no wish to disturb anyone's peace of mind . . . With a certain rude contentment he covers himself in the hairy cloak of our ape-genealogists and praises Darwin as one of the greatest benefactors of mankind—but it confuses us to see that his ethics are constructed entirely independently of the question: 'What is our conception of the world?' Here was an opportunity to exhibit native courage: for here . . . he ought to have boldly derived a moral code for life out of the *bellum omnium contra omnes* and the privileges of the strong. (UI 7)

Strauss had accepted a world of *bellum omnium contra omnes,* but was unable to explain how the characteristic qualities of humanity could have arisen in such a world, or how ethics are at all possible in a post-Darwinian universe:

> Strauss has not yet even learned that no idea can ever make men better or more moral, and that preaching morals is as easy as finding grounds for them is

difficult; his task was much rather to take the phenomena of human goodness, compassion, love and self-abnegation, which do in fact exist, and derive and explain them from his Darwinist presuppositions. (UI 7)

The distinction between Nietzsche and a rationalist of the type of Strauss is therefore clear: Strauss found the tenets of religion no longer credible, and believed that Darwin had demonstrated the truth of the evolution hypothesis, but continued to think and act as if nothing else had changed; but Nietzsche, when he arrived at the same conclusions, grasped the fact that everything else had changed, that the universe had ceased to possess any meaningful reality.

By attacking Strauss, Nietzsche had, in a negative way, committed himself to attempting the task Strauss had shirked: that is, to ask 'what is our conception of the world' after Darwin? The second *Meditation—On the Use and Disadvantage of History for Life*—approaches this question obliquely through a consideration of the most marked characteristic of his age when compared with past ages: its historical consciousness. The initial thought is that knowledge of the past is a burden to man (UII 1). It might be that happiness would be better promoted by ignorance of the past; in any event, forgetfulness of the past is a necessary concomitant of happiness and action (UII 1). But men cannot forget the past for more than a few moments at a time; they cannot become perfectly 'unhistorical', as the animals are; so they must learn to 'overcome' the past and to think 'supra-historically':

> . . . historical men believe that the meaning of existence will grow ever clearer in the course of its *process* . . . supra-historical men . . . see no salvation in this process; for them, rather, the world stands complete and has achieved its end in every single moment. (UII 1)

Mankind, Nietzsche says, is still young and it is a mistake to think of 'human nature' as a fixed quality. But just such a supposition lies behind the excess of historical consciousness from which the age suffers; and behind this supposition is a hangover from the Christian era and the influence of Hegel:

> . . . the human race is a tough and persistent thing and will not permit its progress to be viewed in terms of millennia, or indeed hardly in terms of hundreds of millennia . . . What is there in a couple of thousand years (or in other words the space of 34 consecutive generations of 60 years each) which permits us to speak of the 'youth' of mankind at the beginning and the 'old age' of mankind at the end? Is there not concealed in this paralysing belief that humanity is already declining a misunderstanding of a Christian theological idea inherited from the Middle Ages, the idea that the end of the world is coming,

that we are fearfully awaiting the Last Judgment? Is the increasing need for historical judgment not that same idea in a new dress . . . ? (UII 8)

> The belief that one is a late-comer of the ages is, in any case, paralysing and depressing; but it must appear dreadful and devastating when such a belief one day by a bold inversion raises this late-comer to godhood as the true meaning and goal of all previous events . . . Such a point of view has accustomed the Germans to talk of a 'world-process' and to justify their own age as the necessary result of this world-process. [This has been the effect of] the enormous and still-continuing influence [of Hegelian philosophy]. (UII 8)

Hegel has led modern man to call 'his way of living . . . "the full surrender of his personality to the world-process"' and to think of himself as the 'final target of the world-process'; and to the influence of Hegel has now been added that of Darwin:

> . . . now the history of mankind is only a continuation of the history of animals and plants; even in the profoundest depths of the sea the universal historian still finds traces of himself as living slime . . . He stands high and proud upon the pyramid of the world-process. (UII 9)

'Overproud European of the 19th century, you are raving mad!' Nietzsche exclaims. 'Your knowledge does not perfect nature, it only destroys your own nature' (UII 9). The cry is directed against those who had hailed Darwin as a saviour when in reality he had reduced them to worthlessness. Hegel and Darwin between them are going to lead in the near future to a nihilistic collapse of all values:

> If the doctrines of sovereign becoming, of the fluidity of all concepts, types and species, of the lack of any cardinal distinction between man and animal— doctrines which I consider true but deadly—are thrust upon the people for another generation with the rage for instruction that has by now become normal, no one should be surprised if . . . individualist systems, brotherhoods for the rapacious exploitation of the non-brothers, and similar creations . . . appear upon the stage of the future. (UII 9)

Against this approaching nihilism, Nietzsche sets the 'supra-historical' ideal:

> [The virtuous man] always rises against the blind power of facts, against the tyranny of the actual, and submits himself to laws that are not the laws of historical flux. He always swims against the tide of history, either by fighting his passions, as the nearest brute actualities of his existence, or by dedicating himself to honesty. (UII 8)

The time will come when one will prudently refrain from all constructions of the world-process or even of the history of man; a time when one will regard not the masses but individuals, who form a kind of bridge across the turbulent stream of becoming. These individuals do not carry forward any kind of process but live contemporaneously with one another, . . . they live as that Republic of Genius of which Schopenhauer once spoke . . . No, the *goal of humanity* cannot lie in its end but only *in its highest specimens.* (UII 9)

The production of these, Nietzsche thinks, is clearly a function of culture; and as an object lesson in how to create a living culture we have before us, as ever, the Greeks:

The God of Delphi cries to you . . . his oracle: 'Know thyself!' . . . There were centuries during which the Greeks found themselves faced by a danger similar to that which faces us: the danger of being overwhelmed by what was past and foreign, of perishing through 'history' . . . their culture was for a long time . . . a chaos of foreign, Semitic, Babylonian, Lydian, Egyptian forms and ideas, and their religion a battle of all the gods of the East . . . The Greeks gradually learned to *organise the chaos* by following the Delphic teaching and thinking back to themselves, that is, to their real needs . . . Thus they . . . did not long remain the overburdened heirs and Epigoni of the entire Orient . . . This is a parable for each one of us: he must organise the chaos within him by thinking back to his real needs . . . Thus he will discover the Greek idea of culture . . . —the idea of culture as a new and improved physis. (UII 10)

'Organising the chaos' is another way of describing Apollo's victory over Dionysus, but it is still a metaphor and to that extent unhelpful: Nietzsche is unable to say what is actually involved. Yet the cardinal concepts of his mature philosophy are already present in the *Meditation* on history, even if they are still unrelated: the concept 'organising the chaos' leads to the chapter 'Of Self-Overcoming' in *Zarathustra*, in which the will to power is first described; the idea that 'the *goal of humanity* cannot lie in its end but only *in its highest specimens*' leads to the *Übermensch*, the man who has organized the chaos within him; the outlook of the supra-historical man leads to the eternal recurrence. He has also been brought up more sharply than before against his typical problem of the 'true but deadly'. Darwinism is true but represents a calamity; the teaching that reality is 'becoming' and never is, is also true, but likewise a calamity. Neither can be denied: ultimately both will be surmounted.

The third *Meditation—Schopenhauer as Educator*—takes up the thought that the 'highest specimens' of mankind are its meaning, and that each individual may realize the 'Greek idea of culture . . . as a new and improved physis' by 'thinking back to his real needs'.

> The man who does not wish to belong to the mass needs only to cease taking himself easily and to follow his conscience, which calls to him: 'Be yourself! All you are now doing, thinking, desiring, is not you yourself!' (UIII 1)

> But how can we find ourselves again? How can man know himself? . . . The youthful soul should look back on life with the question: What have you truly loved up to now, what has drawn your soul aloft, what has mastered it and at the same time blessed it? Set up these things . . . before you and perhaps they will give you . . . the fundamental law of your own true self . . . for your real nature lies not buried deep within you but immeasurably high above you . . . There are other means of finding oneself, . . . but I know of none better than to think on one's educators. (UIII 1)

The essay that follows contains Nietzsche's thoughts on *his* 'educator', Schopenhauer. Significantly enough, there is hardly a word about Schopenhauer's philosophy; the emphasis is upon his independence of mind and situation, and his intellectual courage:

> I profit from a philosopher only in so far as he can be an example to me . . . But this example must be supplied by his outward life and not merely in his books . . . Kant clung to his university, submitted himself to its regulations, . . . so it is natural that his example has produced, above all, university professors and professorial philosophy. (UIII 3).

> Where there have been powerful societies, governments, religions, public opinions—in short, wherever there has been tyranny—there the solitary philosopher has been hated; for philosophy offers an asylum to man into which no tyranny can force its way. (UIII 3)

During the era of disintegration and tyranny which Nietzsche never doubted was coming, the philosopher of the type of Schopenhauer would preserve the 'image of man':

> For a century we have been preparing for an absolutely fundamental convulsion . . . Who is there to guard and champion *humanity* . . . amid the dangers of our period? Who will set up the *image of man* when men . . . have fallen to the level of the animals or even of automata? (UIII 4)

There have, he says, been three 'images of man' devised in the modern age, and he names them after Rousseau, Goethe and Schopenhauer. Rousseau's man is essentially the revolutionary, Goethe's the contemplative man. Schopenhauer's man is he who *'voluntarily takes upon himself the suffering involved in being truthful'* (UIII 4):

> . . . he who would live according to Schopenhauer . . . would seem more like a Mephistopheles than a Faust . . . All that exists that can be denied deserves to be denied; and being truthful means to believe in an existence that can in no way be denied . . . To be sure, he will destroy his earthly happiness through his courage; he will have to be an enemy to those he loves and to the institutions which have produced him; he may not spare men or things, even though he suffers when they suffer; he will be misunderstood and for a long time thought an ally of powers he abhors; . . . he will have to descend into the depths of existence with a string of curious questions on his lips: Why do I live? What lesson have I to learn from life? How have I become what I am and why do I suffer from being what I am? . . . He who regards his life as no more than a moment in the evolution of a race or of a state or of a science . . . has not understood the lesson of existence. (UIII 4)

The 'lesson of existence' is that only great individuals have any significance, and the great individual is he who is more than animal—more than man, *'Übermensch'*, in Nietzsche's later terminology:

> As long as anyone desires life as a pleasure he has not raised his eyes above the horizon of the animal, for he only desires more consciously what the animal seeks through blind impulse. But that is what we all do for the greater part of our lives . . . But there are moments *when we realise this:* . . . we see that, in common with all nature, we are pushing towards man as towards something that stands high above us. (UIII 5)

> —and who are they who can raise us up? They are those true *men, those who are no longer animal, the philosophers, artists and saints;* nature, which never makes a leap, has made her one leap . . . in creating them. (UIII 5)

> Mankind must work continually to produce individual great human beings— this and nothing else is its task . . . For the question is this: how can your life, the individual life, retain the highest value, the deepest significance? . . . Only by your living for the good of the rarest and most valuable specimens. (UIII 6)

> [Whoever does this] places himself within the circle of *culture*, [and says] I see above me something higher and more human than I am; let everyone help me to attain it, as I will help everyone who knows and suffers as I do: so that at last the man may appear who feels himself perfect and boundless in knowledge and love,

perception and power, and who in his completeness is at one with nature, the judge and evaluator of things. (UIII 6)

The bulk of the fourth *Meditation—Richard Wagner in Bayreuth*—is at this remove of greater biographical than intrinsic interest: not *what* Nietzsche wrote but *that* he wrote about Wagner in 1875 and published his essay in 1876, to coincide with the first Bayreuth Festival. The essay is unreservedly laudatory in tone, and Nietzsche's 'explanation', in *Ecce Homo,* is that in this and the essay on Schopenhauer he was really writing about himself. 'The essay "Wagner in Bayreuth" is a vision of my own future', he says (EH–U 3); and again:

> . . . what I heard in Wagner's music in my youth had nothing at all to do with Wagner . . . The proof of this . . . is my essay 'Wagner in Bayreuth': in all the decisive psychological passages I am the only person concerned—one may unhesitatingly insert my name or the word 'Zarathustra' wherever the text contains the word Wagner . . . Wagner himself had an idea of this: he failed to recognise himself in the essay. (EH–GT 4)

This claim is quite unacceptable, and the statement that Wagner failed to recognize himself in the essay is untrue. Nietzsche sent it to him in July 1876, and both he and Cosima were delighted with it. (So was King Ludwig, to whom Wagner sent a copy.) Wagner wrote to Nietzsche almost at once: 'Friend! Your book is prodigious! However did you learn to know me so well?' In any case, the student of Wagner is more likely to admire the insight into his personality displayed in the essay than to believe it is Nietzsche, and not Wagner at all, who is being described.

From the point of view of Nietzsche's philosophy there is one element of the essay which is of the highest importance, and which makes it a bridge between his early writings and *Human, All Too Human:* the attribution of Wagner's creative energy to his desire for power. In the *Meditation* on history he had suggested that the process then called 'organising the chaos' through which the Greeks had become an integrated and living culture might also operate in each individual person, viewed as a kind of state with conflicting drives and emotions within him. We can see, with hindsight, that he had already approached near to the conception of the desire for power as the ruling idea in a state and in an individual, but the concept was still obscured by the Apollonian–Dionysian dualism. In *Richard Wagner in Bayreuth* he alters his perspective: he had seen Wagner close up and he was able to venture a *psychological* account of Wagner's development. With Wagner he had seen a desire for power transformed into artistic creativity not as a distant or half-metaphorical phenomenon but as an actual occurrence:

> When the *ruling idea* of his [Wagner's] life—the idea that an incomparable amount of influence . . . could be exercised through the theatre—seized hold on him, it threw his whole being into the most violent ferment . . . this idea appeared at first . . . as an expression of his obscure personal will, which longed insatiably for *power and fame.* Influence, incomparable influence—how? over whom?—that was from now on the question and quest that ceaselessly occupied his head and heart. He wanted to conquer and rule as no artist had done before, and if possible to attain with a single blow that tyrannical omnipotence for which his instincts obscurely craved. (UIV 8)

As a consequence Wagner became a genius of the theatre, not stopping until he had created an entire little world in which his word was law.

Nietzsche nowhere suggests that this origin of Wagner's art is in any way discreditable, since he had directed his lust for power into purely ideal channels. The history of the nineteenth century might have been very different had Wagner sought power through politics or the army: he had the makings of a second Napoleon in him—which was precisely his great value to the psychologist in Nietzsche.

7

Sorrento and an End in Basel

> . . . it was during the years of my lowest vitality that I *ceased* to be a
> pessimist: the instinct for self-recovery *forbade* to me a philosophy of
> indigence and discouragement. (EH–I 2)

1

The breach with Wagner was by the autumn of 1876 virtually an accomplished fact. Nietzsche met him only once more: at Sorrento in November of
that year. It was a chance meeting. When Nietzsche left Bayreuth on the 27th
August he did so in the company of Paul Rée, with whom he had established a
close friendship. (As Rée was a Jew this friendship was held against him at
Wahnfried.) The state of his health made it obvious he would be unable to go
straight back to work; he asked for sick leave and on the 15th October was
released from all duties for a year. In anticipation of this he had left with Rée
on the 1st for the small spa of Bex, in Canton Waadt, where they stayed until
the 20th: his health had by then settled into the rhythmic cycle of sickness and
recovery which was to persist for the remainder of his life. Towards the end
of their stay in Bex they were joined by the young novelist Albert Brenner,
and the three went off on the 20th to Genoa and thence by boat to Naples;
there they were met by Malwida, who took them to a villa she had rented
outside Sorrento—the Villa Rubinacci—where they stayed until the following spring.

Malwida's account of her adventurous life can be read in her *Memoirs of an
Idealist*. By the time Nietzsche met her at Bayreuth in 1872 she had become a
kind of universal aunt to the younger generation of writers and artists of the
German-speaking world: she had an enormous circle of acquaintances most of
whom were people she had helped in one way or another, and it was quite in

character that she should have offered the three young men[1] a place to work and relax during the winter months. The villa stood on the coast a fifteen-minute walk from Sorrento with a view over the open sea to Naples and Vesuvius. 'We live . . . in the quarter in which there are only gardens and villas and garden-houses,' Brenner wrote to his family.[2] 'The entire quarter is like a monastery.' Later Nietzsche himself wrote to Reinhard von Seydlitz, a writer and painter with whom he was acquainted: 'We lived together in the same house and moreover we had all our higher interests in common: it was a kind of monastery for free spirits.' The 'secular monastery' which he had discussed with Rohde had, for a short time, become a reality.

Rée and Brenner stayed until the middle of the following April, Nietzsche until May; all three worked on their books, Nietzsche sometimes dictating to Brenner, who, as the youngest, had a number of 'duties' to perform, including announcing the date at lunch and getting up first in the morning. Nietzsche was unwell for much of the time, although the mild winter climate gradually effected an improvement.

It happened that Wagner and his family were also in Italy. On the 14th September, with the first festival behind them, they had come away on a long holiday, and on the 5th October they arrived in Sorrento, staying until the 7th November. Wagner met Nietzsche several times: they indulged in long talks, as they had in the Tribschen days—Wagner doing most of the talking, Nietzsche the listening—and outwardly there was harmony. Inwardly, however, Nietzsche was saddened by the impressions he received from his former idol. Wagner, he repeats in his letters of this and a slightly later time, is *old* and cannot now change his ways. It was not simply a matter of years: Wagner was only 63 and only seven years older than he had been when Nietzsche had first met him; but he was mentally old and his mind was rigidly made up on all conceivable questions. He was beginning to immerse himself in the subject of his last great creation, *Parsifal:* and while, as Newman says, there is nothing 'senile' in this opera—'Into no other work of his had Wagner ever put such severely critical thinking. He . . . was engaged on the creation of a musical world undreamed of till then not merely by others but by himself'[3]—yet it is unmistakably the work of an old man in a way that Verdi's *Falstaff,* for instance, is not. In its emphasis upon suffering and pity, its turning away from action and change towards resignation, its extreme slowness of pace, and in the garrulousness of its longest role, Gurnemanz (which recalls that of Prospero), it reveals the hand of a man who is conscious of producing his last work and

---

[1]Nietzsche was 32, Rée 26, Brenner not quite 21.
[2]His letters are printed in Bernoulli: op. cit., vol. I, pp. 198 ff.
[3]Newman: op. cit., vol. 4, p. 581.

who therefore makes of it a last will and testament. For all its Christian vocabulary and trappings, *Parsifal* is Wagner's truly Schopenhaueran work, and to hear him speaking of it must have brought home to Nietzsche how distant they had grown from one another.

After Rée and Brenner had left on the 10th April Nietzsche and Malwida must have got down to considering Nietzsche's future career seriously. Two things seemed at that time to be quite clear: he must leave Basel and he must find a wife. He had already spoken or written to Elizabeth on the latter topic; and on the 25th April he wrote again:

> Now, the plan which Frl. von M. thinks we should keep immovably before our eyes, and in which you must help, is as follows: We are convinced that in the long run I shall have to give up my Basel university life, that if I continued there it would be at the cost of all my more important designs and would involve a complete breakdown in my health. Naturally, I shall have to remain there during next winter, but I shall finish with it at Easter 1878, provided we bring off the other arrangement, i.e. marriage with a suitable and necessarily well-to-do woman. 'Good *but* rich', as Frl. von M. says . . . This project will be pushed ahead this summer, in Switzerland, so that I could come back to Basel already married. Various persons have been invited to come to Switzerland, among them several names that will be quite unfamiliar to you, e.g. Elise Bülow from Berlin, Elsbeth Brandes from Hanover. From the point of view of intellect, I still find Nat. Herzen the best qualified.[1] Your praise of little Frl. Köckert of Geneva was very impressive! . . . But I still have my doubts: and what are her means?[2]

All this seems definite enough; but none of it was to be carried through. Nietzsche was due to return to Basel in the autumn (of 1877), and it was clearly his (or more probably Malwida's) idea that he should pass the intervening time in Switzerland where, through Malwida, he would meet various young ladies and inspect them with a view to making one of them his wife. There is no evidence that he did this; on the contrary, in a letter to Malwida of the 1st July, after he had been travelling in Italy and Switzerland for six months or so, he says he still has that 'pleasant duty' before him. He has also changed his mind about Basel:

> I am determined to return to Basel and to resume my old activities. I can't endure not to feel *useful* and the Baselers are the only people who let me feel

---

[1] Natalie Herzen was a daughter of Alexander Herzen. Malwida had been private tutor to Natalie's sister Olga. The other candidates for matrimony had no doubt also been suggested by Malwida.
[2] Fräulein Köckert was the daughter of a Geneva banker, and Nietzsche's inquiry as to her means gives us an idea of what he and Malwida meant by 'rich' when applying the term to a possible wife.

I am. What has made me ill is all this thinking and scribbling; as long as I was genuinely a *scholar* I was well; but then there came along all that nerve-shattering music and metaphysical philosophy [i.e. Wagner and Schopenhauer] and I started worrying about a thousand things that have nothing to do with me. So I want to be a teacher again. If I can't endure it, I'll die in harness.

But this was only a passing mood. In August he wrote to Overbeck more realistically: '*One thing* I can see now with perfect clarity: in the long run an academic existence is impossible for me.'

And so it proved to be. On the 1st September he set up house again in Basel with Elizabeth, Gast making a third as 'secretary and friend', and tried to resume his academic career; but by the end of the year he was forced to relinquish his duties as a teacher at the High School and concentrate entirely on his lectures. In the middle of June 1878 Elizabeth returned to Naumburg, and Nietzsche rented a house on the edge of town so that he would be compelled to walk to work and so, he thought, get some strengthening exercise. During the winter semester 1878–79 he seemed to have recovered somewhat, but at Easter he felt the need for a 'cure' at Geneva. This was so unsuccessful that he returned to Basel in a worse condition than ever before. Now he began to pay the price of nearly a decade's neglect of his health. Granted the fundamental cause of his illness was incurable, nonetheless the disabling symptoms would have yielded to careful treatment. This treatment he always neglected: instead of resting he worked; instead of behaving cautiously in every period of improvement he acted each time as if he were finally cured; instead of allowing the recuperative powers of his body time to act he swallowed medicines. He enjoyed walking and swimming and therefore allowed himself to believe that walking and swimming were good for him. In short, he did everything calculated to aggravate the disease, and in April 1879 it got the better of him: for several weeks he was in a constant state of collapse, racked by attack after attack of the most agonizing headaches, his eyes almost useless from pain and his stomach in continual revolt. In a panic, Overbeck wired to Elizabeth that her brother was in urgent need of assistance, and when she arrived she found him half-dead with pain and exhaustion.

On the 2nd May he asked to be relieved of his duties at the university for good: he was finished with teaching. On the 14th June he was retired on a pension and left Basel with Elizabeth. They went first to Schloss Bremgarten, a resort near Bern, and soon afterwards to Overbeck's mother-in-law's in Zurich. There Nietzsche stayed until he had recovered sufficiently to be capable of deciding what his next move should be.

2

On the 3rd January 1878 Wagner sent Nietzsche a copy of the recently-published text of *Parsifal*. The following May *Human, All Too Human* appeared, and Nietzsche sent Wagner a copy. The two men were now worlds apart. To Seydlitz Nietzsche wrote on the 11th June:

> His [Wagner's] endeavours and mine are going in opposite directions. This is painful enough to me—but in the service of truth one must be prepared for any sacrifice. If he only knew of all I have *against* his art and his aims he would consider me one of his worst enemies—which, as is well known, I am not.

On the 31st May he told Peter Gast that *Human, All Too Human* 'is under a sort of *ban* at Bayreuth, and the great excommunication appears to have been extended to its author too'. Wagner's reaction to the book was, however, characterized more by sorrow than anger

> From what you wrote, [he wrote to Overbeck on the 24th May,] I gather that our old friend Nietzsche is now keeping himself at a distance. Certainly some very striking changes have been taking place in him: yet whoever has witnessed him in the psychical convulsions to which he has been subject for years must almost say that the long-feared catastrophe which has struck him down was not altogether unexpected. I have done him the kindness . . . of *not* reading his book, and my greatest wish and hope is that one day he will thank me for this.

On the 19th October he again wrote to Overbeck asking for news of Nietzsche, whom he speaks of as a dear friend whose mind has cracked but for whom there is still some faint hope of recovery. In the interim a mild attack on *Human, All Too Human* had appeared under Wagner's name in the August number of the *Bayreuther Blätter*.[1]

In the letter to Gast just referred to, Nietzsche remarks on the 'curious estrangement of many friends and acquaintances' following the publication of *Human, All Too Human*. (This is clearly Nietzsche's 'keeping himself at a distance' referred to by Wagner seen from the other side.) Among these estranged friends was Rohde, who was quite frank in his dislike of the new book. He told Overbeck that what he found exasperating was Nietzsche's ability to 'adopt any possible standpoint at will' and that he then 'boasts of

---

[1]It is contained in the third of the articles called *Public and Popularity*. The *Bayreuther Blätter*, founded in February 1878, was the magazine of the Wagnerian party: it was edited by Hans von Wolzogen, but the master-mind and controlling hand were of course Wagner's own.

what seems to us a defect, that is, of freedom from any *compulsion* to see the world in any particular light'. The Wagnerians in general, and Cosima in particular, looked upon the book as a scarcely-credible betrayal of the Master.

Much of this is, of course, explicable purely as the effect of novelty, and Wagner's letter is a useful control for measuring the substance of later contemporary assertions that this or that book of Nietzsche's exhibited signs of insanity: if Wagner could think this of *Human, All Too Human* we cannot be surprised if lesser men could think it of *The Gay Science* or *Beyond Good and Evil*. Rohde's objection is well taken and shows that, unlike Wagner, he had read the book with some application. (Wagner's statement that he had not read it does not signify much: he must either have dipped into it or been told what it was about.) What Rohde objects to, however, is Nietzsche's very virtue at this time: his dialectical skill in experimenting with points of view. This seems to Rohde purely capricious; what he cannot see is that it constitutes a philosophical method: that will become apparent only when it has produced results.

III

1879–1889

. . . people find difficulty with the aphoristic form: this arises from the fact that the form is *not taken seriously enough.* An aphorism, properly stamped and moulded, has not been 'deciphered' when it has simply been read; rather, one has then to begin its *exegesis,* for which is required an art of exegesis. (GM *Vorrede*)

8

The Turning-Point

It is a war, but a war without powder and smoke, without warlike attitudes, without pathos and contorted limbs—all this would still have
been 'idealism'. One error after another is calmly laid on ice; the ideal is
not confuted—*it freezes* . . . Here for example 'the genius' freezes; on
the next corner 'the saint' freezes; 'the hero' freezes into a thick icicle; at
last 'faith', so-called 'conviction', freezes; 'pity' also grows considerably
cooler—almost everywhere 'the thing-in-itself' freezes. (EH–MA 1)

I

The collapse of Easter 1879 was the turning-point of Nietzsche's life. From
then onwards he was incapacitated for normal social life, released from daily,
weekly, seasonal routine, and driven back into himself. He had always tried to
avoid responsibilities and obligations which might conflict with the sense he
had of being reserved for some special mission: now the matter was taken out
of his hands and whether he desired it or not he was apart and alone. It is clear
now that this is what his nature required. He was essentially a solitary man,
and those who have pitied him for his isolation should have asked themselves
why, if he really disliked it, he did not end it. Within very wide bounds he
could have lived wherever he wished, but in fact he established himself nowhere. The closest he came to a permanent residence was a single room in the
house of the Bürgermeister of Sils-Maria, a village in the Ober-Engadine,
where he spent several winters. At other times he was in Genoa, Nice, Venice,
Turin, or travelling between them, and in Switzerland and Germany. He lived
in hotel rooms and lodgings, and his only property was the clothes he wore,
the paper he wrote on, and a large travelling-trunk in which they were kept.
Until his meeting with Lou Salomé in 1882 he had still been keeping an eye
open for a possible wife; but the outcome of his wooing of that young lady

convinced him he was fated for solitude. Sometimes, to be sure, he felt sorry for himself, particularly when reminded that others could find contentment in marriage and family: he succumbed to a wave of self-pity, for instance, when Rohde sent him a picture of his newly-born child in February 1884:

> I don't know how it happened, [he replied,] but as I read your last letter, and especially when I saw the picture of your child, it was as if you were clasping my hand and gazing at me in a melancholy way . . . as if to say: 'How is it possible that we now have so little in common and live as if in different worlds, when once . . . !' And so it is, friend, with all the people I love: everything is *over*, past, forbearance; people still see me, they speak so as not to stay silent. . . . But their eyes tell me the truth: and they say to me (I hear it well enough!): 'Friend Nietzsche, now you are *completely alone!*' That is really what it has come to . . . Oh friend, what a senseless withdrawn life I live! So alone, alone! So without 'children'!' (Letter of the 22nd February 1884)

Three and a half years later, sending Rohde a copy of the *Genealogy*, he complained: 'I now have 43 years behind me, and I am just as much alone as I was as a child' (letter of the 11th November 1887).

Outbursts of this kind, however, seem to refer to the sort of solitude to which, had he wished, he could have put an end. I have suggested that his inability to settle down anywhere might have originated in the death of his father; I would now add that intellectually as well as emotionally he needed solitude. This fact emerges, I believe, from the manner of thinking and style of writing revealed in his books, which are essentially a species of *talking to oneself*. Much of his work was not only thought out but written down while walking, in small notebooks which would fit into a pocket; it would not be surprising if it was also spoken aloud, with gesticulations. Something of the sort is implicit in the whole tenor of his writings. This is how I imagine him during his mature years: he is a man whose mind is full, overfull, of ideas; he is constantly finding ways of expressing them which, as he says in his letters, surprise and delight him; he spends much of each day walking, and at night he sits crouched over his table; and all the time he is talking to himself. He loves his own company, for with no one else can he enjoy such entertaining conversation. Sometimes he contradicts himself, but what would conversation be without contradiction? He argues, he grows angry, he laughs at himself; he postures and exposes himself as a posturer; he announces he is the freest of free-thinkers, and retorts that free-thinking is mere destructiveness. Gradually a philosophy emerges, *his* philosophy: none of it is of any use to anyone, no one is even interested in it; but *one day*—so he tells himself—mankind will open its eyes and see that a new world has been discovered: that is why he so often stays in the city of Columbus. With that thought he consoles himself for being his only comprehending auditor, and in the meantime he goes on talking. The tone of his voice suggests intimacy and a common understanding that thinking and talking are the most pleasurable of pastimes. The exhortatory tone is sometimes there (principally in *Zarathustra*) and, in the Prefaces and in *Ecce Homo*, self-laudation passes the bounds of good sense and good taste; but the prevailing mode is that of heightened conversation.

His real biography is from now on his books: not only in the broad sense in which this is true of any professional writer but in the special sense that he spent the greater part of his time metaphorically (or, as I think, at times actually) talking to himself, and that his books are an artistically-improved reproduction of what he said. In addition, we have the mass of notes and jottings which he did not publish, by means of which we can see him at work refining, weeding-out, rejecting what he considered superfluous and setting aside what he considered inadequately thought through.

By the end of June 1879 Nietzsche had benefited sufficiently from the care of Overbeck's mother-in-law to feel capable of leaving Zurich for a locality more suited to his invalid condition. He chose to go to the Ober-Engadine, and as soon as he arrived he realized he had found a combination of clear air, solitude and grand scenery which exactly suited him. To Elizabeth he wrote on the 24th: 'It is as if I had entered the Promised Land'. He stayed at St. Moritz, and there he began to think about how he was to get well. The obvious place for a prolonged convalescence was Naumburg, which, since his departure from Basel, was again the only town he could call home; and in fact it had already been arranged for him to spend the coming autumn and winter there. He was also having ideas about the kind of life he should lead from then on.

> You know that I prefer a simple and natural way of living, [he wrote to his mother on the 21st July,] . . . and that is also the only remedy for my state of health. Some real *work* which takes time and is some *trouble* to do, without placing a strain on the head, is what I need. Didn't father say I'd be a gardener one day? I'm quite inexperienced in it, I know, but not otherwise stupid and you will have to show me what to do at first.

To return to Naumburg and 'cultivate one's garden' must have seemed a pleasant idea during the painful months of this summer: he was still the victim of repeated attacks of migraine and exhaustion (he suffered severe attacks on 118 days of 1879), he was living on an invalid's diet, and his eyes were a constant source of pain and discomfort. Yet he was quite incapable of persisting for long in any way of life that did not 'place a strain on the head'. Except during the worst periods of his illness he was working throughout the spring and summer on completing *Human, All Too Human.* The first supplement, *Assorted Opinions and Maxims,* had appeared in February and the second and final supplement, *The Wanderer and His Shadow,* was finished by the first week of September. It was published in 1880.

It is clear that writing was by now a compulsion over which he had little control; indeed, it had probably been so since his discovery, in the summer of 1876, of the form of the long aphorism—the form into which his thoughts and stylistic genius fitted as a hand into a glove. Perhaps it has not been sufficiently remarked how extraordinary this form is, or how extraordinary was the strength of Nietzsche's devotion to it: the possibility of constructing a philosophy of lasting value out of a multitude of fragments would seem problematical if Nietzsche had not done it. Evidently he had no choice: the transformation his style and thought underwent as soon as he began to employ this form is proof of its congeniality.

(What are usually referred to as 'aphorisms' in Nietzsche's work are passages varying in length from a single sentence to a short essay of several pages. The aphoristic works in the sense the word acquires in Nietzsche—i.e. *Human, All Too Human, Assorted Opinions and Maxims, The Wanderer and His Shadow, Daybreak, The Gay Science* and *Beyond Good and Evil*—include between them 2,650 aphorisms. In *Zarathustra,* the *Genealogy, The Wagner Case, The Anti-Christ* and *Ecce Homo* the text is more continuous, but aphoristic forms of expression obtrude themselves again and again. *Götzen-Dämmerung*—in this as in other respects an epitome of Nietzsche's mature work—includes a chapter of short and a chapter of long aphorisms (G I and IX). The posthumous compilation called *The Will to Power* contains 1,067 aphorisms of widely varying length and other material from the *Nachlass* greatly increases this number.)

Sickness could not stop him working: it may be that, on the contrary, it compelled him to work; that writing was, in his own language, a species of 'self-overcoming'. He suggests as much in a letter of the 11th September to Peter Gast from St. Moritz accompanying the manuscript of The *Wanderer and His Shadow,* which Gast was to copy for the printer:

I am at the end of the 35th year of my life, [he writes;] for 1,500 years they called this period the 'mid-point of life'; Dante had his vision at this time and speaks of it in the opening words of his poem. But I, at the mid-point of life, am so 'in the midst of death' that it may take me hourly . . . To that extent I feel like an old man; and I am also like one in that I have *done* my life's work [i.e. *Human, All Too Human* and its two supplements] . . . Continual and painful suffering has not up to this moment subdued my spirit [*Gemüt*]; sometimes it even seems to me that I feel more cheerful and benevolent than at any time in my life . . . Read this latest manuscript through, dear friend, and ask yourself if any trace of suffering or depression can be discovered in it: I *think it cannot,* and this I think to be a sign that what lies behind these views of mine must be *strength,* and not the weakness and weariness which those who dislike me will look for.

The painful conditions under which he wrote are sufficient evidence of the compulsive character of the work:

The manuscript you received from St. Moritz was so dearly bought that perhaps no one would have written it at such a price who could have avoided writing it, [he told Gast in a letter of the 5th October from Naumburg. He has received Gast's fair copy of *The Wanderer and His Shadow,* but] I often shudder when I read it . . . on account of the ugly memories it calls up . . . I read your copy and I find it hard to understand what I have written—my head is so weary.

In September he left St. Moritz with Elizabeth and after visiting Chur came back to Naumburg, where he stayed until February of the following year. With the completion of *The Wanderer and his Shadow* he had resolved to '*take a rest* from thinking' (letter to Gast of the 11th September), and in the above-quoted letter from Naumburg he tells Gast:

You wouldn't believe how faithful I am being to my programme of thoughtlessness; and I have good reason to be faithful to it, for 'behind thought stands the Devil'—a raging attack of pain.

This may have been so; but the period of inactivity could not have lasted long, for by 1881 the 575 sections of *Daybreak* were ready for publication, and these are a selection from a larger body of work. We are probably safe in thinking that whenever he had a good day he soon also had a pen in his hand.

2

Section 3 of *Human, All Too Human* announces the change in the method by which Nietzsche intends to pursue his inquiries:

Appreciation of unpretentious truths. It is the mark of a higher culture to value the little, unpretentious truths which have been discovered by means of rigorous method more highly than the advantageous and dazzling errors which arise in metaphysical and artistic ages and men.

The nature of the problem underlying the very diverse investigations of *Human, All Too Human* and its two sequels is exposed in section 10:

> As soon as the origin of religion, art and morality is so described that it can be perfectly understood without the postulation of *metaphysical interference* . . . the greater part of our interest in the purely theoretical problem of the 'thing-in-itself' and 'appearance' ceases to exist. For . . . with religion, art and morality we do not touch upon 'the nature of the world in itself'; we are in the realm of 'ideas', no 'intuition' can take us any farther.

Realization of the nature of the problem brings with it that of the 'task' before which Nietzsche and the rest of mankind stand:

> Since the belief that a God directs the fate of the world has disappeared . . . mankind itself must set up oecumenical goals embracing the entire earth . . . if mankind is not to destroy itself through the conscious possession of such universal rule, it must first of all attain to an unprecedented *knowledge of the preconditions of culture* as a scientific standard for oecumenical goals. Herein lies the tremendous task facing the great spirits [*Geister*] of the coming century. (MA 25)

How are the problem and the task to be approached? Nietzsche says that *Human, All Too Human* is devoted to 'reflection on the human, all too human—or, according to the learned expression, psychological observation' (MA 35). He at once explains what he understands by psychology and why it is probable that psychological investigation will be of help in explaining the world in non-metaphysical terms:

> [Psychology is] that science which inquires into the origin and history of the so-called moral sensations. [Paul Rée had written in his *Origin of the Moral Sensations:* 'Moral man is no closer to the intelligible (metaphysical) world than physical man.'] This proposition, hardened and sharpened beneath the hammer-blow of historical knowledge, may perhaps at some future time serve as the axe which is laid at the root of the 'metaphysical need' of man. Whether this will be *more* of a curse than a blessing, who can say? It will in any case have the weightiest consequences; at once fruitful and fearful, it will look out upon the world with that Janus-face possessed by all great perceptions. (MA 37)

Mankind is proud of its 'moral sensations' because these seem the surest guarantee that a 'higher world' impinges on the lower: if our ideas of right and wrong are not God-given, whence are they? In section I (quoted in chapter 5) Nietzsche gave as his view that the 'good' qualities are *sublimated* 'bad' ones.

The 'bad' quality he proceeds to investigate is the desire for power, and he asks: what good qualities can be explained as sublimated desire for power? This approach was suggested to him by his knowledge of Greece:

> The artists of Greece, the tragedians for example, poetised in order to conquer; their whole art is unthinkable apart from the contest: Hesiod's good Eris, ambition, gave their genius its wings. (MA 170)

> [The Greek philosophers] possessed a sturdy faith in themselves and in their 'truths' and with it they overthrew all their neighbours and predecessors; every one of them was a violent and warlike *tyrant* . . . which was what every Greek wanted to be . . . To be a lawgiver is a more sublimated form of tyranny. (MA 261)

and of the psychology of Wagner:

> Influence, incomparable influence—how? over whom?—that was from now on the question and quest that ceaselessly occupied his head and his heart. (UIV 8)

Let us be clear which of Nietzsche's ideas on power are novel and which are no more than a restatement of Hobbes's dictum: 'I put for a general inclination of all mankind, a perpetual and restless desire for power after power, that ceaseth only in death.' It is hardly open to question that a thirst for power of some kind is a natural thirst in man, or that it can often be satisfied by quite modest acquisitions. With this obvious fact Nietzsche was not very much concerned, although its very obviousness is an aid to making his philosophy credible. What interested him was the possibility that actions and sentiments not obviously connected with a desire for power were in fact prompted by it. To Hobbes power means political power, which is ultimately reducible to brute force; to Nietzsche power is a psychological need which men will strive to satisfy in indirect ways if direct satisfaction is denied them. Such a conception is similar to that embodied by Dickens in the figure of Uriah Heep:

> Father got made a sexton by being umble. 'Be umble, Uriah', says father to me, 'and you'll get on. It was what was always being dinned into you and me at school; it's what goes down best. Be umble', says father, 'and you'll do.' And really I ain't done bad . . . I'm very umble to the present moment, Master Copperfield, but I've got a little power.

Uriah is intended as a conscious hypocrite, and Dickens does not believe all humility is feigned; nor does Nietzsche maintain that all humility is hypocrisy consciously entertained. But the thought that Uriah's apparent humility is actually a device for achieving a little power—that is, the reverse of what it seems—is the same as that behind Nietzsche's aphorism:

> *St. Luke 18, 14 improved.* He that humbleth himself wants to be exalted. (MA 87) (Luke has 'He that humbleth himself shall be exalted'.)

Human, All Too Human advances no general propositions concerning the origin of humane qualities in the desire for power; faithful to his new method, Nietzsche merely investigates individual cases. He suggests that gratitude may be a refined form of revenge (MA 44); that the weak and suffering may desire to arouse sympathy because this gives them the feeling they 'have at least one *form of power* despite their weakness: the *power to hurt*' (MA 50); that justice— one of the good qualities 'which do in fact exist', as he had told David Strauss—may be understood as an arrangement between forces of approximately equal power (MA 92); that those who offer gratuitous advice do so with the aim of exerting power over him they advise (MA 299); that teasing is a public exhibition of power over the person teased (MA 329); that the acquisition of knowledge is accompanied by the feeling of pleasure because it is also accompanied by the feeling of enhanced power (MA 252); that truth is preferred to untruth because in the realm of thought '*power* and *fame* are hard to maintain on the basis of error or lies' (VMS 26).

But there is another aspect to the question of power. Nietzsche has already offered the suggestion that the individual is a kind of state and the cultured individual one who brings the 'chaos' within him to order in the way the Greeks did on a national scale. Since this would involve having power over oneself, he considers whether self-control may not be an aspect of the power-drive:

> There exists a *defiance of oneself* of which many forms of asceticism are among the most sublimated expressions. For certain men feel so great a necessity to exercise their strength and lust for power that, in default of other objects or because their efforts in other directions have always miscarried, they at last hit upon the idea of tyrannising over certain portions of their own nature. (MA 137)

> . . . the saint exercises that defiance of oneself which is a near relation to lust for power and which gives the sensation of power even to the most solitary. (MA 142)

This 'defiance of oneself' was later to seem to Nietzsche the most important aspect of the desire for power.

Morality as such—the judgment that this kind of action is good, that evil—is also tentatively explained in terms of a power relationship:

Two-fold pre-history of good and evil. The concept good and evil has a two-fold pre-history. *Firstly,* in the soul of the ruling tribes and castes. He who has the power to requite good with good, evil with evil, and actually practises requital and is therefore grateful and revengeful is called good; he who is powerless and cannot requite is considered bad. As a good man one belongs to 'the good', a community with a sense of common interest, because all the individuals in it are bound together by the concept of requital. As a bad man one belongs to 'the bad', to a swarm of subjugated, powerless men which has no sense of common interest. The good are a caste, the bad a mass. For a long time, good and bad are much the same as noble and base, master and slave. On the other hand, one does not view the enemy as bad: he can requite. In Homer, the Trojan and the Greek are both good. Not he who harms us but he who is contemptible counts as bad. . . . *Then,* in the soul of the subjugated and powerless. Here every other man is considered an enemy, as ruthless, exploiting, cruel and cunning, whether he be noble or base. Evil is the characterising expression for man, even for imagined beings, for example a god . . . Signs of goodness, helpfulness, sympathy are . . . received as refined wickedness. (MA 45)

Not strictly congruent with this theory, but later to be reconciled with it, is a development of the idea that good is sublimated evil and essentially involved with it:

All good motives . . . , whatever exalted names we may give them, have grown up from the same roots as those we suppose are poisoned; between good and evil actions there is no difference of kind, but at the most one of degree. Good actions are sublimated evil ones; evil actions are coarsened and brutalised good ones. The individual's sole desire is for self-satisfaction, and it is this (together with the fear of its loss) which asserts itself under all circumstances, . . . whether in vain, revengeful, impulsive, wicked or cunning actions, or in deeds of sacrifice, of pity or of knowledge . . . many actions are called evil when they are only stupid, because the degree of intelligence which decided for them was very low. Indeed, as yet *all* actions are in a certain sense stupid, for the highest degree of human intelligence which can at present be attained will certainly be exceeded in the future: and then all *our* actions will, in retrospect, seem as circumscribed and thoughtless as the actions and judgments of still-surviving primitive peoples appear to us. (MA 107)

The cyclops of culture. When we behold those deeply-furrowed hollows in which glaciers have lain, we think it hardly possible that a time will come when a wooded, grassy valley, watered by streams, will spread itself out upon the same spot. So it is too in the history of mankind: the most savage forces beat a path, and are mainly destructive; but their work was nonetheless necessary, in order that later a gentler civilization might raise its house. The frightful energies—

those which are called evil—are the cyclopean architects and road-makers of humanity. (MA 246)

To behave morally is to obey a certain code, i.e. morality is *custom:*

> To be moral, virtuous, ethical, means to obey a long-established law or tradition. Whether one obeys gladly or reluctantly is immaterial: it is enough that one obeys. He is called 'good' who acts according to custom as if by nature, as the result of a long inheritance, and therefore easily and gladly . . . To be evil is to be 'not bound by custom' (immoral), to have bad habits,[1] to fight against tradition, however reasonable or stupid this tradition may be. (MA 96)

Custom is essentially that which is good for the *community:*

> The origin of custom can be traced to two ideas: 'the community is of greater value than the individual' and 'a lasting advantage is to be preferred to a transient one'; from which arises the conclusion that the lasting advantage of the community is to take unconditional precedence over the advantage of the individual. (VMS 89)

Because morality is custom, conscience consists in the commands we have been given as children:

> The content of our conscience is that which was, without any given reason, regularly *demanded* of us in our childhood by people we honoured or feared. (WS 52)

Nietzsche in fact explains conscience in much the same way as Freud was later to do: as the 'super-ego'.

The essential purpose of *Human, All Too Human* is to explain reality without reliance upon metaphysical ideas, and by explaining it to arrive at a knowledge of the 'preconditions of culture'. Its method is 'experimentalism'. Its general tendency is towards the abolition of the 'higher qualities' (i.e. those for which a supra-terrestrial origin might be supposed) through understanding them as transformations of 'lower' qualities (i.e. those which people have in common with the animals). The particular quality which appears to offer the greatest scope for development is the desire for power. In these respects *Human, All Too Human* is a genuine first stage in a quite specific and easily comprehensible Nietzschean philosophy.

---

[1] The verbal connection between morality and custom is much closer in German than in English. In the original of the present passage, custom = *Sitte*, immoral = *unsittlich*, bad (i.e. immoral) habits = *Unsitte.*

9

The Wanderer

We have left the land and taken to our ship! We have burned our bridges—more, we have burned our land behind us! Now, little ship, take care! The ocean lies all around you; true, it is not always roaring, and sometimes it lies there as if it were silken and golden and a gentle favourable dream. But there will be times when you will know that it is infinite and that there is nothing more terrible than infinity . . . Alas, if homesickness for land should assail you, as if there were more *freedom* there—and there is no longer any 'land'! (FW 124)

1

'My existence is a *fearful burden*,' Nietzsche wrote to his doctor, Otto Eiser of Frankfort am Main, in January 1880: 'I should have thrown it off long ago had I not been making the most instructive tests and experiments in the intellectual-moral field precisely in this condition of suffering and almost complete renunciation—this joy in seeking for knowledge carries me to heights where I overcome all torments and all hopelessness. On the whole I am happier than ever before in my life: and yet! continual pain; for many hours of the day a feeling much like seasickness; a semi-paralysis which makes it hard for me to talk, alternating with furious attacks (the last one had me vomiting for three days and nights, I longed for death).'

Three months in Naumburg had worked no improvement, and his idea now was to go south, where the weather was always fine and he could spend most of his waking hours walking—he had still not lost his faith in the curative effect of muscular activity. The only difficulty presented by this plan was that, in his ailing condition, he might need the ministrations of a companion; and it may have been Paul Rée, who paid a long visit to Naumburg in January, who called to mind that Peter Gast was at that time living in Venice.

125

Gast's singular devotion to Nietzsche was well known to their Basel acquaintances, and Rée no doubt felt justified in thinking the faithful Peter the man they were looking for. So it happened that on the 26th Gast received from Rée an unexpected gift of 200 marks, together with a letter telling him what the money was for. Nietzsche, said Rée, was coming south and would be staying at Riva: perhaps Gast would like to keep him company; if so, train fare and expenses were enclosed. Gast was annoyed at this high-handed suggestion: he was struggling to gain recognition as a composer, and during 1880–81 he was at work on many musical plans (some of them originating with Nietzsche), and it angered him that his associates were interested in him only in his capacity as Nietzsche's 'secretary and friend'.[1] But, as always, his love for Nietzsche overcame less worthy feelings, and he agreed to Rée's proposal.

He still had to wait to hear when his duties would commence. On the 4th February Franziska wrote him that her son was not leaving yet because of the bad weather, and it was not until the 19th that he heard again, this time from Nietzsche himself, who was already in Riva. Thither Gast faithfully repaired, arriving on the 23rd in pouring rain and snow. The following morning Nietzsche came to his room at half-past five with the information that, if they intended to get any walking done that day (and he *did* intend to get some done), they had better start then and there, as all the signs were that more rain and snow were on the way. 'Exacting Samaritan service' is how Gast describes to his Austrian friend his activities at Riva from then until the 13th March, when he and Nietzsche set off for Gast's home in Venice. He foresaw that he would be in constant demand, and so it turned out: on the 15th he scribbled in haste:

> I am writing these lines in a café; I have got away from Nietzsche for a few minutes. Yesterday I absolutely could not write; when I got home I simply *fell* into bed. Straight out again this morning. You have no idea of the exertions . . . Nietzsche's presence costs me.

At the end of March the strange pair were joined by an Italian friend named Minutti, who himself promptly fell ill. Gast complained on the 8th April:

> That I didn't write yesterday is due entirely to the total lack of time from which I now suffer. I am fed up with listening to the patients complaining the whole day long. If I finally lose patience with this dog's life, I shall leave Venice . . . and let the sick tend the sick as the dead are supposed to bury the dead. I shall soon be sick myself.

[1]For the letters from which we learn of Gast's activities and feelings at this time, see Chapter 6.

He did not leave, although his work as a composer was almost at a stop. On the 11th May he wrote:

> Here it rains almost without ceasing. How Nietzsche—who is sensitive to every cloud that appears in the sky—is faring, you may imagine.

In a letter of the 24th September Gast tells how he had to spend five or six hours a day with Nietzsche, reading and talking:

> You have no idea what I endured . . . , how many a night I lay down and tried to sleep and when I thought about what had happened during the day, and saw that I had done nothing for myself and everything for other people, I was often seized with such rage that I threw myself into contortions and called down death and damnation on Nietzsche. I have hardly ever felt so bad as I did during this time. . . . Then, when I had at last managed to get to sleep at four or five in the morning, Nietzsche would often come along at nine or ten and ask if I would play Chopin for him.

It must have been with a sigh of relief that he saw his friend off on the train for Marienbad on the 29th June. To admire the fine mind and intellectual energy that were Nietzsche's was one thing; to have charge of the tormented frame in which they were enclosed clearly another: Nietzsche himself realized what a trial he had been to Gast and wrote apologetically from Marienbad. Back among hills and forests, he says, he is more his old self, and is again hard at work 'zealously digging in my moral mines' (letter of the 18th July). But the fine weather he was seeking was still eluding him:

> I am still in Marienbad, [he wrote to Gast on the 20th August.] . . . it has rained every day since the 24th July, often all day long. Rainy skies, rain in the air, but fine walks in the woods.

In the same letter he reveals how greatly his alienation from Wagner was still affecting him:

> I . . . suffer dreadfully if I have to do without sympathy, and nothing for example can compensate me for having lost the sympathy of Wagner during recent years. How often I dream of him, and always we are back together in our former intimacy. There was never an angry word spoken between us, but very many cheerful and encouraging ones; and perhaps I have never laughed together with anyone more than with him. All that is over—and what good is it that in many things I am in the *right* in *opposition* to him! As if that could wipe away the memory of this lost sympathy! . . . it seems so ridiculous to want to be in the right at the cost of love.

There is no need to comment on the inaccuracy of his memory: here, as in *Ecce Homo,* he is recalling a total impression, and in retrospect the quarrels with Wagner seem of no importance.

At the beginning of September he returned to Naumburg, where he stayed for five weeks, leaving on the 8th October on a second quest for Italian sunshine: this time he went to Stresa on Lake Maggiore, calling at Basel on the way and enjoying a reunion with Overbeck. At Stresa his health suffered a setback, and after staying only a few weeks he travelled on to Genoa, where he spent the winter. His condition was wretched but he was learning to live with it:

> All my effort now is bent upon realising an ideal garret-solitude [*Dachstuben-Einsamkeit*], in which all the necessary and simplest demands of my nature, as I have been taught them by much, much pain, can receive their due, [he wrote to Overbeck in November.] And perhaps I shall achieve it! The daily battle against headache and the laughable diversity of my ailments demands such an amount of attention that I am running into the danger of becoming *petty*—but this is a counterweight to those very general, very high-flying tendencies that have such power over me that without some counterweight to them I would become a fool. I recover from a very bad attack, and hardly has the two-day incapacitation been shaken off than my folly again goes running after quite unbelievable things, from the time I wake up onwards . . . Help me to retain this seclusion . . . for a good length of time I have to live without people, and in a city whose language I do not know; I *have* to—I repeat it; don't worry about me! I live as if the centuries were nothing and follow my thoughts without paying heed to the date or the newspapers.

His 'garret-solitude' in Genoa was a miserable time. The winter of 1880–81 was a hard one, and he had little money to spare for the luxury of keeping warm: 'Often my limbs are frozen', he wrote to Overbeck on the 22nd February. In the spring he took up with Gast again, and spent a month with him at Recoaro from the end of April to the end of May; after Gast's departure he stayed on until the middle of June and then returned to St. Moritz. On the 23rd of that month Overbeck received a letter from a new resort: Sils-Maria, in the Ober-Engadine. 'I know of nothing more suited to my nature than this piece of high land', Nietzsche wrote; and indeed in the high Alpine village of Sils-Maria he had found the place which came nearest in his later years to being a permanent residence. He lodged in a room attached to the house of the Bürgermeister and took his meals at the village hotel, and all around was the mountain and forest solitude which was always more congenial to him than a garret-solitude in a city. Naturally, things were not quite perfect:

Even *here* I have much to endure, [he wrote;] the summer this year is hotter and more full of electricity [!] than usual, which is detrimental to me.

But on the whole Sils-Maria won his approval, and we should note again that his aim was not to avoid isolation but to seek it: the inhabitants of the village were unsophisticated peasants to whom he was only a long-staying tourist, and he was in all essentials quite alone.

He had been on his wanderings for two years now, and his health had improved hardly at all: doubtless the shortcomings of medicine in the 1880s were in part responsible, but where the greater part of the blame for his lack of progress really lay is made apparent by a letter of mid-July from Sils-Maria to his mother. She has been perplexed and worried by his continual sickness and, it would seem, reproaching him for not taking better care of himself. He tries to reassure her, but his protestations, if read in the knowledge of how sick he actually was, are the reverse of reassuring:

There could never have been a man to whom the word 'depressed' applied less, [he wrote.] Those who divine more of my life's task and its ceaseless demands think me, if not the *happiest* of men, at least the *most courageous*. I have weightier things to consider than my health, and therefore I am ready to bear that too. My appearance is in any case excellent; as a result of all the marching about I do my muscular system is almost that of a soldier; stomach and abdomen in order. My nervous system is, considering the tremendous exertions it has to make, splendid and an object of astonishment to me, very subtle and very strong . . . It is very difficult to diagnose what is wrong with my brain; regarding the scientific materials necessary for this I am better placed than any doctor. Indeed, it offends my pride as a man of science when you suggest new cures and even say that I am 'paying no attention to my illness'. Trust me a little more in this matter! I have been treating myself for only two years, and if I have made mistakes it has always been because I have at last given in to the pressing advice of others and put it to the test . . . In any case, every sensible doctor has made it clear that I could be cured only after a *long* passage of time, and above all I must try to free myself from the bad after-effects of all those false methods of cure with which I have been treated for so long . . . I intend to be my own doctor from now on, and people shall say of me that I was a *good* doctor . . . Anyone who could grasp how I am able to unite a regard for my recovery with the furthering of my great tasks would be doing me no small honour. I am living not only very bravely but in the highest degree reasonably and sustained by a wide medical knowledge and incessant observation and investigation.

It is the same story as during the Basel years: any form of cure which means an interruption of work is 'false'; only by working can he be cured, consequently only *he* can effect a cure, for only he knows how he should work. It is hard to take seriously the reference to his own 'medical knowledge', for he must have realized this was non-existent, and that he should call attention to the first-rate condition of his 'muscular system' and nervous system typifies the irrelevance of virtually all his 'observations and investigations' into his disease. If we seek the basic reason Nietzsche was perpetually ill from about 1872 onwards, we have it in the fact that he made no serious effort to follow medical advice; and if we ask ourselves why he did not, the answer, I think, is that he was convinced from the first that he was incurable and feared he would die before he had written all he wanted to write: the compulsive character of his work which I mentioned earlier probably has its roots in this fear.

He stayed at Sils-Maria until the 1st October, when he returned to Genoa for the winter: however uncomfortable Genoa might have been, an Alpine winter would probably have been too much for him. His second stay in Genoa lasted until the end of the following March. These months were occupied with work later included in *The Gay Science,* and it seems no coincidence that its greater stylistic individuality and exuberance compared with the preceding works should have appeared at the same time as he discovered the 'antithesis' and stylistic counterweight to the still-dominant Wagner: Bizet's *Carmen.* He first saw it in November, and repeated the experience the following month; and he wrote Gast on the 5th December:

> I have heard *Carmen* for the second time—and again I had the impression of a *Novelle* of the first rank . . . For me this work is worth a journey to Spain—a work in the highest degree southerly!—Do not laugh, old friend; with my 'taste' I am not easily misled so completely . . . I've been really ill, but recovered through *Carmen.*

In a letter to which this is a reply Gast had told him something about Wagner's activities, and Nietzsche assures him: 'From time to time (why is it so?) it is *almost a necessity* for me to hear some general and definite news about *Wagner,* and best of all from you!' The second Bayreuth festival, devoted to launching *Parsifal,* was already being planned, and although, in common with the rest of the world, he had not seen Wagner's last opera,[1] he had read the text and the

---

[1] He never did see it, as it was retained at Bayreuth during the remainder of his life and he would not have been welcome there. He heard the orchestral prelude to the opera in January 1887 (in Monte Carlo) and was frank in his admiration of it: 'Has Wagner ever written anything *better?*' he wrote to

antithesis *Parsifal–Carmen* took on a symbolic significance for him which he later exploited to the full.

He had already decided not to attend the festival of 1882, although he placed some importance on Elizabeth's going: probably it was his thirst for news of what Wagner was doing. The letter of the 10th February 1882 in which he tells her how to go about getting tickets also contains an account of his health which reveals how bizarre his existence had become. Paul Rée was paying him a visit, but Nietzsche's condition was making it hard to enjoy:

> On the first day things were very good; I endured the second by taking all the tonics I had; on the third, exhaustion, in the afternoon a fainting fit; that night I had an attack; the fourth day I spent in bed; on the fifth I got up again, only to lie down again in the afternoon; on the sixth and afterwards perpetual headache and weakness.

The completed work of the years 1880–82 comprises *Daybreak* and *The Gay Science*. The manuscript of *Daybreak* went to Gast for copying in the early days of 1881, and the book appeared in June; *The Gay Science* occupied most of the winter of 1881–82, and in his letter to Lou Salomé of the 2nd July 1882 Nietzsche says that the previous day the last part of the manuscript was completed 'and therewith the work of six years (1876 to 1882), my entire "free-thought"!'

As the author of *The Birth of Tragedy* and the polemic against Strauss he had enjoyed a certain brief celebrity; as the author of *Human, All Too Human, Daybreak* and *The Gay Science* he was unnoticed and unknown: these masterworks aroused scarcely a ripple of interest outside Nietzsche's immediate circle. The fact is, even now, not altogether explicable. Viewed simply as 'literature', *Daybreak* was the most notable publication of 1881, *The Gay Science* of 1882, in the German-speaking world: the language of *Daybreak* is a model of what can be achieved in modern German in the way of conciseness and clarity, and *The Gay Science* exhibits a stylistic virtuosity unsurpassed in that language. In these works not only Nietzsche but German itself had found a new voice. Why the custodians of the tongue, who a few years previously had been hailing the pedestrian work of David Strauss as a 'classic', failed to recognize the appearance of the greatest master of German prose since Goethe is a mystery; but if one seeks a clue to Nietzsche's own immense self-appreciation it is to be found in this lack of appreciation by others. He was

Gast on the 21st; its directness of statement and psychological certainty 'cut through the soul like a knife'. There is no contradiction between this and the denunciations of *Der Fall Wagner:* it was no part of Nietzsche's case to suggest that Wagner was not a composer of genius.

beginning at this time to evince an excitement in his own work that was to grow stronger as the years passed:

> Ideas have arisen on my horizon the like of which I have never seen before [he wrote to Gast on the 14th August 1881 from Sils-Maria (the reference is to the idea of the eternal recurrence, which had come to him that same month).] I shall certainly have to live a *few* years more! . . . The intensity of my feelings makes me shudder and laugh—a couple of times I couldn't leave my room for the ludicrous reason that my eyes were inflamed . . . Each time I had been weeping too much on my walks the day before, not sentimental tears but tears of rejoicing; and as I wept I sang and talked nonsense, filled with a new vision . . . if I were unable to draw strength from myself, if I had to wait for applause, encouragement, consolation, where would I be? what would I be? There were certainly moments and whole periods in my life (e.g. the year 1878) when a robust word of encouragement, a hand-clasp of agreement would have been the refreshment of refreshments—and it was just then that everybody left me in the lurch . . . Now I no longer expect it and I experience only a certain troubled surprise when, for example, I think of the letters I receive nowadays—it is all so insignificant . . . what people say to me is considerate and well-meant, but distant, distant, distant.

2

'With this book I open my campaign against morality,' Nietzsche wrote in *Ecce Homo* of *Daybreak* (EH–M 1), but the tone of the book is not as aggressive as this claim suggests: nowhere else, in fact, is he so calm and clear-sighted and so free from quirks and excesses as he is here. *Human, All Too Human* and its sequels were overloaded with undeveloped ideas, which gives them the air of compendia rather than of individual works, but by the time he wrote *Morgenröte* Nietzsche had sorted out from this mass of suggestions those which he felt were likely to lead to some concrete conclusions: what chiefly engrossed him was the idea that morality had developed out of the desire for power and the fear of disobedience, and *Morgenröte* is mainly devoted to an examination of morality in this light.

The first difficulty about the 'problem of morality' that Nietzsche faces is that hitherto it has not been thought a problem at all. In the preface to the second edition of 1886 he attributes the failure of all preceding philosophies to this cause:

> Why is it that from Plato onwards every philosophical architect in Europe has built in vain? . . . The correct answer would probably have been that all philoso-

phers were building under the misguiding influence of morals, . . . that they were apparently aiming at certainty, at 'truth', but in reality at '*majestic moral structures*'. (M *Vorrede* 3)

The universal idea is that morals are something 'given', that they exist as part of the known world; but this is not so:

When man gave a gender to all things he did not think he was playing, but that he had gained a deep insight: . . . In the same way, man has connected every-thing with morals, and dressed the world in an *ethical significance*. One day this will have no more value than the belief in the masculinity or femininity of the sun has today. (M 3)

Mankind prides itself on its morality and denies it to the animal world; morality is one of the principal guarantees of the divine origin of man. But the animal world does not see the situation in the same light:

We do not consider animals moral beings. But do you suppose animals consider us moral beings?—An animal which could speak said: 'Humanity is a prejudice from which we animals at least are free.' (M 333)

Yet if morality is conceived of as custom, the animals *do* have a morality—and it is the same morality men have:

Animals and morals. The practices demanded in polite society: careful avoidance of the ridiculous, the offensive, the presumptuous; the suppression of one's virtues as well as of one's strongest inclinations; self-adaptation, self-deprecation, submission to orders of rank—all this is to be found as social morality in a crude form even in the depths of the animal world, and only at this depth do we see the purpose of all these amiable precautions: one wishes to elude one's pursuers and be favoured in the pursuit of one's prey. For this reason the animals learn to master themselves and alter their form, so that many, for example, adapt their colouring to the colouring of their surroundings . . . Thus the individual hides himself in the general concept 'man', or in society, or adapts himself to princes, classes, parties, opinions of his time or place: and all the subtle ways we have of appearing fortunate, grateful, powerful, enamoured, have their easily-discoverable parallels in the animal world . . . The beginnings of justice, as of prudence, moderation, bravery—in short of all we call the *Socratic virtues*—are *animal:* a consequence of that drive which teaches us to seek food and elude the enemy . . . It is not improper to describe the entire phenomenon of morality as animal. (M 26)

Not only is this an attempt, by now instinctive with Nietzsche, to account for the 'metaphysical' qualities in a non-metaphysical way, but almost a piece of 'Darwinism': men have evolved from the animals, and so has their morality; the beginning of morality is fear and desire for power, and these men share with the whole animal world:

> Is the *origin of morality* not to be sought in such revoltingly petty conclusions as: 'what harms *me* is *evil* (harmful in itself); what profits *me* is *good* (beneficent and profitable in itself) . . .'? *O pudenda origo!* (M 102)

Morality, as it is usually understood, does not exist:

> If only those actions are moral . . . which are performed for the sake of another and only for his sake, then there are no moral actions! (M 148)

> I deny morality as I deny alchemy, that is, I deny their premises; but I do *not* deny that there have been alchemists who believed in these premises and acted according to them. I also deny immorality: *not* that countless people *feel* themselves to be immoral, but that there is any *true* reason so to feel. It goes without saying that I do not deny—unless I be a fool—that many actions called immoral ought to be avoided and resisted, or that many called moral ought to be done and encouraged—but I think the one should be encouraged and the other avoided *for other reasons than hitherto.* (M 103)

A morality establishes itself through becoming custom, and this is the origin of civilization: '*First rule of civilization* . . . : any custom is better than no custom' (M 16). Nietzsche proposes two fundamental grounds why people act according to custom: from fear and from desire for power; and *Daybreak* contains a large number of experiments with both. 'All actions may be traced back to evaluations, all evaluations are either *original* or *adopted*—the latter being by far the most common,' he writes. 'Why do we adopt them? From fear' (M 104). Thus he suggests that mankind developed the faculty of sympathy ('feeling with') from its onetime need to understand the meaning of the behaviour of other people and animals:

> . . . man, on account of his delicate and fragile nature the most timid of all creatures, has learned from his *timidity* that sympathy and quick understanding of the feelings of others (and of animals). Throughout long millennia he saw a danger in everything strange and living: at the sight of it, he straightaway copied the features and posture and drew a conclusion concerning the kind of evil intention behind these features and this posture . . . Joy and pleasant surprise, finally the sense of the ridiculous, are the later progeny of sympathy and the much younger siblings of fear. (M 142)

Similarly, he supposes that the security which is the product of moral behaviour as usually understood is the object of that moral behaviour:

> Behind the basic law of the current moral code—'moral actions are actions
> prompted by sympathy for others'—I see the social effect of timidity hiding in
> an intellectual mask: it desires, first and foremost, that *all the dangers* which life
> once held should be removed from it, and that *everyone* should assist in this with
> all his might: hence only those actions which tend towards the common security
> and society's sense of security are to be accorded the predicate 'good'! (M 174)

In an early aphorism, in which fear and custom are directly connected, Nietzsche gives a definition of the 'immoral' man that goes a long way towards
explaining his employment of the term 'immoralist' to describe himself: referring to '*the principal law:* morality is nothing else but (therefore *no more than!*)
obedience to custom', he goes on to say:

> The free man is immoral because he is *determined* in everything to depend upon
> himself and not upon some tradition: in every primitive state of mankind, 'evil'
> signified the same thing as 'individual', 'free', 'arbitrary', 'unaccustomed', 'un-
> foreseen', 'incalculable'. . . . What is tradition? A higher authority which is
> obeyed not because it commands what is *useful* but because it *commands* . . .
> Originally everything was custom, and he who wanted to raise himself above it
> had to become a law-giver and medicine-man and a kind of demi-god: that is to
> say, he had to *make customs* . . . Those moralists who, following in the footsteps
> of *Socrates*, offer the *individual* a morality of self-control and temperance as a
> means to his own *advantage,* as his personal key to happiness, *are the
> exceptions*— . . . they detached themselves from the community, as immoral
> men, and are in the profoundest sense evil. Thus to a virtuous Roman of the old
> stamp every *Christian* who 'considered first of all his *own* salvation' appeared
> evil. (M 9)

'Progress' in the moral sphere therefore means the changes that have been
wrought by men initially thought evil:

> . . . history treats almost exclusively of . . . *bad men* who have later been *declared
> good men!* (M 20)

> There is a continual moiling and toiling going on in morality—the effect of
> *successful crimes* (among which, for example, are included all innovations in
> moral thinking). (M 98)

'In the glorification of "work"', he writes, 'I see . . . fear of the individual.
Fundamentally one believes . . . that work is the best policeman' (M 173).

Because the individual is the antithesis of the group—whether the group be a primitive tribe or a modern state—and consequently the only source of immorality (i.e. disobedience to custom), he is dreaded by those to whom custom is sacred.

In time Nietzsche was to abandon the conception of fear as a positive force in the sense implied in *Daybreak* and to think of it as the negative aspect of the desire for power: that is, as identical with the feeling of powerlessness, of being subject to the power of someone or something else. Even in *Daybreak*, because of its more positive effect power begins to appear a more fruitful field of investigation than fear. 'Neither necessity nor desire,' he says, echoing Hobbes, '—no, the love of power is the demon of mankind' (M 262), and he makes a number of suggestions concerning the origin of morality in the love of power; e.g.:

> *Wherein we are most subtle.* Because *things* (nature, tools, property of every kind) were thought for many thousands of years to possess life and soul, with the power to hurt . . . , the feeling of powerlessness has been much greater . . . among men than it ought to have been: . . . But because the feeling of powerlessness and fear has been so strong, . . . the *sense for power* has become so *subtle* that in this respect man can vie with the most delicate balance. It has become his strongest instinct; the means which have been discovered to create this sense almost constitute the history of culture. (M 23)

> Oh, how much superfluous cruelty and vivisection have proceeded from those religions which invented sin! And from those people who desired by means of it to gain the highest enjoyment of power! (M 53)

> *Towards a natural history of rights and duties.* Our duties—are the rights of others over us . . . My rights—are that part of my power which others have not merely conceded me, but which they wish me to preserve . . . rights are recognised and guaranteed degrees of power . . . The rights of others constitute a concession on the part of our sense of power to the sense of power of those others. (M 112)

> To strive for distinction is to strive for ascendancy over one's neighbour, be it only a very indirect one or one only felt or even dreamt. (M 113)

> If a war proves unsuccessful, one always asks who was to 'blame' for it . . . Guilt is always sought in cases of failure; for failure always brings with it a depression of spirits, the sole remedy for which is instinctively applied: a fresh excitement of the *sense of power*—and this can be found in the *condemnation* of the 'guilty'. This guilty one is not even a scapegoat for the guilt of others: he is a sacrifice to the weak, humiliated and depressed, who want to demonstrate in some way that

they still have some strength left. To condemn oneself can also be a means towards restoring the feeling of strength after a defeat. (M 140)

However much advantage and vanity . . . may be involved in *great politics*, the strongest tide that carries it forward is the *need for the sense of power* . . . When man feels the sense of power he feels and calls himself *good:* and at the same time those upon whom he needs to *vent* his power feel and call him *evil!* (M 189)

The unbounded ambition . . . to be the 'unraveller of the world' filled the thinker's dreams: . . . Thus philosophy was a kind of exalted struggle for the tyrannical lordship of the spirit. (M 547)

Field-dispensary of the soul. What is the strongest remedy? Victory. (M 571)

The last quotation establishes the connection—which Nietzsche was to find of increasing significance—between happiness and the feeling of power: 'The first effect of happiness is the *sense of power*' (M 356), he writes; and further:

[There are] two kinds of happiness (the feeling of power and the feeling of surrender). (M 60)

. . . happiness, conceived as the liveliest sense of power, has perhaps nowhere on earth been greater than in the souls of superstitious ascetics. (M 113)

Even more important for the development of the theory of the will to power is the reference to power as a means to self-mastery:

We are still on our knees before *strength* . . . and yet when the degree of *honour* is fixed, only the *degree of rationality in strength* can be decisive: one must measure to what extent even strength has been overcome by something higher, in the service of which it now stands as tool and instrument! . . . perhaps the most beautiful still appears only in the dark, and sinks, scarcely born, into eternal night—I mean the spectacle of that strength which empolys genius *not for works* but *for itself as a work;* that is, for the its own constraint, for the purification of its imagination, for the imposition of order and choice upon the influx of tasks and impressions. (M 548)

The passage is not ideally lucid, and Nietzsche still speaks of strength's being 'overcome by something higher' although he has already lost the right to this kind of expression; but it was to be through an understanding of this aspect of the power-drive that he was later able to suggest a solution to the problem of the meaning of man:

Formerly one sought to arrive at a sense of the grandeur of man by pointing to his divine *origin:* this has now become a forbidden path, for at its gateway stands the ape . . . Now one seeks in the opposite direction: the way man is *going* shall serve as a proof of his grandeur and kinship with God. Alas, this is of no use either! At the end of this path stands the funeral urn of the *last* man . . . However highly man may have developed . . . a transition to a higher order is no more possible to him than it is possible for the ant or the earwig at the end of their 'earthly course' to rise up to kinship with God and to eternity. The becoming drags the having-been along behind it. (M 49)

3

The Gay Science has usually been seen as the climax of Nietzsche's 'Socratic' period, the period in which he still trusted in reason and logic. With *Thus Spoke Zarathustra* he is supposed to have suffered a change, to have become irrational, praising and commending evil and deliberately reversing all canons of judgment out of cynical cussedness: in a word, he is thought to have become insane. There exists no justification for this view. The positive assertions of *Zarathustra* and its successors are a consequence of the critical experiments of *Human, All Too Human, Daybreak* and *The Gay Science,* and not a contradiction of them. Moreover, the 'Socratic' books are by no means homogeneous in style: even in *Human, All Too Human* the cold, spare manner sometimes gives way to a passionate diction which foreshadows that of *Zarathustra; Daybreak* employs a style altogether warmer and more expansive; while in *The Gay Science* Nietzsche achieves a very wide range of expression, from the bare 'scientific' exactitude of *Human, All Too Human* to the exalted and impassioned exhortation of *Zarathustra.* The last section of the original edition of *The Gay Science* is almost identical with the opening of *Thus Spoke Zarathustra,* and the language of the aphorism in which the eternal recurrence is first mentioned (FW 341) is very close to that of the corresponding passage in *Zarathustra* (Z III 2 2). Neither the style nor the thought of *Zarathustra* is a freak appearance in Nietzsche's work.

In *The Gay Science* Nietzsche continues the experimentation of the preceding works, but his final conceptions—the will to power, the superman and the eternal recurrence—are all present in embryo. In addition, the ultimate basis of all this experimenting, the disappearance of the metaphysical world, is kept clearly in mind. The new cosmic situation of mankind is expressed in memorable form in a parable called 'The Madman':

Have you not heard of that madman who lit a lantern in the bright morning hours, ran to the market place and cried incessantly: 'I am looking for God! I am looking for God!'—As many of those who did not believe in God were standing together there he excited considerable laughter. Have you lost him then? said one. Did he lose his way like a child? said another. Or is he hiding? Is he afraid of us? Has he gone on a voyage? or emigrated?—thus they shouted and laughed. The madman sprang into their midst and pierced them with his glances. 'Where has God gone?' he cried. 'I shall tell you. *We have killed him*—you and I. We are all his murderers. But how have we done this? How were we able to drink up the sea? Who gave us the sponge to wipe away the entire horizon? What did we do when we unchained this earth from its sun? Whither is it moving now? Whither are we moving now? Away from all suns? Are we not perpetually falling? Backwards, sidewards, forwards, in all directions? Is there any up or down left? Are we not straying as through an infinite nothing? Do we not feel the breath of empty space? Has it not become colder? Is more and more night not coming on all the time? Must not lanterns be lit in the morning? Do we not hear anything yet of the noise of the gravediggers who are burying God? Do we not smell anything yet of God's decomposition?—gods too decompose. God is dead. God remains dead. And we have killed him. How shall we, the murderers of all murderers, console ourselves? That which was holiest and mightiest of all that the world has yet possessed has bled to death under our knives—who will wipe this blood off us? With what water could we purify ourselves? What festivals of atonement, what sacred games shall we need to invent? Is not the greatness of this deed too great for us? There has never been a greater deed—and whoever shall be born after us, for the sake of this deed he shall be part of a higher history than all history hitherto.'—Here the madman fell silent and again regarded his listeners; and they too were silent and stared at him in astonishment. At last he threw his lantern to the ground and it broke and went out. 'I come too early,' he said then; 'my time has not yet come. This tremendous event is still on its way, still travelling—it has not yet reached the ears of men. Lightning and thunder require time, the light of the stars requires time, deeds require time after they are done before they can be seen and heard. This deed is still more distant from them than the most distant stars—*and yet they have done it themselves.*'—It has been related further that on that same day the madman entered divers churches and there sang a *requiem aeternam deo*. Led out and quietened, he is said to have retorted each time: 'What are these churches now if they are not the tombs and sepulchres of God?' (FW 125)

'God is dead' but the fact has not yet been realized or accepted: people still think in a way that would be appropriate only if God were still a reality:

After Buddha was dead, his shadow was for centuries still pointed out in a cave—an immense, frightful shadow. God is dead: but, men being what they are, perhaps there will for millennia still be caves in which his shadow is pointed out.—And we—we still have to conquer his shadow too! (FW 108)

The nature of this 'shadow' is outlined in the following section: mechanistic and humanistic properties transferred to 'nature', the idea of 'nature' itself as a realm of order and purpose:

> Let us be on our guard against saying there are laws in nature. There are only necessities: there is no one to command, no one to obey, no one to transgress. (FW 109)

'When,' he exclaims, 'shall we have nature entirely undeified?'

Morality, deprived of any metaphysical origin or supernatural sanction, cannot have any 'everlasting worth' but must be the consequence of a 'necessity' felt by those who frame and live by it: there are, in fact, *moralities* but there is as yet no *morality:*

> Wherever we encounter a morality, there we find a valuation and an ordering of rank of the human drives and actions. These valuations and orderings of rank are always the expression of the needs of a community and herd: . . . By means of morality the individual is led into being a function of the herd and into ascribing value to himself only as a function. Since the conditions for the maintenance of one community have been very different from those of another there have been very different moralities. (FW 116)

As a consequence, modern morality abounds in the self-contradictions which arise when a certain specific morality is imagined to constitute morality in general:

> A man's virtues are called *good* not with regard to the effects they produce on him himself but with regard to the effects we suppose they will produce on us and on society . . . For otherwise it must have been seen that virtues . . . are mostly *injurious* to their possessors, as impulses which rule in them too vehemently . . . If you possess a virtue, an actual perfect virtue (and not merely a faint impulse towards a virtue!)—you are its victim! But that is precisely why your neighbour praises your virtue! . . . The 'neighbour' praises selflessness because *he derives advantage from it!* . . . The basic contradiction in that morality which is highly honoured at present is here indicated: the *motives* which prompt this morality are in opposition to its *principle!* (FW 21)

The 'self-overcoming' of Christian morality and belief, as Nietzsche conceived it, is just this recognition that what has been called moral is, by its own standards, not moral at all:

One sees precisely *what* has gained victory over the Christian God: Christian morality itself, the concept of truthfulness taken more and more strictly, the confessional-subtlety of the Christian conscience translated and sublimated into the scientific conscience, into intellectual cleanliness at any price. (FW 357)

That this may lead to the nihilism against which Nietzsche is trying to fight is a new instance of the 'true but deadly': he speaks of the 'dreadful alternative' of the coming generation:

> . . . either do away with your venerations or—*with yourselves!*' The latter would be nihilism; but would the former not also be—nihilism?—This is *our* question-mark. (FW 346)

Not until he had formulated his theory of the will to power was he able to venture an answer to this question.

As all moralities are of relative value only, good and evil must be distinguished relatively and not absolutely: there exists no warrant for repudiating evil actions as such—on the contrary, they are as valuable as good actions, since the latter evolve from the former:

> The strongest and most evil spirits have hitherto advanced mankind the most: they have again and again rekindled the sleeping passions—all ordered society lulls the passions to sleep—they have again and again reawoken the sense of comparison, of contradiction, of delight in the new, the hazardous, the untried; they have compelled mankind to set opinion against opinion, ideal against ideal. Generally it has been by force of arms, by overturning boundary-stones, by violating piety: but also through new religions and moralities! . . . The new . . . is under all circumstances the *evil*, . . . only the old is the good! The good men of every age are those who dig down deep into the old ideas and bear nourishment with them, the agriculturalists of the spirit. But every soil at last becomes exhausted and the ploughshare of evil must return again and again . . . the evil impulses are just as useful, indispensable and preservative of the species as the good: only their function is different. (FW 4)

Once again it is the idea of conflict as the dynamic force of culture: conflict is 'evil', but without conflict there is no culture:

> Examine the lives of the best and most fruitful men and peoples, and ask yourselves whether a tree, if it is to grow proudly into the sky, can do without bad weather and storms: whether unkindness, and opposition from without, whether some sort of hatred, envy, obstinacy, mistrust, severity, greed and violence do not belong to the *favouring* circumstances without which a great increase even in virtue is hardly possible. (FW 19)

Hesiod's 'good Eris'—the impulses of envy, greed and enmity directed towards competition—is still the reigning goddess of culture. Nietzsche had already, in *Human, All Too Human*, accounted for the existence of the 'good' Eris by calling her a sublimation of the 'bad' one, but, although he keeps this idea in view in *The Gay Science:*—

> Where weak eyesight can no longer recognise the evil impulses as such on account of their refinement, there mankind establishes the realm of the good (FW 53)

—he is unable to give any account of sublimation as an actual event: this account must wait upon his theory of the will to power.

Yet he is advancing towards that theory. In an early aphorism called 'Towards a theory of the sense of power' he suggests that good and ill actions both derive from the power-drive:

> By doing good and doing ill one exercises one's power over others . . . By *doing ill* to those over whom we still have to make our power felt . . . By *doing good* . . . to those who are in some way dependent upon us . . . ; we want to increase their power because in doing so we increase our own . . . Whether we make sacrifices in doing good or ill does not change the ultimate value of our actions; even if we stake our life, as a martyr does for the sake of his church—it is a sacrifice to *our* longing for power . . . He who feels 'I am in possession of the truth', how many possessions does he not let go in order to retain this feeling! What does he not throw overboard in order to keep himself 'on high'—that is, *above* others who lack the 'truth'! (FW 13)

Love too, the so-called unegoistic passion, derives from the desire to exercise the greatest degree of power over the loved one:

> Our neighbour-love—is it not an impulse towards new *property?* . . . Our joy in ourselves seeks to preserve itself by again and again transforming some new thing *into ourselves*—this is what possessing means . . . When we see anyone suffering we are glad to seize the opportunity thus presented to take possession of him; the benevolent and sympathising person, for example, does this, and he too calls the desire for a new possession awakened in him 'love' . . . Sexual love, however, betrays itself most clearly as impulse towards property: the lover wants unconditional sole possession of the person he desires, he wants unconditional power over her soul as over her body, he wants her to love him alone and to dwell and rule in her soul as what is highest and most desired . . . one is surprised that this ferocious greed and injustice of sexual love should have been glorified and

deified to such an extent at all times, that out of this love, indeed, the concept of love as the opposite of egoism should have been derived, when it is perhaps precisely the most unconstrained expression of egoism. (FW 14)

Renunciation—that is, asceticism—is now attributed to a desire for power:

What does the renouncer do? He strives after a higher world, he wants to fly farther and longer and higher than all men of affirmation—*he throws many things away* that would hinder him in his flight, and among them several things that are not valueless, not unpleasant to him: he sacrifices them to his desire for the heights. (FW 27)

The superman and the eternal recurrence also make preliminary appearances in *The Gay Science.* The picture of the superman is as yet vague, but certain traits are distinctive: Nietzsche is feeling his way towards an 'image of man' which embodies the power-impulse and somehow employs it as a creative force. In a rather strange aphorism he directly connects the 'elevation' of man with the 'death of God':

There is a lake which one day denied itself the power to flow away and threw up a dam at the place where it formerly flowed away: since then, this lake has risen higher and higher . . . perhaps man will rise higher and higher from that time when he no longer *flows out* into a god. (FW 285)

Elevation through some kind of constraint, through exercising one's power against oneself: this is the tendency of his thought at this time:

To 'give style' to one's character—a great and rare art! He practises it who surveys all that his nature presents in strength and weakness and then moulds it to an artistic plan until everything appears as art and reason, and even the weaknesses delight the eye. Here a large amount of second nature has been added, there a piece of original nature removed . . . It will be the strong, imperious natures which experience their subtlest joy in exercising such a control, in such constraint and perfecting under their own law. (FW 290)

When we read this we realize that he is still speaking the language of *On the Future of our Educational Institutions, The Birth of Tragedy* and the *Untimely Meditations;* that there is no discontinuity of direction between his early and later philosophy; and that throughout the destructive period of *Human, All Too Human* and *Daybreak* he has kept in mind the positive aim of all his inquiries: to establish a new meaning for man in a world become meaningless. The disappearance of divine sanction for moral values, he says again, implies that man must make his own values and that somehow these values must find a basis:

> Let us *limit* ourselves . . . to the purification of our opinions and evaluations and to the *creation of our own new tables of values*. . . . We . . . *want to become them who we are*—the new, the unique, the incomparable, those who make their own laws for themselves, those who create themselves! (FW 335)

Making laws for ourselves and creating ourselves is as yet a mysterious occupation: we do not yet know by what power we can do it. But in another aphorism Nietzsche makes it clear that he still has in mind the driving force of *The Birth of Tragedy:* passion controlled; and the dynamic agency of progress: conflict. Men must learn to 'live dangerously':

> I greet all the signs that a more manly, warlike age is coming, which will, above all, bring valour again into honour! For it has to prepare the way for a yet higher age, and assemble the force which that age will one day have need of—that age which will carry heroism into knowledge and *wage war* for the sake of ideas and their consequences. To that end many brave pioneers are needed now . . . : men who know how to be silent, solitary, resolute, . . . who have an innate disposition to seek in all things that which must be *overcome* in them: men to whom cheerfulness, patience, simplicity and contempt for the great vanities belong just as much as do generosity in victory and indulgence towards the little vanities of the defeated: . . . men with their own festivals, their own work–days, their own days of mourning, accustomed to and assured in command and equally ready to obey when necessary, equally proud in the one case as in the other, equally serving their own cause: men more imperilled, men more fruitful, happier men! For believe me!—the secret of realising the greatest fruitfulness and the greatest enjoyment of existence is: to *live dangerously!* Build your cities on the slopes of Vesuvius! Send your ships out into uncharted seas! Live in conflict with your equals and with yourselves! Be robbers and ravagers as long as you cannot be rulers and owners, you men of knowledge! The time will soon be past when you could be content to live concealed in the woods like timid deer! (FW 283)

The language of this aphorism may stand as an example of Nietzsche's 'embattled' style. Those few passages in which he employs the vocabulary of war have done more harm to his reputation and led to more misunderstanding than all his other writings put together. Quoted out of context they sound like—indeed, they often amount to—incitement to armed conflict: in context, they usually amount to little more than what he had written as a schoolboy at Pforta: 'Strife is the perpetual food of the soul'—and usually (as in the above quotation) his war vocabulary is associated with that most unwarlike pursuit, philosophy. This is, indeed, the clue to *why* he saw fit to introduce warlike expressions into his writings. German philosophy had got on well with the established order in Germany—but philosophers ought not to get on well with the established order; hitherto German philosophers had written books and done no harm—but philosophers ought not to do no harm; the passionate, active man is admirable but he cannot think—the philosopher must add to his ability to think the ability to act, he must endow his thought with passion, he must live his philosophy and not only think it, he must become a warrior, a robber, a ravager, of knowledge: this, it seems to me, is what Nietzsche means when he associates philosophy with war. The *locus classicus* for Nietzsche on war is the chapter 'Of War and Warriors' in *Zarathustra:* the familiar lines are:

> You should love peace as a means to new wars. And the short peace more than the long . . . You say it is the good cause that hallows even war? I tell you: it is the good war that hallows every cause. War and courage have done more great things than charity. (Z I 10)

Less familiar are the lines that give these warlike expressions the meaning he intends:

> And if you cannot be saints of knowledge, at least be its warriors. They are the companions and forerunners of such sainthood . . . You should seek your enemy, you should wage your war—a war for your opinions. And if your opinion is defeated, your honesty should still cry triumph over that! You should love peace as a means to new wars . . . etc.

Another line of approach to the superman is that the development of individuals has now become easier since the belief in a single God has disappeared:

> Monotheism, . . . this rigid consequence of the teaching of a standard man— therefore the belief in a standard God, beside whom other gods were no more than false and fraudulent—has been perhaps the greatest danger facing mankind hitherto: mankind was threatened with that premature inertia which, so far as we can see, other species of animals reached long ago. (FW 143)

Nietzsche arrived at the theory of the eternal recurrence as a consequence of two requirements: the need to explain the world and the need to accept it. The former is a general requirement of all philosophically-inclined minds, the latter a special requirement of a philosopher whose inquiries seemed to be leading to nihilism: to understand the necessary character of all phenomena—

even, or especially, the 'evil'—would be to avoid the logically absurd posture of 'rejecting' a world that cannot be other than it is. Nietzsche's picture of the 'evil' passions as the 'cyclops of culture' had gone some way towards this, but now he sees the problem in more personal psychological terms:

> What? The ultimate goal of science is to create for man the greatest possible amount of pleasure and the least possible amount of pain? But suppose pleasure and pain were so linked together that he who *wants* to have the greatest possible amount of the one *must* have the greatest possible amount of the other also . . . ? And perhaps that is how things are! The Stoics, at any rate, thought so, and were consistent when they desired to have the least possible amount of pleasure in order to have the least possible amount of pain from life. (FW 12)

Two aphorisms express in a more forthright manner than ever before the world as Nietzsche then saw it—a world of appearance with no possibility of a 'break-through' to any 'higher reality'—and his resolution to see this world as it had to be seen: as 'acceptable':

> *Consciousness of appearance.* In what a marvellous and new and at the same time terrible and ironic relationship with the totality of existence do I feel myself to stand with my knowledge! I have *discovered* for myself that the old human and animal world, indeed the entire prehistory and past of all sentient being, works on, loves on, hates on, thinks on in me—I have suddenly awoken in midst of this dream but only to the consciousness that I am dreaming and that I *have* to go on dreaming in order not to be destroyed: as the sleepwalker has to go on dreaming in order not to fall. What is 'appearance' to me now! Certainly not the opposite of some kind of being—what can I possibly say about being of any kind that is not a predicate of its appearance! Certainly not a dead mask placed over an unknown 'x', which could, if one wished, be removed! Appearance is for me the active and living itself, which goes so far in its self-mockery as to allow me to feel that there is nothing here but appearance and will-o'-the-wisp and a flickering dance of spirits—that among all these dreamers I too, the 'man of knowledge', dance my dance, that the man of knowledge is a means of spinning out the earthly dance and to that extent one of the masters-of-ceremonies of existence, and that the sublime consistency and unity of all knowledge is and will be perhaps the supreme means of *preserving* the universality of dreaming and the mutual intelligibility of all these dreamers, and thereby the *continuance of the dream.* (FW 54)

> I want to learn more and more to see what is necessary in things as the beautiful in them—thus I shall become one of those who make things beautiful. *Amor fati:* may that be my love from now on! I want to wage no war against the ugly. I do not want to accuse, I do not want even to accuse the accusers. May *looking*

away be my only form of negation! And, all in all: I want to be at all times hereafter only an affirmer [*ein Ja-sagender*]! (FW 276)

This last passage was written on New Year's Day 1882; six months earlier the ideas circulating within him coalesced into the conception of the eternal recurrence. It was the ultimate fruit of his study of the Greeks, and it became the fundamental idea of *Zarathustra*. The moment when it flashed into his consciousness was preserved in his memory until he wrote about it in *Ecce Homo*:

> . . . the *idea of the eternal recurrence*, the extremest formula of affirmation that can ever be attained—belongs to the August of the year 1881: it was scribbled down on a piece of paper, with the postscript: '6,000 feet beyond man and time'. (EH–Z 1)

It provided Nietzsche with a new picture of a non-metaphysical reality, a reconciliation of 'becoming' with 'being', a goal for mankind. As it appears in *The Gay Science* the idea is simply a suggestion, a 'what if?': its full implications could be established only after the theory of the will to power and the superman had been clearly formulated: in the meantime, this 'what if?' stood at the end of *The Gay Science* as a bizarre puzzle to all who read it:

> *The heaviest burden.* What if a demon crept after you one day or night in your loneliest solitude and said to you: 'This life, as you live it now and have lived it, you will have to live again and again, times without number; and there will be nothing new in it, but every pain and every joy and every thought and sigh and all the unspeakably small and great in your life must return to you, and every-thing in the same series and sequence—and in the same way this spider and this moonlight among the trees, and in the same way this moment and I myself. The eternal hour-glass of existence will be turned again and again—and you with it, you dust of dust!'—Would you not throw yourself down and gnash your teeth and curse the demon who thus spoke? Or have you experienced a tremendous moment in which you would have answered him: 'You are a god and never did I hear anything more divine!' If this thought gained power over you it would, as you are now, transform and perhaps crush you; the question in all and every-thing: 'do you want this again and again, times without number?' would lie as the heaviest burden upon all your actions. Or how well disposed towards your-self and towards life would you have to become to have *no greater desire* than for this ultimate eternal sanction and seal? (FW 341)

10

Lou Salomé

Whom does woman hate most?—Thus spoke the iron to the magnet: 'I
hate you most, because you attract me but are not strong enough to draw
me towards you.' (Z I 18)

1

By the summer of 1882 Nietzsche had, in a sense, already started writing *Thus
Spoke Zarathustra*. The foundations of the book had been laid in the series
from *Human, All Too Human* to *The Gay Science,* and in the last work the
specific outlook and tone of *Zarathustra* appear in many passages.[1] Part One of
Zarathustra was put on to paper in February 1883. These facts should help us
to see the 'affair' of Lou Salomé in its proper perspective. At the time, Nietzsche thought it very important, and his disappointment at its failure threw
him off balance for a while: but there is no ground for thinking it changed him
in any way or that his work from 1883 onwards would have been any different
in its essentials if he had never met Lou Salomé.

After staying for about a month with Nietzsche in Genoa, Paul Rée left on the
13th March (1882) and shortly afterwards turned up in Rome, where, at
Malwida's house there he encountered Lou Salomé and fell in love with her.
Lou (properly Louise) was born in St. Petersburg in 1861, daughter of a
Russian general of Huguenot extraction. Determined to live a life of independence she had left Russia in September 1880 in the company of her mother to
study at the university of Zurich; there she fell ill and a friend gave her a letter
of introduction to Malwida and the suggestion she should go to Rome to

[1]E.g. sections 115, 121, 124, 125, 153, 183, 267, the eight questions and answers of 268–75, and book
four entire (276–342).

recuperate. She arrived at Malwida's in January 1882, and was staying with her when Rée arrived.

Rée proposed marriage to her, but she declined and counter-proposed that they should live and study together 'as brother and sister', with a second man for company. This idea surprised Rée (and outraged Malwida when she heard of it), but he accepted it and suggested Nietzsche as the third party. Nietzsche had left Genoa on the 29th March and gone to Messina, where he stayed for three weeks:[1] his health was very low, and he was probably on his way back to Germany to consult his doctor when he appeared in Rome towards the end of April. He was surprised to learn from Malwida that Rée was also in Rome and in the company of the young lady Rée had mentioned in a letter to him of the middle of March. He met them both and was at once smitten with Lou as Rée had been. A couple of days after their meeting, Rée told Lou that Nietzsche had asked him to propose to her on his behalf. Lou was interested in Nietzsche as the third for their *ménage-à-trois*—to which idea he had agreed with alacrity—but neither then nor later was she interested in him as a husband. He was rejected; the 'study plan', however, was still on, with Vienna as the suggested venue.

Nietzsche seemed to be content with this arrangement, but secretly he had not given up hope of winning Miss Salomé, and after a short holiday tour in Italy and Switzerland with her, her mother and Rée (during which they visited Orta and its famous Monte Sacro), he again proposed, this time in person and this time, it appears, very soberly and earnestly. Lou told him she was not interested in marriage, not only with him but with anyone, and that she wanted to live the life of an independent woman. With this reply he again appeared content and to be satisfied with their plans to live and study together in Vienna.

This second proposal took place in Lucerne on the 13th May. From the 23rd May to the 24th June he was in Naumburg; Lou and Rée had gone off to stay with Rée's mother in Stibbe, in West Prussia. The events of the summer are not very clear. In an undated letter to Overbeck from Naumburg Nietzsche says:

> So far as the summer goes, everything is still very uncertain. I am keeping quite quiet here [i.e. about Lou Salomé]. I am absolutely determined to keep my sister out of it; she could only confuse things (and herself most of all).[2]

---

[1]On Nietzsche's trip to Messina see the Postscript.

[2]The letter of April to Elizabeth from Rome, telling her about Lou, is a falsification; see Karl Schlechta's edition of Nietzsche (Munich 1960), vol. III, pp. 1408 ff.

To Lou he wrote on the 10th June:

> I have such high hopes of our plan to live together that all . . . things secondary to that make little impression on me.

Some time during the month at Naumburg he did tell Elizabeth about Lou. How much he told her we do not know; probably he said merely that the young lady was a possible 'disciple' whom he would like to get to know better, and that for this he needed Elizabeth's help. Elizabeth was due to visit Bayreuth that summer to attend the first performances of *Parsifal*, and it was arranged that Lou should accompany her; afterwards they were to proceed to the Thuringian resort of Tautenburg, where Nietzsche would already be installed. At Tautenburg the three would spend three weeks relaxing and talking, and (Nietzsche must privately have thought) Elizabeth would gradually be initiated into the 'immoral' plan for the coming winter. He went off to Tautenburg on the 25th June, and on the 2nd July he wrote to Lou:

> Now the sky above me is bright! Yesterday it seemed as if it must be my birthday: *you* sent me your assent [i.e. to come to Tautenburg], the best present anyone could have given me—my sister sent me some cherries, Teubner [a printer] sent the first three proof-sheets of the *Gay Science*, and in addition to all this the last part of the manuscript of the *Gay Science* was completed, and therewith the work of six years (1876 to 1882), my entire 'free-thought'! . . . So far as the winter goes I am thinking *seriously and exclusively* of Vienna: my sister's winter plans are quite independent of mine . . . I don't want to be lonely any more; I want to learn to be human again. Alas, in *this* field I have almost everything still to learn!

Elizabeth and Lou arrived at Tautenburg on the 7th August; they had already quarrelled and Elizabeth had made up her mind that Lou was the wrong sort of woman to associate with Fritz and must be disposed of. The three weeks at Tautenburg hardened her in that opinion, and on the day Lou left, the 26th, there was a row between brother and sister which led to Nietzsche's leaving the following day. He went to Naumburg, and at the beginning of September he wrote to Elizabeth (apparently in reply to a letter she had written to their mother):

> I am sorry to hear you are still thinking about that scene, which I would gladly have spared you. But look at it from this point of view: through this scene there came to *light* what would perhaps otherwise have remained hidden for a long time: that L. had an *indifferent* opinion of me and was *somewhat mistrustful* of me; and when I weigh the circumstances of our association, she had perhaps a

right to that (taking into account the effect of certain incautious remarks of our friend Rée). But now she certainly thinks *better* of me—and *that* is the main thing, is it not, my dear sister?

So far as Elizabeth was concerned it was *not* the main thing: the main thing was to get Fritz out of the immoral woman's clutches. She wrote their mother telling her she refused to come back to Naumburg while her brother was there, and explaining why: Fritz was now associating with an immoral woman, Lou Salomé; there had been disgraceful behaviour and more was planned. Nietzsche was now subjected to a further righteous scene, this time with his mother, as an outcome of which he left Naumburg in a hurry and went to Leipzig. A letter to Overbeck from there explains what had happened:

> Unhappily, my sister has developed into a mortal enemy of Lou. She has been full of moral indignation from beginning to end and says she finally understands what my philosophy is all about. She wrote my mother that she saw my philosophy come to life at Tautenburg and was shocked: *I* love evil, she says, but *she* loves good . . . In short, I have Naumburg 'virtue' against me; it has come to a real *breach* between us—and my mother too so far forgot herself as to say something that made me pack my case and go to Leipzig next morning.[1]

Lou and Elizabeth were very different in nature, and it was never likely they would get on well together; but, even if he understood this, Nietzsche underestimated his sister's possessiveness and her obtuseness about his 'philosophy'. Elizabeth, for her part, quite misunderstood the situation with which she was confronted: she believed, and never ceased to believe, that the freethinking and free-living Miss Salomé was 'chasing' her brother and had ensnared him; whereas the truth was that Lou was indifferent to Nietzsche as a man. She admired him as a thinker and talker and enjoyed his company only slightly less than he enjoyed hers; but the *emotion* was all on Nietzsche's side.

If he had reckoned without Elizabeth's hatred for Lou, he had also reckoned without Rée's love for her. When Rée and Lou came to Leipzig at the beginning of October Rée had already decided, so it seems, that Nietzsche must be excluded from any future plans involving himself and Lou: he was too dangerous a rival. The three weeks spent at Leipzig were outwardly cheerful enough. The *ménage-à-trois* was now to be set up in Paris; Nietzsche had been making inquiries for suitable accommodation, and he was mildly puzzled when, at the end of the month, Lou and Rée left for Stibbe without any

---

[1]From a later letter we learn that she had said he was a 'disgrace to his father's grave', a remark which, if my reading of Nietzsche's feelings towards his dead father is accurate, would have been enough to drive him away in baffled rage.

definite date for another meeting having been fixed. At the beginning of
November Gast arrived in Leipzig, and during the following fortnight spent
in his company Nietzsche gradually realized he had been ditched. When the
fact was finally borne in upon him he fled back to Italy in rage and despair. He
was in Basel for Overbeck's birthday on the 15th November, but went straight
on to Genoa; incapable of settling there again he transferred to Rapallo, where
he stayed, alone, until the 23rd February of the following year.

2

There is no simple formula to sum up the state of his mind during the ten
months or so he required to grow calm again. He was a proud man, and the
thought that he had devoted himself to Lou Salomé—a girl of 21—as he had
to no other woman and that she had then calmly walked out maddened him: it
was his pride, first and foremost, which was wounded. But a letter from Rée
trying to explain matters could make him see the affair in a more reasonable
light:

> But, my dear friend, [he wrote in reply (towards the end of November),] I
> thought you would feel quite the *reverse* and be quietly glad to have got *rid* of
> me! There have been a hundred times this year, from Orta onwards, when I felt
> you had 'paid too much' for your friendship with me. I have already filched
> much too much of *your* Roman discovery (I mean Lou)—and it always seemed
> to me, that is in Leipzig, that you had a right to be a little withdrawn from me.
> Think as well of me as you can, dear friend, and ask Lou to do the same. I belong
> to you both, from the heart . . . We shall see one another from time to time,
> won't we?

Then he began to brood on the events of the past summer and autumn, and
reproachful and spiteful letters would go out to Lou and Rée. Here is one
dated mid-December:

> Don't let my outbreaks of 'megalomania' or 'wounded vanity' bother you too
> much—and if I should one day happen to take my own life in some fit of
> passion, there wouldn't be anything in that to worry about overmuch. What are
> my fantasies to you! . . . Just bear clearly in mind that I am, after all, a semi-
> madman totally confused by solitude. I came to this (as I think) *reasonable* view
> of the situation after I had taken—from despair—an enormous dose of opium.
> Instead of losing my senses through it I seemed at last to *come* to them. To be
> sure, I was really ill for a week.

This may have happened, but there is no need to believe it actually did: the object of the letter is to warn the miscreants that their victim might be driven to suicide—and how would they feel then? A letter of Christmas Day 1882 to Overbeck reveals the depths of sickness and despair Nietzsche had by then plumbed:

> I have suffered from the disgraceful and anguishing recollections of this past summer as from a kind of madness . . . They involve a conflict of contrary emotions which I am not equal to . . . If only I could sleep! But the strongest sleeping-draughts help as little as do the six to eight hour walks I take. If I cannot find the magic formula to turn all this—muck to *gold,* I am lost . . . I now mistrust everybody: I sense in everything I hear contempt towards me . . . Yesterday I broke off all correspondence with my mother: I couldn't endure it any longer . . . My relationship with Lou is at its last painful gasp: at least, that is what I think today . . . Sometimes I think of renting a small room in Basel, visiting you now and then and attending lectures. Sometimes I think of doing the opposite: of driving my solitude and resignation to the ultimate limit and—

There speaks in this cry not only the voice of the sick and suffering man but also the voice of the artist, the man who turns muck into gold. *Zarathustra* is, in one of its aspects, a hymn to solitude and its hero the loneliest man in literature. Robinson Crusoe has his Friday, his chest of tools and his hopes of rescue; but Zarathustra has only his eagle and his serpent: he is 'out of humanity's reach' in very truth, alone even when he walks in the market-place. Nietzsche had entitled the last chapter of *Human, All Too Human* 'Man Alone with Himself'; now, in *Thus Spoke Zarathustra*, he attempts a representation at length of a man alone with himself: at first choosing solitude, then growing weary of it, seeking companions to banish it, discovering that he is alone even when surrounded by followers, accepting solitude as his lot, retreating into it and at last praising and glorifying it. Even when ostensibly talking to others Zarathustra sounds as if he were addressing himself: an effect of the well-known laconism of his style. What is unclear in *Zarathustra* is so because Nietzsche is assuming in the reader a background of knowledge similar to his own: if the reader has read the series from *Human, All Too Human* to *The Gay Science* he will share that background; if not, not. In any event, *Zarathustra* appears to care little whether he is understood or not, and he himself is the only listener to whom he imparts the ultimate secret of the eternal recurrence. Having broken with his family because of his association with Lou and Rée, and then having been deserted by them too, Nietzsche felt he was now truly alone in the world, and his health was such that, ridiculously, he could neither die nor live: had he not been an artist, we can feel tolerably certain that around the turn of the year he would have put an end to an existence grown to a painful absurdity. Being an artist he was able, instead, to translate the pains of solitude into pleasures, and in the figure of Zarathustra—who, like all imagined personages, is and is not his author—to create a type of man who desires solitude because it is his natural element.

The first part of *Zarathustra* is decisive for the tone and mood of the whole book. Nietzsche chose to open it by repeating almost literally the conclusion of *The Gay Science,* thus establishing the connection between his new work and his 'free-thought' which his critics have been at pains to deny. The superman and the will to power are introduced, and the criticism of contemporary society is of unexampled ferocity. The style is exuberant and exotic in the highest degree, and the thought is sometimes lost in a welter of metaphor and rhetoric. Sexual imagery is very abundant, and we have Nietzsche's own word for it that his vocabulary was not always under his control: there is certainly a hit-or-miss element in the manner, although the matter is sound and considered enough, deriving as it does from six years' cogitation.

It is painful to descend from the heights of *Zarathustra* to the realities of life in the following months. A reconciliation with Elizabeth led to a visit to Rome, where she was staying with Malwida, from the 4th May to the 16th June. There Nietzsche allowed himself to become convinced that Rée had been plotting against him from the beginning, and that Lou's defection was a consequence of Rée's misrepresentations. Elizabeth was already conducting a campaign against Lou Salomé of a kind that gives us a new idea of the meaning of female spite: letters were flying in all directions, and since Lou was then living unmarried with Rée in Berlin efforts were made to have her deported back to Russia as an immoral person. It cannot be doubted that, to his great discredit, Nietzsche was a party to this, or that he encouraged his sister to make trouble for both Lou and Rée by writing to their relations revealing the life they were leading. It is in these months of 1883 that Nietzsche's mentality is hardest to understand. It is best illustrated by his letters. The most important of them are unfortunately inexactly dated, and we can only guess at their precise order. In one addressed to Georg Rée, Paul's brother, dated 'summer 1883', he announces that further traffic with Paul Rée is 'beneath *my dignity*'—this is why he is writing to Georg instead. He has discovered that Lou Salomé had all along been 'only the mouthpiece' for Paul, who had behaved behind his back 'like a sneaking, slanderous, mendacious rogue'.

It is he who speaks of me as a low character and common egoist, who desires to use everything only for his own ends, . . . who reproaches me with having, behind the mask of ideals, pursued the filthiest designs on Frl. Salomé, . . . who dares to speak contemptuously of my intellect, as if I were a lunatic who doesn't know what he is doing.

As for Lou herself, she is 'a dried-up, dirty, ill-smelling monkey with false breasts'. Do we catch the gentle tones of Elizabeth in this brief account of what Rée is supposed to have said about him? It is hard to think from whom he could have learned such information if not from here. We know a lot about Rée's character, and this kind of spiteful talk is foreign to it; but it is not foreign to Elizabeth's, and all in all one is inclined to believe that she made it up, with the aim of turning her brother into a willing ally in her campaign against the hated Lou Salomé. Nietzsche was, of course, very foolish to believe her—as he later confessed. Her reaction to his flirtation with his young admirer had been fantastically extravagant: one might imagine that never before in human history had a man and a woman been alone together, and her continued proceedings against Lou *after* Nietzsche was disaffected from her suggest a neurotic obsession—long before the year 1883 was out, Nietzsche had come to his senses and seen that what Rée had done was no more than what he himself had wanted to do, and that it had simply been ill-luck that both had fallen in love with the same woman; but Elizabeth maintained her feud with Lou until her death in 1935. (Lou died in 1937.)

At the end of June Nietzsche went back to Sils-Maria and almost at once wrote the second part of *Zarathustra*.[1] It is in no way inferior to the first part and seems the product of a mind at a different level of culture from the one that spat out, in a letter to Malwida dated August:

> According to all I have now discovered—alas, *far too late*—these persons Rée and Lou are not worthy to lick the soles of my boots.—Pardon this all-too-masculine figure of speech! It has been a protracted misfortune for me that this Rée, a liar and sneaking slanderer to the core, has crossed my path.

Two letters to Overbeck show balance returning. One, dated simply 'Sils-Maria summer 1883', is a direct contradiction of the August letter to Malwida:

> My relations and I—we are too different from one another. The precaution I thought necessary last winter of receiving no more letters from them can no

---

[1] He maintains in *Ecce Homo* that the first two parts of *Zarathustra* were each written in ten days, but in *Ecce Homo* he consistently exaggerates the speed at which he could work. *Götzen-Dämmerung*, for example, was, he claims, 'a work of so few days that I hesitate to reveal their number' (EH–G 1), yet it can be shown that he was engaged upon it over a period of two months, if not longer. The exact time in which parts one and two of *Zarathustra* were written must therefore remain uncertain.

longer be maintained. (I am not hard enough for that.) But every contemptuous word directed against Rée or Frl. Salomé makes my heart bleed: it seems I am ill-equipped to be an enemy.

Late in August he visited Overbeck and after returning wrote him that he now felt 'a genuine hatred for my sister', who had so worked upon him that

at last I have become a victim of a pitiless revengefulness, while my innermost thought is against all revenge and punishment . . . It is no longer even advisable for me to write letters to my sister—except the most harmless kind . . . Perhaps my most fateful step in this whole affair was to become reconciled to her—I can see *now* that she took that as a justification for her revenge on Frl. Salomé.

This, really, was the end of the affair. Nietzsche returned to his former way of life and never met Lou or Rée again, although he sometimes had sentimental thoughts about them: writing to Overbeck from Nice on the 7th April 1884, for instance, he says that he is hoping to gather a few friends around him there, including 'perhaps even Dr. Rée and Frl. Salomé, with whom I should like to put right what my sister has put wrong.' If one wishes to apportion blame the task is easy: everyone was to blame. But perhaps Nietzsche himself was to blame most of all. Elizabeth, the cloistered, religiously-minded spinster, with her narrow code of morals and vindictive hatred for a woman less inhibited and freer than she was, knew no better than to pursue such a woman with all the spite outraged virtue could summon up; Nietzsche did know better, but instead of restraining he abetted her. He must have felt some shame at this, for to the end he laid the responsibility on his sister. 'I should like to put right what my sister has put wrong,' he says, but no one can believe he was a mere tool in Elizabeth's hands: the relationship between them was not of that kind, for he was always the dominant personality. Ultimately, if his affair with Lou Salomé ended in a welter of mud-slinging and abuse, *he* was to blame.

It should be added that the student who looks to the principals in the affair for further enlightenment is disappointed. Nietzsche himself, whenever he refers to Lou in his letters—which is not very often—plays down his emotional involvement, and speaks of her simply as a friend. There is only one overt reference to her in *Ecce Homo*, and this is only to correct a supposed misunderstanding concerning the authorship of the poem *Hymn to Life*, which Nietzsche set to music in 1882 and which, he says, was not by him but by 'a young Russian lady, Fräulein von Salomé, with whom I was then friendly' (EH–Z 1).

Lou Salomé's book *Friedrich Nietzsche in seinen Werken*, published in 1894, is silent on the subject of the events of 1882–83, and her memoirs, post-humously published in 1957, are equally unenlightening. Asked, many years afterwards, whether Nietzsche had kissed her on the trip to Monte Sacro she replied that she didn't remember.

The eternal recurrence had been held in reserve to form the climax of *Zarathustra:* it is introduced in the third part, written during January 1884 at Nice. In terms of poetic power the sixteen chapters which form this part excel anything Nietzsche had written before: the occasional tumbles into bathos are no more than the occupational hazard of a writer who attempts to stretch language to the pitch of expressiveness essayed here. The fourth part, written in the autumn and winter of 1884–85, was intended as the first of a second group of three parts. It is markedly inferior in style and contains no new ideas, and Nietzsche was wise to call a halt to the work: the glowing conclusion of the third part is the book's true climax and the seal upon what was by then a complete philosophical outlook on the world.

11

Zarathustra

I taught them all *my* art and aims: to compose into one and bring together what is fragment and riddle and dreadful chance in man. (Z III 12)

Between *The Gay Science* and *Thus Spoke Zarathustra* Nietzsche arrived at the hypothesis that all actions are motivated by the desire for power. Employing Schopenhauer's terminology he called this principle the 'will to power', and by means of it he now tried to give a picture of a possible reality deprived of all metaphysical support.

The will to power is introduced in the chapter called 'Of the Thousand and One Goals': hitherto there have been many peoples, consequently many 'goals'—i.e. moralities; the reason each people has had its own morality is that morality is will to power—not only power over others but more essentially power over oneself:

Zarathustra has seen many lands and many peoples: thus he has discovered the good and evil of many peoples. Zarathustra has found no greater power on earth than good and evil. No people could live without evaluating; but if it wishes to maintain itself it must not evaluate as its neighbour evaluates. Much that seemed good to one people seemed shame and disgrace to another: thus I found. I found much that was called evil in one place was in another decked with purple honours . . . A table of values hangs over every people. Behold, it is the table of its overcomings; behold, it is the voice of its will to power. What it calls hard it calls praiseworthy; what it accounts indispensable and hard it calls good; and that which relieves the greatest need, the rare, the hardest of all—it glorifies as holy. Whatever causes it to rule and conquer and glitter, to the dread and envy of its neighbours, that it accounts the sublimest, the paramount, the evaluation and the meaning of all things. (Z I 15)

Morality, understood as being identical with custom, is now visualized as the *self-overcoming* of a people: a herd turns its desire for power *against itself*, it conquers itself, it learns to obey self-imposed commands, and in obeying becomes 'a people'. From the beginning of his philosophical writings Nietzsche had always felt justified in applying to the individual the same criteria as he applied to a state; he had always viewed the individual as a kind of miniature state, with the same drives at work and the same needs. Consequently, in the second part of *Zarathustra* he applies his theory of the will to power to the individual:

> *Of Self-Overcoming* . . . I have followed the living creature, I have followed the greatest and smallest paths, that I might understand its nature . . . wherever I found living creatures, there too I heard the language of obedience. All living creatures are obeying creatures. And this is the second thing: he who cannot obey himself will be commanded . . . But this is the third thing I heard: that commanding is more difficult than obeying . . . In all commanding there appeared to me to be an experiment and a risk: and the living creature always risks himself when he commands. Yes, even when he commands himself: then also must he make amends for his commanding. He must become judge and avenger and victim of his own law. How has this come about? thus I asked myself. What persuades the living creature to obey and to command and to practise obedience even in commanding? . . . where I found a living creature, there I found will to power; and even in the will of the servant I found the will to be master. The will of the weaker persuades it to serve the stronger; its will wants to be master of those weaker still: this delight alone it is unwilling to forgo. And as the lesser surrenders to the greater, that it may have delight and power over the least of all, so the greatest, too, surrenders, and for the sake of power stakes—life . . . And where sacrifice and service and loving glances are, there too is will to be master. There the weaker steals by secret paths into the castle and even into the heart of the more powerful—and steals the power. And life told me this secret: 'Behold', it said, 'I am that *which must overcome itself again and again*. To be sure, you call it will to procreate or impulse towards a goal, towards the higher, more distant, more manifold: but all this is one and one secret. I would rather perish than renounce this one thing: and truly, where there is perishing and the falling of leaves, behold, there life sacrifices itself—for the sake of power! . . . and you too, you enlightened man, are only a path and footstep of my will: truly, my will to power walks with the feet of your will to truth! . . . Only where life is, there is also will: not will to life, but . . . will to power! The living creature values many things higher than life itself; yet out of this evaluation itself speaks—the will to power!' Thus life once taught me: and with this teaching do I solve the riddle of your hearts, you wisest men . . . You exert power with your values and doctrines of good and evil, you assessors of values . . . But a mightier power and a new

overcoming grow from out your values . . . And he who has to be a creator in good and evil, truly, has first to be a destroyer and break values. Thus the greatest evil belongs with the greatest good . . . (Z II 12)

To see how completely this theory is a development of Nietzsche's earlier experiments one must recall what he had written about obeying and commanding, about self-sacrifice for the sake of power, about the interdependence of good and evil:

Those capacities which are dreadful and accounted inhuman are, indeed, perhaps the fruitful soil out of which alone all humanity in impulse, act and deed can grow. ('Homer's Contest')

[The virtuous man] always rises against the blind power of facts, against the tyranny of the actual, and submits himself to laws that are not the laws of historical flux . . . either by fighting his passions, as the nearest brute actualities of his existence, or by dedicating himself to honesty. (UII 8)

St. Luke 18, 14 improved. He that humbleth himself wants to be exalted. (MA 87)

There exists a *defiance of oneself* of which many forms of asceticism are among the most sublimated expressions. (MA 142)

When man feels the sense of power, he feels and calls himself good. (M 189)

. . . philosophy was a kind of exalted struggle for the tyrannical lordship of the spirit. (M 547)

. . . the spectacle of that strength which employs genius *not for works* but *for itself as a work;* that is, for its own constraint . . . (M 548)

. . . valuation and an ordering of rank of the human drives and actions . . . are always the expression of the needs of a community and herd. (FW 116)

The strongest and most evil spirits have hitherto advanced mankind the most: . . . the evil impulses are just as useful, indispensable and preservative of the species as the good. (FW 4)

With the aid of the will to power Nietzsche was now able to see the Darwinian struggle for existence as a special case of the struggle for domination:

To want to preserve oneself is the expression of a state of distress, of a limitation of the true basic drive of life, which aims at *extension of power* and with this in view often enough calls in question self-preservation and sacrifices it . . . in nature, the rule is not a state of distress but one of superfluity and prodigality, even to the point of absurdity. The struggle for existence is only an *exception,* a temporary restriction of the basic will of life; the struggle, great and small, turns everywhere on ascendancy, on growth and extension, on power, according to the will to power, which is precisely the will of life. (FW 349—in book five of FW, written after Z)

Physiologists should think again before positing the drive to self-preservation as the cardinal drive in an organic being. A living thing wants above all to *vent* its strength—life itself is will to power—: self-preservation is only one of the indirect and most frequent *consequences* of it.—In short, here as everywhere be on your guard against *superfluous* teleological principles!—such as is the drive to self-preservation. (J 13)

He can now try to explain what he had criticized David Strauss for refusing to explain: the origin of the 'good' qualities in the 'evil', in the world as it appeared after Darwin. 'Good' qualities are sublimated passion, and passion now means will to power:

Once you had passions and called them evil. But now you have only your virtues: they grew from out your passions . . . Once you had fierce dogs in your cellar: but they changed at last into birds and sweet singers. From your poison you brewed your balsam; you milked your cow, affliction, now you drink the sweet milk of her udder. (Z I 5)

For virtue to be possible, the 'evil' passions must be allowed to flourish, for they are the only source of virtue, the only driving power; hence Nietzsche's enmity towards those who would extirpate the passions because they are dangerous: he does not deny that the will to power is dangerous, but it must be controlled, 'sublimated', not weakened and destroyed:

It does not suffice that the lightning no longer does harm. I do not want to conduct it away: it shall learn—to work for *me.* (Z IV 13 7)

This is why he condemns weakness, however it may be disguised—for example, as 'moderation':

It is not your sin, but your moderation that cries to heaven, your very meanness in sinning cries to heaven! (Z I *Vorrede* 3)

Great wickedness, even, is preferable to weakness, because it gives ground for hope: where there is a great crime there is also great energy, great will to power, consequently the possibility of 'self-overcoming'. One has misunderstood Nietzsche completely unless one realizes that he visualized the overcoming of *self* as the most difficult of all tasks, as well as the most desirable; that he considered the will to power to be the only drive alive in man; that a strong will to power was needed for the hardest task; and that therefore the man of strong but ungoverned will to power was preferable to the man whose will to power was weak, although the former was certainly more 'dangerous'. Because 'good' is sublimated 'evil', evil has a positive value, and the extirpation of the evil impulses would not leave the good behind—the good would vanish too. To abolish the 'good Eris' is to abolish mankind, which has grown to be what it is through contest. Therefore: 'rather . . . a Cesare Borgia than . . . a Parsifal' (EH III 1): rather an evil man than one whose goodness consists in not doing evil, in *not being able* to do evil. Anyone who thinks Nietzsche admired Cesare Borgia *as such* has not understood him on this point: the men he admired were those whose will to power was strong but sublimated into creativity, men who had 'become them who they are', *Übermenschen:*

> *I teach you the superman.* Man is something that should be overcome. What have you done to overcome him? All creatures hitherto have created something beyond themselves: and do you want to be the ebb of this great tide, and return to the animals rather than overcome man? . . . The superman is the meaning of the earth. Let your will say: The superman *shall be* the meaning of the earth! I entreat you, my brothers, *remain true to the earth.* (Z I *Vorrede* 3)

The superman is he who achieves in himself what nations once achieved when they raised themselves from the level of herds:

> Can you furnish yourself with your own good and evil and hang up your own will above yourself as a law? Can you be judge of yourself and an avenger of your law? . . . you yourself will always be the worst enemy you can encounter; you yourself lie in wait for yourself in caves and forests. (Z I 17)

All creatures desire power but only man is able to desire power over himself; only man has the requisite amount of power to achieve *self*-mastery.[1] The distinction between man and animal, obliterated by Darwin, is restored—and without recourse to the supernatural; moral values, deprived of divine sanc-

---

[1] An explanation of how mankind achieved its superiority in this respect is attempted in *Towards a Genealogy of Morals:* see Chapter 12 of the present volume.

tion, now receive a new, naturalistic sanction: quanta of power; human psychology is now understood in terms of power; 'good' is now understood as sublimated 'evil', the evil and the good passions being essentially the same, i.e. will to power. The new outlook is summarized in concisest form in *The Anti-Christ:*

> What is good?—All that heightens the feeling of power, the will to power, power itself in man. What is bad?—All that proceeds from weakness. What is happiness?—The feeling that power *increases*—that a resistance is overcome . . . (A 2)

All men desire happiness because all desire the feeling of increased power; the greatest increase of power brings the greatest happiness; that which demands the greatest power is the overcoming of oneself; the happiest man is the man who has overcome himself—the superman.

The whole sense of the philosophy which produced the superman makes it clear that what is being held up here as a new 'image of man' to stand against the growing nihilism of modern Europe—a man who is no longer animal; and it is suggested that the 'goal' of mankind is to 'produce supermen'—that is, to transform itself into the no-longer-animal. Man will then have a positive value, the term 'man' will possess a specific connotation as distinct from the animal world in general, and it will then be possible once again to speak of 'good and evil' as 'eternal' qualities—as value judgments valid for the whole world because determined by a genuinely higher being:

> When I visited men, I found them sitting upon an old self-conceit. Each one thought he had long since known what was good and evil for man . . . I disturbed this somnolence when I taught that *nobody yet knows* what is good and evil—unless it be the creator. But he it is who creates a goal for mankind and gives the earth its meaning and its future: he it is who *creates* the quality of good and evil in things. (Z III 12 2)

It is in this sense that the superman can be called 'God's successor':

> Once you said 'God' when you gazed upon distant seas; but now I have taught you to say 'superman'. God is a supposition: but I want your supposing to reach no further than your creating will. Could you *create* a god? But you could surely create the superman . . . God is a supposition: but I want your supposing to be bounded by conceivability. Could you *conceive* a god?—But may the will to truth mean this to you: that everything shall be transformed into the humanly-conceivable, the humanly-evident, the humanly-palpable . . . And you your-

selves should create what you have hitherto called the World . . . Neither in the incomprehensible nor in the irrational can you be at home. (Z II 2)

In the universe in which Nietzsche grew up God was the highest being, and man, raised above the animals by the divinity breathed into him by God and sustained in his elevation by divine grace, was promised that the life he led was eternal, death being only a transition from one state of existence to another. During his twenties he was compelled to accept a universe which was the contrary of all this: there was no highest being, men were essentially continuous with the animals, and death was the end. Unable to deny the scientific basis of this world-picture, he came to see in his thirties that the 'death of God' meant that a new description of reality was called for in which the metaphysical world could find no place. In his forties he put forward three hypotheses which, whether he intended it or not, offered naturalistic substitutes for God, divine grace and eternal life: instead of God, the superman; instead of divine grace, the will to power; and instead of eternal life—the eternal recurrence.

The will to power and the superman evolved as a consequence of the need to account for certain implications of a non-metaphysical reality; but the eternal recurrence is the consequence of a non-metaphysical reality *as such:* it springs from the fact that—as Nietzsche saw it—the metaphysical world is nothing but a contradiction of the world of appearance, the metaphysical plane nothing more than an antithesis to the mundane plane, and the very idea of a metaphysical reality part of the world of phenomena; and that is why he considered it the crown of his philosophy. At first Zarathustra fears the eternal recurrence and does everything he can to delay the day when he must recognize its possible truth. At length, in the third part of the book, he relates a nightmare in which he has imagined eternity as a gateway with two paths leading from it in opposite directions:

Behold this gateway . . . : it has two aspects. Two paths come together here; no one has ever reached their end. This long lane behind us: it goes on for an eternity. They are in opposition to one another, these paths; they abut on one another. The name of the gateway is written above it: 'Moment'. But if one were to follow them further and ever further: do you think . . . that these paths would be in eternal opposition? . . . Behold this moment! . . . From this gateway Moment a long, eternal lane runs *back:* an eternity lies behind us. Must not all things that *can* run have already run along this lane? Must not all things that *can* happen *have* already happened, been done, run past? And if all things have been here before: what do you think of this moment . . . ? Must not this gateway, too, have been here—before? And are not all things bound fast together in such a way that this moment draws after it all future things? *Therefore*—draws itself too? For all things that *can* run *must* also run once again forward along this long lane. And this slow spider that creeps along in the moonlight, and this moonlight itself, and I and you at this gateway whispering together, whispering of eternal things—must we not all have been here before?—and must we not return and run down that other lane out before us, down that terrible long lane—must we not return eternally? (Z III 2 2)

It is not until near the end of the third part that Zarathustra gains the courage to view this idea in the cold light of day, and even then it is his emblematic animals, his eagle and his serpent, who have to spell out to him what the recurrence means in all its details:

Sing and bubble over, O Zarathustra, heal your soul with new songs, so that you may bear your great destiny, that was never yet the destiny of any man! For your animals well know, O Zarathustra, who you are and must become: behold, *you are the teacher of the eternal recurrence*, that is now *your* destiny! . . . Behold, we know what you teach: that all things recur eternally, and we ourselves with them, and that we have already existed an infinite number of times before and all things with us. You teach that there is a great year of becoming, a colossus of a year: this year must, like an hour-glass, turn itself over again and again, so that it may run down and run out anew. So that all these years resemble one another, in the greatest things and in the smallest, so that we ourselves resemble ourselves in each great year, in the greatest things and in the smallest. And if you should die now, O Zarathustra: behold, we know too what you would then say to yourself . . . 'Now I die and decay . . . and in an instant I shall be nothingness . . . But the complex of causes in which I am entangled will recur—it will create me again! . . . I shall return, with this sun, with this earth, with this eagle, with this serpent—*not* to a new life or a better life or a similar life: I shall return eternally to this identical and self-same life, in the greatest things and in the smallest, to teach once more the eternal recurrence of all things.' (Z III 13 2)

The premise behind the eternal recurrence is that the metaphysical world is an 'idea' belonging to the phenomenal world; i.e. does not exist: appearance *is* reality; when we deduct everything that can be called appearance we have nothing left over; consequently there can be no 'breakthrough' to another 'level' of reality—such expressions have no meaning, for however 'deep' we go we cannot get out of the world of phenomena.

From this thought to the thought that everything is repetition is a short step. To speak of a 'timeless world' is merely to use the characteristically negative language of metaphysics: the 'metaphysical world' is simply the negation of the actual world; the actual world exists in time, therefore one of the attributes of the metaphysical world must be timelessness (just as it is 'disembodied', i.e. spaceless). If we can never break out of the reality we perceive, then we are bound to a reality one of whose attributes is time; i.e. time is not an 'illusion' masking a 'timeless reality'. Another of the attributes of the reality to which we are bound is 'becoming': reality is 'becoming' and never is. Since reality 'becomes' *in time,* if a final state were possible it would have been achieved a long time ago; but empirically this is not so. Moreover, if there is no end-state there cannot have been a first-state either, since this would also have been a static condition, a 'being'. Empirically, our existence is temporal and unstable: time is real and change is real, and we know nothing of an existence in which time and change are absent. Now, if we are unable to posit either a beginning or an end to time, there must be a temporal infinity behind us and ahead of us; reality must be of endless duration, never breaking through to a state in which there is no duration. But we cannot say with the same certainty that the number of possible forms in which our ever-changing reality appears is infinite. Common sense suggests that it is not: however large a kaleidoscope one makes, and however many pieces of coloured paper one puts into it, the number of possible arrangements will not be infinite; the point will inevitably be reached when the number of possible arrangements, and the number of possible orders in which these arrangements appear, will have been exhausted and the series will begin to repeat itself.

The comparison between a 'becoming' reality and a kaleidoscope may seem inept, but in fact it exactly represents Nietzsche's picture of what 'becoming' entails. He refused to allow God or metaphysics to enter his thought by the back-door: having rejected God, he refused to admit some unverifiable principle which would turn out to be God in disguise. The failure of other 'free-thinkers' to take comparable precautions excited only his scorn: he attributed their behaviour to cowardice. But the world viewed as 'becoming' in the usual sense, as becoming *something,* as purposeful becoming—what would that be but God and metaphysics all over again? Can it be shown that there is any direction in nature? That the changes which we recognize as happening everywhere and constantly are governed by any laws or tending towards any goal? Is there anything in the universe we can recognize as a directing force? Nietzsche's answer was No; nothing of the sort can be demonstrated to exist: on the contrary, if the universe *had* a goal that goal would already have been reached. 'The total nature of the world is . . . to all eternity chaos' (FW 109)—for who is there, or what is there, to bring it to order? Every ordering principle, whether it be God, or 'nature', or 'history', must be imposed upon the flux of phenomena from outside—yet this 'outside' is still phenomenon. 'Becoming' is for Nietzsche utterly random change: *this* is the ultimate consequence of the 'death of God' which others had refused to draw, the inevitable result of the disappearance of the 'regulating finger of God' from the world; and it is to this that he alludes when he says that mankind must fix its *own* goal, for unless men make a purpose for themselves they will continue to live as they have lived hitherto—in chaos.

Nietzsche envisages the universe as a kaleidoscope of changes, and however many different states it is possible for this universe to fall into, their number must be finite. But time is infinite, so the present state of the universe must be a repetition of a previous state, as must the state which preceded it and the state which succeeds it: all events must recur an infinite number of times.

The consequence for the life of anyone who realizes this, says Nietzsche, is that the knowledge crushes him, unless he can attain to a supreme moment of existence for the sake of which he would be content to relive his whole life. The evil and pain in his life then become a positive good, since they were necessary for the achievement of this one supreme moment: if one event were subtracted, everything following would be different. The life to aim for is the life containing the greatest amount of joy—and joy is the feeling that power increases, that an obstacle is overcome. The superman, therefore, as the man whose will to power has increased the most by overcoming the most, is the most joyful man and the justification of existence. Such a man will affirm life, love life and say Yes even to misery and pain, because he realizes that the joy he has known would not have been possible apart from the pain he has known; and as he will not be dismayed at the idea that the joy of his life will be repeated endlessly, neither will he flinch from the knowledge that its pain must be repeated too:

> Did you ever say Yes to one joy? O my friends, then you said Yes to *all* woe as well. All things are chained and entwined together . . . if ever you said: 'You please me, happiness, instant, moment!' then you wanted *everything* to return! (Z IV 19 10)

The sensation of the increase of power, the sensation of joy, is itself the strongest advocate of the eternal recurrence, for joy *wants* eternity:

> O Man! Attend!
> What does deep midnight's voice contend?
> 'I slept my sleep,
> 'And now awake at dreaming's end:
> 'The world is deep,
> 'Deeper than day can comprehend.

'Deep is its woe,
'Joy—deeper than heart's agony:
'Woe says: Fade! Go!
'But all joy wants eternity,
'—wants deep, deep, deep eternity!'
                    (Z III 15 3; IV 19 12)

12

The Solitary

To live alone one must be an animal or a god—says Aristotle. There is
yet a third case: one must be both—a *philosopher*. (G I 3)

1

After the completion of *Zarathustra* Nietzsche felt as if a weight had been
lifted from him. The matter and the peculiar expressive manner of that book
had been accumulating within him since his days at Pforta and had at length
found impassioned release. The aftermath was not a feeling of exhaustion but
one of freedom and new vigour. He now had a working hypothesis—the will
to power—and he proceeded to develop it in a series of books comparable with
the pre-*Zarathustra* trilogy: *Beyond Good and Evil* (1886), *Towards a Genealogy of Morals* (1887) and *Twilight of the Idols* (written 1888, published 1889).
Stylistically these works are as different from *Human, All Too Human* as
Human, All Too Human is from *The Birth of Tragedy*. There has been a
marrying of the clarity and concision of the 'free-thinking' period with the
passion of *Zarathustra*, and the child is a style of passionate conciseness that is
seen to have been the style he was aiming for all along:

To create things upon which time tries its teeth in vain; in form and in *substance*
to strive after a little immortality—I have never been modest enough to demand
less of myself. The aphorism, the apothegm, in which I am the first master
among Germans, are the forms of 'eternity'; my ambition is to say in ten
sentences what everyone else says in a book—what everyone else does *not* say in
a book. (G IX 51)

The aphoristic form is gradually abandoned, but the spirit of aphorism—the
summation of a lengthy process of thought in a single striking sentence—

remains. In this sense *Götzen-Dämmerung*, the shortest of Nietzsche's important works, is an aphoristic summary of his entire thought.

The background to these publications (and to the short books of 1888 to be discussed later) is the unpublished material intended for what was to have been Nietzsche's major undertaking of the post-*Zarathustra* years: a large-scale summary of his work called variously *The Will to Power* and *The Revaluation of all Values*. The appearance after his death of a collection of notes and aphorisms under the former title has created confusion concerning his intentions regarding this work; the truth of the matter will be outlined in Chapter 14 below.

From 1883 to 1888 he spent the summer in Sils-Maria and the winter in Nice; the intervening seasons he spent mainly with Gast or at Naumburg, where he returned at the beginning of September 1883. If his idea was to resume his old footing with his mother and sister it was misconceived: the visit led to a general worsening of relations. Elizabeth's animus against Lou Salomé had not cooled in the least, and their mother's view of the 'affair' was entirely that of her daughter, through whose eyes she saw it: as already remarked, Nietzsche was notably inhibited where the expression of emotion was concerned, and this inhibition—which is far from uncommon and often passes under the name of delicacy—had restrained him from talking to his mother about Lou and his feelings for her. The Naumburg judgment on him at this time was that he no longer associated with 'respectable people', their conception of respectability being such that it excluded Lou Salomé and Paul Rée but included the then notorious anti-Semitic leader Dr. Bernhard Förster, to whom Nietzsche learned to his consternation Elizabeth had just become engaged. His sense that his two closest relatives understood him not at all was quickened by their insistence he should think of returning to the life of a university. He was still full of *Zarathustra* and dreaming of even greater things to come, and the suggestion that he might abandon this for the sake of a university post—assuming his health made it possible—was the least acceptable that could be imagined. He left Naumburg at the beginning of October and went back to Genoa. His health, he wrote to Overbeck on the 22nd, was 'unbelieveably low', and at the end of November he travelled to Nice: he now thought that what he needed was 'dry air', and he had heard Nice possessed a good supply. He found the city suited him and stayed there until the 20th April of the following year.

With the summer heat coming on he thought about returning to Sils-Maria, but before doing so he paid a visit to Peter Gast at Venice, with whom he stayed from the 21st April until the 12th June. Gast played him his newly-completed comic opera *The Lion of Venice;* Nietzsche was delighted with it, and determined to exert himself more to procure performances of Gast's music when and where he could. A two-week visit to Overbeck at Basel, from the 15th June to the 2nd July, was spoiled by Nietzsche's being ill the whole time; when he recovered he set out for Sils-Maria, arriving on the 16th July—after calling at Piora, near Airolo, and Zurich—and staying there until mid-September.

The most memorable event of these months was a visit from Heinrich von Stein (the 26th to the 28th August), a visit which Nietzsche counted as a sign he was exercising some influence within the Wagnerian camp. Stein had gone to Wahnfried in October 1879 at the age of 22 to act as tutor to Wagner's son Siegfried, and was co-editor (with Glasenapp) of the massive *Wagner-Lexikon* (1883), a monument to the days when Wagner was taken seriously as a thinker. After Wagner's death in February 1883 he had been one of the most active workers at Bayreuth, although his subsequent appointment as a teacher at Halle and Berlin universities occupied an increasingly large amount of his time. His book *Helden und Welt* appeared in 1883, and Wagner's last published work was an *Open Letter* to von Stein designed as an introduction to it. By 1884 Nietzsche's name was a blasphemous expression at Bayreuth, and it is therefore somewhat surprising that Stein should have read *Zarathustra* and then written to its author asking if he could come and see him. Nietzsche recalls the visit in *Ecce Homo:* Stein, he says,

> once appeared for three days at Sils-Maria, . . . explaining to everyone that he had *not* come for the Engadine. This excellent man, who with the whole impetuous artlessness of a Prussian Junker had waded into the Wagnerian swamp, . . . was during those three days as if transported by a storm-wind of freedom, like one suddenly raised to *his own* heights and given wings. I kept telling him it was a result of the fine air up here, that everyone felt the same, that you couldn't stand 6,000 feet above Bayreuth and not notice it—but he wouldn't believe me. (EH I 4)

Afterwards he alone of the Bayreuth garrison maintained relations with Nietzsche and there was a lively correspondence between them; his early death in June 1887 robbed Nietzsche of one of his few sympathizers in Germany.

The month of October was spent at Zurich, and here Nietzsche met Gottfried Keller, whom he considered the greatest German poet since the death of Heine and, indeed, the only German poet then living. He also got in touch with the Zurich *Kapellmeister* Friedrich Hegar and persuaded him to try out the overture to Gast's *Lion*, which the Zurich orchestra played with Nietzsche as the sole auditor. Hegar's opinion of the music was that it was too full of brass and woodwinds; Gast placed too little faith in the strings and wanted 'everything to be trumpeted out'. (See Nietzsche's letter to Gast of the 8th October.) Nietzsche's efforts on behalf of Gast's music continued during the following years: in June 1886 he obtained through his Leipzig friends a performance of Gast's Septet at the Gewandhaus, and he sent Gast's scores to various conductors and musicians, among them Bülow and Joachim. He even had the idea of approaching Brahms on the subject: he had heard Brahms had shown 'a lively interest' in *Beyond Good and Evil,* and it occurred to him that he might be able to turn this interest to Gast's advantage. (See his letter to Gast of the 18th July 1887. But nothing came of the idea.)

By December he was back in Nice, and for the following eighteen months his life was virtually devoid of outward incident. By 1885 he was living only to write: his nature had become almost perfectly self-centered and he had reduced his contact with the exterior world to the minimum necessary for survival. His health was showing no sign of improvement, and his eyes, which had always suffered the most not only from his complaint but also from his manner of 'curing' it by work, were worse than ever before: during the winter 1884–85 he approached blindness.

On the 8th April 1885 he left Nice for Venice, where he stayed with Gast until the 6th June; on the 7th he arrived in Sils-Maria and stayed there in his farmhouse room until mid-September, when he travelled north to Naumburg. There he spent six weeks, paying occasional visits to Leipzig, and in November he returned to Nice, via Munich and Florence. He was in Nice for the winter of 1885–86, and then, in mid-May, went back to Naumburg, again using his home as a stepping-off place for trips to Leipzig.

It was during one of these that he met Rohde for the last time. The former friends now lived as if in different worlds, and the impression Nietzsche made on Rohde was remembered by the latter until he recorded it in 1889:

> He was surrounded by an indescribable atmosphere of *strangeness*, by something that seemed to me completely uncanny. There was something in him which I had not known before, and much that had formerly distinguished him was missing. As if he came from a land where no one else lives.[1]

We should remember that when Rohde penned this description he had just heard of Nietzsche's mental collapse, and that this is likely to have coloured his language; but even when we have taken this into account, it remains true that Nietzsche did present a strange and in some ways uncanny figure at this period

---

[1]Letter to Overbeck of the 24th January 1889, quoted in Podach: *Gestalten um Nietzsche,* p. 59.

of his life. He had become, in a clearly definable way, 'abnormal': he was without some of the characteristics of social man which constitute 'normality' and which are developed through the necessity of living in a certain minimal degree of harmony with other people. The solitary life he had been leading and his preoccupation with his illness and his work had distanced him from the 'normal' world to which Rohde belonged.

It is to Rohde too that we owe an insight into how antipathetic Nietzsche's later work could seem to an intelligent scholar of the 1880s. In August 1886 Nietzsche sent him a copy of the newly-published *Beyond Good and Evil,* and in a long letter to Overbeck of the 1st September[1] Rohde unburdens himself of the feeling of annoyance and exasperation that must have been rankling within him for years. He has read the book, he says, with 'great ill-humour'. Its contents are mostly 'discourses of an over-surfeited man after dinner', replete with an 'offensive disgust with everything and everyone'. The philosophy is 'as paltry and almost childish' as the politics is 'absurd and ignorant of the world'. There are some 'clever aperçus' and 'ravishing dithyrambic passages', but everything is capricious. The point of view is constantly changing, but Rohde is 'no longer able to take these eternal metamorphoses seriously': they are no more than 'hermit's visions' and 'mental soap bubbles'. Worse than all this, *Beyond Good and Evil* serves up again 'the eternal *proclamation* of frightful things, hair-raising audacities of thought, which then, to the bored disappointment of the reader, *never come!*' 'This', says Rohde, 'is unspeakably offensive to me.' Everything in the book 'runs like sand through the fingers', and above it all stands 'the gigantic vanity of the author'. What Nietzsche needs, Rohde concludes, is to get a real job: 'then he would realize what this fumbling about with things of all kinds is worth: nothing whatever.'

Nietzsche was in Sils-Maria again from the beginning of July to the 25th September; then, after a month at Genoa and Ruta, he returned to Nice on the 22nd October and stayed there until the 2nd April 1887. By the middle of the following June he was back in Sils-Maria, where he remained until the middle of September; a month with Gast in Venice separated this from the winter season in Nice, from the middle of October to the 2nd April. Again his existence was almost eventless: his struggle with his bad health and continual and obsessive writing filled all his days.

One description of his appearance during 1887 will suffice to show what, outwardly, he was reduced to. It is given us by Paul Deussen, who visited him at Sils-Maria in the autumn of that year while on a holiday trip with his wife. Deussen had not seen him for fourteen years:

---

[1] Quoted in *Gestalten um Nietzsche,* p. 55.

What a change had taken place in him during this time, [he writes.][1] There was no longer the proud bearing, the elastic step, the flowing speech of former years. He seemed to drag himself along wearily, and his speech was often slow and halting. Perhaps it was one of his bad days. 'My dear friend', he said sadly, pointing to the clouds passing overhead, 'I need a blue sky above me if I am to collect my thoughts.' Then he led us to his favourite spot. I can still recall with particular clarity a grass plot close beside a cliff and looking down on a rushing mountain stream. 'Here', he said, 'is where I like best to lie and where I have my best ideas.' We were staying at the modest Hotel zur Alpenrose, where Nietzsche usually had his lunch, which consisted as a rule of a chop or something similar. We went back there to rest for an hour. The hour was hardly over before our friend was back at our door, asking very gently if we were still tired, apologising in case he had come too early, etc. I mention this because such excessive solicitude and consideration were previously not to be found in Nietzsche's character and seemed to be significant of his present condition. The following morning he led me to his lodgings, or, as he said, to his cave. It was a simple room in a farm house . . . The furnishings were the most simple imaginable. To one side stood his books, most of them well known to me from earlier days, then followed a rustic table with coffee cups, egg shells, manuscripts and toilet articles thrown together in confusion, which continued past a boot-jack with a boot in it to the still-unmade bed.'

During the years we have been considering, Nietzsche's relations with women were outwardly correct, and belie any suggestion of misogyny to be found in his writings. In particular, he developed a small following of intellectual women of the kind whose existence he sometimes appeared to be denying: Meta von Salis, Resa von Schirnhofer, Helene Druscowicz and Helen Zimmern were among them, Meta von Salis being especially friendly. Whether he ever associated with women on any other basis in Genoa, Nice or Sils-Maria we do not know and therefore have no warrant for assuming he did not: the conventional judgment, originating of course with Elizabeth, that he was sexually almost neutral, conflicts with what we know of his earlier years and rests, so far as his later years are concerned, on an absence of evidence; but if he visited prostitutes (as he almost certainly did in Cologne) or other women, what 'evidence' would there be for it? Given Nietzsche's very 'correct' comportment and the absence of any intimates with whom a man might discuss such escapades, it is unlikely there would be any at all. The sexual activity of a solitary man is, if he wishes it to be, the best-hidden portion of his biography, and dogmatizing on the matter is absolutely out of the question. (His sister

---

[1]Deussen: op. cit., pp. 92–93.

would be perhaps the last person to know anything about it.) What is certain is that he had no serious 'affairs' after Lou Salomé, and seems to have abandoned any thought of marriage; but for this the state of his health was at least in part responsible.

In general, Nietzsche's attitude towards women is not to be compressed into a formula. In his writings he is fairly consistent in expressing wariness of the female intellect (not contempt for it, as is often alleged: he had no doubt women could be very 'clever') and a low opinion of female standards of integrity; at the same time he is quite frank in the pleasure he takes in their outward parts and in their ability to be gay and frivolous. 'Man should be trained for war and woman for the recreation of the warrior: all else is folly', says Zarathustra (Z I 18); and provided one understands what is meant by 'war' and 'recreation' this is an accurate enough summary of Nietzsche's ideal of the man-woman relationship. Women are the 'delight of every strong [male] soul', he adds, and at one time or another he personifies Life, Wisdom and Truth as a woman. During the years in which he was personifying the 'life-affirmation of the superman' as Dionysus, he gave Dionysus a companion in Ariadne, and wrote: 'The labyrinthine man never seeks the truth but always and only his Ariadne.' Certainly he had some unkind things to say about women ('Are you visiting a woman? Do not forget your whip!' an old woman advises Zarathustra (Z I 18)—by far the best-known sentence in his works, among women at least), but the total impression is very far from the dislike and fear of them with which he is popularly credited. Essentially, one feels, women were for Nietzsche something strange, mystifying and, above all, tempting; if there is one persistent refrain running through his writings about them, it is that they lure men from the path of greatness, and spoil and corrupt them.

Much more important than any of this, however, is a simple fact which was pointed out by Bernoulli years ago but which is generally lost sight of: although we know of at least one woman whom he loved, we know of no woman who loved him. Let us leave aside the question whether he was 'loveable', i.e. could make some claim to be loved: he himself wrote: 'The demand to be loved is the greatest of presumptions' (MA 523). Men are loved despite their faults, not because they have none. He, however, was loved by none of the women he met—and he met far more, especially in the 1880s, than is usually thought: had he been, who can doubt that many of the spiteful and uncomplimentary things he had to say about them would never have found a place in his works?[1]

---

[1] For more on Nietzsche and feminism, see the Postscript.

Elizabeth's engagement and marriage to Bernhard Förster is of importance in a consideration of Nietzsche's life and thought because it throws into relief his attitude towards anti-Semitism. In his published works he attacks anti-Semitism several times[1] and links it with his general condemnation of racism;[2] he exerts himself in praise of the Jews and Judaism,[3] and his notebooks also contain similar judgments and sentiments. He had no special interest in racism and nationalism, even to attack them, since his philosophy supposes both to be delusions; but his personal circumstances compelled him to take up an attitude towards them, and virtually all his pronouncements about them are to be understood as ripostes to the opinions current in his day and which flourished among some of his closest acquaintances: Elizabeth, Wagner and Cosima, and Bernhard Förster. Nietzsche's reaction to the news that Elizabeth was to marry was not quite so unambiguous as has generally been alleged: together with his well-known letters attacking Förster and criticizing Elizabeth for choosing to marry him are others wishing them both well. What is unambiguous is the strength of his detestation of Förster's opinions and character.

Elizabeth met Förster during 1882, when she was 36, and he accompanied her to the Bayreuth Festival of that year (where they met Lou Salomé). Förster had been a teacher at a Berlin high school since 1870; during the seventies he became a leading figure of the anti-Semitic movement in Germany, and was one of the 'German Seven', a group of anti-Semitic politicians and 'thinkers' whose aim was to 'renew' German life through the exclusion of the Jews. In 1881 he instigated and organized an anti-Jewish petition, claimed to have been signed by 267,000 people, calling for the limitation of Jewish immigration, exclusion of Jews from positions of authority in government and from teaching in schools, and registration of all Jews. Bismarck, to whom the petition was sent, took no notice of this 'cry of distress from the conscience of the German people' (as Förster called it), but Förster asserted that with it 'began the national anti-Semitic movement' in the *Reich*. On the 8th November 1880 he was involved in a scuffle on a tram because of loud anti-Semitic remarks he had been making to a colleague, and as a consequence of this, and of his political activities in general, he was compelled, at the end of 1882, to resign his teaching post. Frustrated by the failure of his petition and now jobless, he turned to colonization as a likely field for his talents, and spent two years conducting an investigation of the German colony of St. Bernardino, in Para-

[1]E.g. MA 475, J 251, A 55.
[2]E.g. FW 377, G I 11, G VIII 3 and 4.
[3]E.g. MA 475, VMS 171 and NCW IV, M 38, J 52, J 250, GM III 22.

guay. In the spring of 1885 he returned to Germany, published his plan for 'German colonies in the Upper La Plata region', married Elizabeth Nietzsche, and at the beginning of 1886 returned with her to Paraguay.

Their colony was called New Germania, and it was a failure from the start, not so much from incompetence, it appears, as from the effects of Förster's dishonesty.[1] The land was owned by the Paraguayan government and leased to Förster on the understanding it would become his property if he had introduced 140 families within two years (from the 17th November 1886, the date of the contract); if this condition was not fulfilled, the government would take the land back and lease it to someone else. Why Förster ever signed so unsatisfactory an agreement is a mystery: as promoter of the colony he not only stood to lose the products of two years' effort but, if the 140 families were not forthcoming, he would be liable to reimburse those which had settled for the cost of their emigration and, specifically, for the price of the land they had bought from him as prospective owner. By July 1888 only forty families had come out and some of these had packed up and gone home again, and Förster was deeply involved in debt. To produce more than 100 families between July and November was impossible, but the undertaking might, somehow, have been quietly wound up had a disaffected colonist, Julius Klingbeil, not published at the beginning of 1889 a 214-page book of 'revelations' about the state of affairs in New Germania. He accused Förster of being totally incapable of organizing a colonial venture, and of practising deception, tyranny and downright theft upon the colonists. He alleged that colonizing families were deprived of their money, forced to purchase what they needed from Förster by a private system of exchange and to live in a kind of barracks while Förster and Elizabeth lorded it over them in a splendidly-constructed house filled with furniture brought from Europe. Klingbeil was inclined to exonerate Förster from full responsibility because he was very evidently under the domination of his wife. Klingbeil's book was in process of being damned as a libel in the *Bayreuther Blätter*[2] when news arrived that Förster was dead. Elizabeth wrote to Bayreuth that he had expired of a 'nervous attack'. 'False friends and the intrigues of enemies broke his heart', she complained. Her vagueness was

---

[1] See the account of C. F. E. Schultze, a genuine colonist, reprinted in Podach: *Gestalten um Nietzsche*, pp. 142 ff. The present account of Förster and Elizabeth in Paraguay is based on that given in Podach's book (see also Chapter 17).

[2] It is symptomatic of the strength of anti-Semitic feeling in Germany at the close of the nineteenth century that, at the time Nietzsche was becoming the most outspoken opponent of Wagner, the pages of the *Bayreuther Blätter* were always open to his sister. *She* was a valued *Parteigenossin* in the war against the Jews.

deliberate: Förster had shot himself through the head to avoid certain bankruptcy and probable prosecution.

Even so brief a sketch of the life of Bernhard Förster suffices to prove that Nietzsche's objection to him was founded upon something more creditable than an egoistic dislike of the man who had taken his sister away. The violence of that objection arose, I believe, not only from his dislike of Förster's whole outlook, but more from the realization that Elizabeth shared it. 'This accursed anti-Semitism . . . is the cause of a *radical* breach between me and my sister,' he wrote to Overbeck on the 2nd April 1884.

Förster was engaged to Elizabeth before he went out to Paraguay for the first time in February 1883, and most of Nietzsche's letters referring to him, and published in the second volume of his letters to his mother and sister, were written between that date and the date of their marriage in 1885; they were clearly designed to prevent the marriage from taking place and not to create difficulty and ill-feeling after the deed had been done. They bring under fire every aspect of the philosophy and outlook that came to a catastrophic climax in National Socialism, and what is most fiercely attacked is anti-Semitism and its corollary, the worship of a pure German race. As to the latter, Nietzsche leaves his opinion in no doubt:

> To enthusiasm for the 'German national character' I have indeed attained very little, but even less to the wish to keep this 'glorious' race *pure*. On the contrary, on the contrary . . . (Letter of the 21st March 1885).

When Elizabeth did marry—on the 22nd May 1885—Nietzsche wished her happiness; but to others he continued to express his detestation of Förster and to emphasize that he had never met him and did not wish to do so; to his mother he wrote that he was glad Förster had seen fit to exile himself to Paraguay and wished others of his kind would do the same. When appeals for money came from New Germania he refused to contribute.

The entry of Förster into his family was not the only connection he had with an active anti-Semite which he feared might be thought compromising to himself. His reputation had already been endangered by his association with the publisher Ernst Schmeitzner, who had brought out *Human, All Too Human* and succeeding works. In 1879 Schmeitzner founded the journal *Antisemitische Blätter* and was a vigorous propagandist against Jewish influence in Germany. Nietzsche had had grave difficulties with him and was anxious to get away from him: his enthusiasm for anti-Jewish agitation had led him to neglect his business, and one consequence was that publication of *Zarathustra* was held up.[1] During 1884–85 Nietzsche had to take legal action against Schmeitzner to obtain payment for the book, and he was relieved when his former publisher, Fritzsch, expressed the wish to buy from Schmeitzner the copyright of all his works and to republish them under his own imprint. This deal was carried through in the summer of 1886, and Nietzsche wrote a preface for the new edition of each of them from *The Birth of Tragedy* to *The Gay Science* (except for the *Untimely Meditations*, which were not reissued). These new editions appeared during 1886–87, and Fritzsch also brought out the first single-volume edition of *Zarathustra*, parts one, two and three. It was while in the process of getting free from Schmeitzner that Nietzsche was confronted by the news that a much more famous anti-Semite was to become not merely his publisher but his brother-in-law.

Fritzsch's optimistic investment notwithstanding, Nietzsche's books made little headway with the public during these years: the first three parts of *Zarathustra* had in fact gone so badly that Schmeitzner had declined to publish the fourth, and we find Nietzsche asking Gersdorff in a rather round-about way if he would lend him the money to have it privately printed (letter of the 12th February 1885). Gersdorff obliged, and part four appeared in a private edition: it was first publicly issued in 1892.

The self-satisfaction and self-laudation which we saw becoming a part of Nietzsche's character at the time of *The Gay Science* made alarming strides during the *Zarathustra* years, as is indeed obvious from the book itself. On the first three parts he wrote to Rohde on the 2nd February 1884:

> It is a sort of abyss of the future, something dreadful, that is in its blissfulness. Everything in it is my own, without model, comparison, predecessor . . . I flatter myself that with this Z. I have brought the German language to perfection. There remained, after Luther and Goethe, yet a third step still to be taken.

At the beginning of May of the same year he told Overbeck:

> That when I approached my 40th year I should be *very much* alone—I have never had any illusion about that . . . I am now, in all probability, the *most independent man in Europe.*

As if this were not sufficient, he announced to Malwida later in the month:

---

[1]A piquant touch is that the printers of the book, Teubner's, were unable to get on with the work because of an order they had in hand for 500,000 hymn books. Nietzsche's comment was that the Christians were evidently trying to kill Zarathustra by anti-Semitism and hymn-singing.

My task is tremendous; but my determination no less so . . . I want to compel men to decisions which will be decisive for the whole human future.

In a letter to von Stein of the 22nd May he explains why he cannot come to Bayreuth to see any of Wagner's operas at the festival theatre:

> . . . the law which stands over me, my *task*, leaves me no time for that. My son Zarathustra may have betrayed to you *what* is going on within me; and if I achieve all I *desire to achieve* I shall die in the knowledge that future millennia will take their highest vows in my name.

The *hubris* of remarks such as these must be accepted as the wild over-compensations of an ailing and half-blind man; they must not be confused with his *philosophy:* if we now turn to that we shall see that *Beyond Good and Evil* and the *Genealogy*—the finished works of these years—are explicable independently of their author's claims for them.

2

Beyond Good and Evil is devoted to an elaboration and explanation of theories put forward in *Zarathustra,* and *Towards a Genealogy of Morals* is described as performing the same service for *Beyond Good and Evil,* so the two books can best be considered together.

The first problem Nietzsche faces is the difficulty involved in saying that the will to power is 'true' if the search for truth is itself prompted by will to power. 'All Cretans are liars', said Epimenides the Cretan. 'Will to truth is will to power', said Nietzsche, the philosopher of the will to power. Both statements are false if true, true if false. Nietzsche sees the paradox inherent in his theory and faces up to it firstly by recognizing that, if life is will to power, the value of truth is problematical:

> *What* is it in us that really wants 'the truth'? . . . Granted we want the truth: *why not rather* untruth? And uncertainty? Ignorance, even?—The problem of the value of truth stepped forth before us. (J 1)

> With all the value which may adhere to the true, the genuine, the selfless, it is possible that a higher and more fundamental value for all life might have to be ascribed to appearance, to the will to deception, to selfishness and to appetite. It might even be possible that *what* constitutes the value of those good and honoured things resides precisely in their being artfully related, knotted and crocheted to those evil, apparently opposed things, perhaps even in their being essentially identical with them. (J 2)

This suggests to him a possible evaluation of power in terms of truth:

> A thing might be true although it were harmful and dangerous in the highest degree; indeed, the basic constitution of existence might be such that one would be destroyed by a complete knowledge of it—so that the strength of a mind might be measured by how much 'truth' it could endure. (J 39)

What is certain, however, is that philosophy must be in some way a means to power and not primarily a means to truth: the philosopher must desire not merely a passive knowing but an active creation of knowledge:

> . . . a philosophy . . . always creates the world after its own image: it cannot do otherwise; philosophy is this tyrannical impulse itself, the most spiritual will to power, to 'creation of the world', to *causa prima*. (J 10)

> The task of true philosophers is *'to create values'* . . . 'Their knowing is *creating*, their creating is a law-giving, their will to truth is—*will to power.*' (J 211)

Secondly, he appeals to the requirement of logic to recognize *one* kind of causality and to exploit it to the limit in an effort to make it responsible for every known effect. According to his own theory that the world is explicable in itself, that it 'works' without any contribution from 'outside', it must be possible to determine its 'intelligible character'—that is, understand it in the form in which it presents itself to our senses—by reference to a basic principle. This principle, he suggests, is will to power; and 'will to truth'—that is, to knowledge of what actually is, genuine 'will to truth'—is an aspect of will to power, since to know is to have power, while to be deceived is to lack power over that in respect of which we are deceived.[1] He put the basis of his argument that one kind of causality must be posited in a long aphorism, J 36:

> Granted that nothing is 'given' as real except our world of desires and passions, that we can rise or sink to no other 'reality' than to this reality of our impulses— for thinking is only the relationship of these impulses to one another—: is it not permitted to make the experiment and ask the question whether this which is given does not *suffice* for an understanding even of the so-called mechanical (or 'material') world? I do not mean as a deception, an 'appearance', an 'idea' (in the Berkeleyan and Schopenhaueran sense), but as possessing the same degree of reality as our emotions themselves—as a more primitive form of the world of emotions in which everything still lies locked in mighty unity, . . . as a *primary form* of life?—In the end, it is not merely permitted to make this experiment: it

---

[1]See also VMS 26, quoted in Chapter 8, section 2.

is commanded by the conscience of *method*. Not to assume several kinds of causality so long as the experiment of getting along with one has not been taken to its ultimate limits . . . : that is a morality of method which one must not repudiate nowadays— . . . one must venture the hypothesis that, wherever 'effects' are recognised, will is operating upon will— . . . Granted finally that one succeeded in explaining our entire instinctual life as the development and ramification of *one* basic form of will—as the will to power, as is *my* theory—; granted that one could trace all organic functions back to this will to power . . . one would have acquired the right to define *all* active force unequivocally as: *will to power*. The world seen from within, the world described and defined according to its 'intelligible character'—it would be simply 'will to power' and nothing else.

If it is proposed that will to power is the basic drive in all life, the question arises: what is the nature of will as such? There still seem to be two forces at work: will, and that will which seeks power; the concept 'will' still exists as a substratum, will in Schopenhauer's sense, a metaphysical basis for life. Nietzsche must dispose of this notion if his philosophy is not to decline into a variant of Schopenhauer's—the will expressing itself not as striving to live but more dynamically as striving for aggrandisement—and he does so in what at first seems a surprising way. There is, he says, no such thing as will. Just as the soul turns out on inspection to be a word for a complicated system of *relationships* and therefore cannot be said to exist, so the will has no discrete existence: there is no force emanating from within the body which can be identified as 'will'. 'Willing' is a product of a complex of sensations; and the sensation of willing is felt when the sensation of command succeeds in dominating the other sensations. What we recognize as 'will' is the act of commanding: there is no substratum of 'will-in-itself' which appears in the *form* of commands. Nietzsche makes clear in the *Genealogy* what he means by denying that will can exist as a separate entity:

> To require of strength that it should *not* express itself as strength . . . is just as absurd as to require of weakness that it should express itself as strength . . . popular morality separates strength from expressions of strength, as if there were a neutral substratum behind the strong man . . . But there is no such substratum; there is no 'being' behind doing, working, becoming: 'the doer' is merely added to the deed—the deed is everything. (GM I 13)

There is no 'being' behind 'doing' and there is no 'will' behind 'willing': both expressions are abstractions, linguistic barriers to apprehending the complicated nature of these phenomena:

Willing seems to me to be above all something *complicated* . . . in every will there is, first of all, a plurality of sensations, namely the sensation of the condition we *leave,* the sensation of the condition towards which we *go,* the sensation of this 'leaving' and 'going' itself, and then an accompanying muscular sensation . . . As feelings . . . can therefore be recognised as an ingredient of will, so, in the second place, can thinking: in every act of will there is a commanding thought— . . . Thirdly, will is not only a complex of feeling and thinking, but above all an *emotion:* and in fact the emotion of command. What is called 'freedom of will' is essentially the emotion of supremacy in respect of him who must obey: 'I am free, "he" must obey'—this consciousness adheres to every will . . . A man who *wills*—commands something in himself which obeys or which he thinks obeys . . . inasmuch as in the given circumstances we at the same time command *and* obey, . . . 'freedom of will' . . . is the expression for that complex condition of joy of the person who wills, who commands and at the same time identifies himself with the executor of the command . . . In all willing it is absolutely a question of commanding and obeying, on the basis . . . of a communal structure composed of many 'souls': on which account a philosopher should claim the right to include willing as such within the field of morality: that is, of morality understood as the theory of the relations of supremacy under which the phenomenon 'life' arises. (J 19)

The nature of will, then, is, in its 'intelligible character', will to power; it appears when a certain relation—the power relation—is established between the elements of a 'social structure', whether that structure be an individual, a nation, or the universe as a whole, life as such. This conclusion is consistent with Nietzsche's conclusion concerning the nature of morality—which he repeats in *Beyond Good and Evil:*

Every morality is . . . a piece of tyranny against 'nature', also against 'reason': . . . The essential and invaluable element in every morality is that it is a protracted constraint . . . The essential thing . . . seems to be . . . a protracted *obedience* in *one* direction. (J 188)

In the *Genealogy* he draws a further conclusion that is important in linking the theory of the will to power with the need to establish a 'meaning' for life. Just as life is will to power, so the 'meaning' of life is the feeling that the will to power is operative, that *something* is subject to the will—no matter what it may be: it is the fact of commanding which counts:

Apart from the ascetic ideal, man, the *animal* man, had no meaning. His existence on earth contained no goal . . . *This* is precisely what the ascetic ideal means: that something was *lacking,* that man was surrounded by a fearful *void*— he did not know how to justify, to account for, to affirm himself, he *suffered* from the problem of his meaning . . . his problem was not suffering itself, but that there was no answer to the crying question '*why* is there suffering?' . . . The meaninglessness of suffering, *not* suffering itself, was the curse which lay over mankind—*and the ascetic ideal gave it meaning!* . . . man was *saved* thereby, . . . he could now *will* something—immaterial to what end, why, with what he willed: *the will itself was saved.* It is quite impossible to disguise from oneself *what* is expressed by every complete will which has taken its direction from the ascetic ideal: this hatred of the human, and even more of the animal, and more still of the material, this horror of the senses, of reason itself, this fear of happiness and beauty, this longing to get away from all appearance, change, becoming, death, wishing, from longing itself—all this indicates—let us dare to grasp it—a *will to nothingness*, a will opposed to life, a repudiation of the most fundamental pre-conditions of life, but it is and remains a *will!* . . . And . . . man would rather will *nothingness* than *not* will. (GM III 28)

'. . . lieber will noch der Mensch *das Nichts* wollen, als *nicht* wollen . . .', the words which close the *Genealogy,* are a reduction into characteristically concise and memorable form of the basis of Nietzsche's final position regarding moral values. He had already established the possibility that a morality might be judged according to its tendency to foster the feeling of increased and more highly-organized power. Those moralities which elevated the claims of the powerless to positions of honour were harmful because they thwarted the claims of power, and consequently those of life itself. Among the debilitating moralities was, Nietzsche thought, the Christian: but Christian morality was the ruling morality in the Europe of his day. Had the weak then triumphed over the strong? And if Christianity had triumphed, must it not therefore be in actuality the stronger morality? How then could it be repudiated as a morality of weakness? Moreover, if the only criterion of the 'good' is power, must not every victorious force be called 'good' simply because it has become victorious? Is this not the 'naked admiration for success' he had condemned in Hegel? These questions were not answered by Nietzsche until he had come to see that man can also will *nothingness*. In this will he recognized the origin of nihilism: an individual, a nation, a civilization deprived of positive goals destroys itself by willing the last thing left in its power to will—its own destruction; and it will will this rather than *not* will. Nietzsche now gained the authority to distinguish between different victorious moralities: that a certain morality had established itself did not imply it was a movement for the enhancement of power—it might be a nihilistic morality, and its triumph the triumph of a will to nothingness. He therefore began to speak of 'life-enhancing' or 'ascending' and 'life-denying' or 'declining' morality, and he was able to condemn the latter without self-contradiction.

The theory of the will to power is now complete, and we are in a position to understand the meaning of the more notorious dicta of *Beyond Good and Evil* and the *Genealogy*.

Still exposing all his ideas at once, as he had done from *Human, All Too Human* onwards, Nietzsche re-emphasizes that conflict and contest are the basis of life, and that the good impulses derive from the bad:

> All psychology has hitherto remained anchored to prejudice and timidities: it has not ventured on to the deep. To conceive of psychology as the morphology and *development-theory of the will to power*, as I conceive it—has never yet entered the mind of anyone else: . . . The power of moral prejudices has penetrated deep into the intellectual world, which is apparently the coolest and least prejudiced: . . . A genuine physio-psychology has to struggle with unconscious resistance in the heart of the investigator; it has 'the heart' against it: even a theory of the mutual dependence of the 'good' and the 'bad' impulses causes, as refined immorality, distress and aversion to a conscience still brave and strong—and even more a theory of the derivation of all good impulses from the bad. When, however, one regards even the emotions of hatred, envy, covetousness, lust for power as life-conditioning emotions, as something which, in the total economy of life, must be present fundamentally and essentially, and which consequently must be furthered if life is to be furthered—he suffers from this conclusion as from seasickness. (J 23)

> That imperious something the people call 'spirit' wants to be master within itself and around itself and to feel itself master: . . . Its needs and capacities are the same as those assigned by physiologists to everything that lives, grows and multiplies . . . Its aim is the incorporation of new 'experiences', . . . growth; more precisely, the *feeling* of growth, the feeling of enhanced power. (J 230)

> . . . life itself is *essentially* appropriation, injury, subjugation of the strange and the weaker, suppression, severity, imposition of its own forms, incorporation and, at the least and mildest, exploitation— . . . Even an organisation within which . . . individuals treat one another as equals . . . will itself—if it be a living organisation and not a dying one—have to do all that towards other organisations which the individuals within it refrain from doing to one another: it will have to be incarnated will to power . . . not from any kind of morality or immorality, but because it *lives*, and because life *is* precisely will to power. (J 259)

Of particular interest in this connection is his attitude towards race:

> The man of an era of dissolution which throws the races together and who therefore contains within him the inheritance of a diversified descent, that is to say contrary and often not merely contrary drives and values which struggle

with one another and rarely leave one another in peace—such a man of late culture and broken lights will, on the average, be a rather weak man: his basic wish is that the war which he *is* should come to an end . . . If, however, the contrariety and war in such a nature should act as one *more* stimulus and enticement to life—and if, on the other hand, there has been inherited and developed . . . a proper mastery and subtlety in conducting such a war within oneself: then there arise those marvellously incomprehensible and inexplicable men, those enigmatic men predestined for victory and the seduction of others, the fairest examples of whom are Alcibiades and Caesar (—with whom I should like to associate the *first* of Europeans according to my taste, the Hohenstaufen Friedrich the Second), and among artists perhaps Leonardo da Vinci. (J 200)

Before the Nazis appropriated his name it was hardly ever doubted that Nietzsche was opposed to 'racism' and that '*Übermenschen*' might appear anywhere, among any people. His ideas on a 'master race', which I shall examine in a moment, are simply part of his general theory of the development of civilization through conflict: in the distant past different races came into conflict; one triumphed over the other and became, in relation to the defeated race, a master race; the defeated became, in relation to their conquerors, a slave race. He never speaks of *the* master race, and clearly he never imagined one existing race to be superior to all others. (Even if he had, one may add in parentheses, he would hardly have designated the Germans that race.) He never uses the word in the sense of 'pure race': for Nietzsche a 'race' was a group of people who had lived together a long time and as a result had certain needs and certain characteristics in common; and it was in this sense that he looked forward to a 'European race', which he hoped might vie in achievement with the most celebrated of all 'mixed races', the Greeks. But his opposition to racism was not merely temperamental bias, or an occasional expression of opinion. Any philosophy which places conflict at the heart of things and sees in it the ladder to perfection must turn its back on 'pure race' as a pure absurdity. Racial mixture would have to be the presupposition of such a philosophy; and the fact that the Greeks were notoriously a chaotic mixture of races seemed to provide him with the sort of evidence he needed that the highest culture proceeds from conflict.

Consideration of Nietzsche's view on race leads to his famous typology of morality and his advocacy of an 'aristocratic' ethic:

In a tour of the many finer and coarser moralities which have ruled or still rule on earth I found certain traits regularly recurring together and bound up with one another: until at length two basic types were revealed and a basic distinction emerged. There is *master morality* and *slave morality*—I add at once that in all higher and mixed cultures attempts at mediation between the two are apparent and more frequently confusion and mutual misunderstanding between them, and sometimes their harsh juxtaposition—even within the same man, within *one* soul. The various moral evaluations have arisen either among a ruling order . . . or among the ruled, the slaves and dependents. . . . In the former case, when it is the rulers who determine the concept 'good', it is the exalted, proud states of soul which are considered distinguishing and determine the order of rank. The noble man separates from himself those natures in which the opposite of such exalted proud states appear: he despises them. It should be noted at once that in this former type of morality the antithesis 'good' and 'bad' means the same thing as 'noble' and 'despicable'—the antithesis 'good' and '*evil*' originates elsewhere. The cowardly, the timid, the petty, and those who think only of narrow utility are despised, as are the mistrustful, . . . those who abase themselves, the dog-like type of man who lets himself be ill-treated, the fawning flatterer, above all the liar—it is the fundamental belief of all aristocrats that the common people are liars . . . It is immediately obvious that designations of moral value were first applied to *men*, and only later and derivatively to *actions:* . . . The noble type of man feels *himself* to be the determiner of values; he does not need to be approved of; he judges 'What harms me is harmful in itself', . . . he *creates values* . . . such a morality is self-glorification. In the foreground stands the feeling of plenitude, of power which seeks to overflow, the happiness of high tension . . . The noble man honours in himself the man of power, and also the man who has power over himself, who understands how to speak and how to keep silent, who enjoys practising severity and harshness upon himself and feels reverence for all that is severe and harsh . . . It is the powerful who *understand* how to honour, that is their art, their realm of invention. Deep reverence for the old and traditional . . . , prejudice in favour of ancestors and against descendants is typical of a morality of the powerful; and when men of 'modern ideas' believe almost instinctively in 'progress' and 'the future' and show an increasing lack of respect for the past, this reveals clearly enough the ignoble origin of these 'ideas' . . . It is otherwise with the second type of morality, *slave morality*. Suppose the abused, oppressed, suffering, unfree, those uncertain of themselves and the weary should moralise: what would their moral evaluations have in common? Probably a pessimistic mistrust of the entire situation of man will find expression, perhaps a condemnation of man together with his situation. The slave is suspicious of the virtues of the powerful: he is sceptical and mistrustful . . . of everything 'good' which is honoured among them . . . On the other hand, those qualities which serve to lighten the existence of the suffering will be brought into prominence and flooded with light: here it is that sympathy, the kind and helping hand, the warm heart, patience, diligence, humility, friendliness, come into honour—for here these are the most useful qualities and virtually the only means of enduring the burden of existence. Slave morality is essentially the morality of utility. Here is the source of the famous antithesis 'good' and '*evil*'—power and dangerousness were felt to exist in the evil, a certain dreadfulness, subtlety and strength which could not be despised. (J 260)

The concept 'master and slave morality' is an attempt to explain how antithetical moral judgments are possible. Before trying to see exactly what is implied in this passage, let us look at those passages in the *Genealogy* which are an elaboration and extension of it:

> . . . the judgment 'good' did *not* originate with those to whom 'goodness' was shown! Much rather it was 'the good' themselves, that is to say, the noble, powerful, high-stationed and high-minded, who felt and established themselves and their actions as good, that is, of the first rank, in contradistinction to all the low, low-minded, common and plebeian. It was out of this *pathos of distance* that they first seized the right to create values and to coin names for values: what had they to do with utility? . . . The pathos of nobility and distance . . . , the protracted and domineering sense of fundamental unity on the part of a higher ruling order in relation to a lower order . . . —*that* is the origin of the antithesis 'good' and 'bad'. (GM I 2)

> The signpost to the *right* track was the question: what was the real etymological significance of the symbols for 'good' which have been coined in the various languages? I found they all led back to the *same conceptual transformation*—that everywhere 'noble', 'aristocratic' in the social sense is the basic concept from which 'good' in the sense of 'with aristocratic soul', 'noble', 'with a soul of a high order', 'with a privileged soul' necessarily developed: a development which always runs parallel with that other in which 'common', 'plebeian', 'low' are finally transformed into the concept 'bad' . . . With regard to a genealogy of morals this seems to me a *fundamental* insight. (GM I 4)

> The slave-revolt in morals begins when *resentment* . . . becomes creative and gives birth to values . . . While every noble morality develops from a triumphant affirmation of itself, slave morality from the outset says No to what is 'outside', what is 'different', what is 'not itself': and *this* No is its creative act . . . its action is . . . reaction . . . The man of resentment . . . has conceived 'the evil enemy', '*the Evil One*', and this indeed is his basic idea, from which he then evolves, as a corresponding and opposing figure, a 'good one'—himself! (GM I 10)

> This is . . . quite the contrary of what the noble man does, who conceives the basic idea 'good' spontaneously . . . out of himself, and only then creates for himself the concept 'bad'. This 'bad' of noble origin and that 'evil' out of the

cauldron of unsatisfied hatred . . . how different these words 'bad' and 'evil' are, although they are both apparently the opposite of the same concept 'good'. But it is *not* the same concept 'good': one should ask rather precisely *who* is 'evil' in the sense of the morality of resentment. The answer, in all strictness, is: *precisely* the 'good man' of the other morality, precisely the noble, powerful man, the ruler. (GM I 11)

One cannot fail to see at the core of all these noble races the animal of prey, the splendid *blonde beast* prowling about avidly in search of spoil and victory; this hidden core needs to erupt from time to time, the animal has to get out again and go back to the wilderness: the Roman, Arabian, Germanic, Japanese nobility, the Homeric heroes, the Scandinavian Vikings—they all shared this need. It is the noble races which have left behind them the concept 'barbarian' wherever they have gone. (GM I 11)

I regard the bad conscience as the serious illness which man was bound to contract under the stress of the most fundamental change he had ever experienced—that change which occurred when he found himself finally enclosed within the walls of society and of peace. . . . All instincts which do not discharge themselves outwardly *turn inwards*— . . . thus it was that man first developed what he afterwards called his 'soul'. The entire inner world . . . acquired depth, breadth, height, in the same measure as outward discharge was *hindered*. Those fearful bulwarks with which the social organisation protected itself against the old instincts of freedom . . . brought it about that all those instincts of wild, free, prowling man turned backwards *against man himself*. Enmity, cruelty, joy in persecuting, in attacking, in change, in destruction—all this turned against the possessors of such instincts: *that* is the origin of the 'bad conscience'. (GM II 16)

. . . the oldest 'state' . . . appeared as a fearful tyranny and went on working until this raw material of people and semi-animals was . . . *moulded*. I employed the word 'state': it is self-evident what is meant—some herd of blonde beasts of prey, a conqueror and master race which, organised for war and with the ability to organise, unhesitatingly lays its terrible claws upon a population perhaps tremendously superior in numbers but still formless and nomad. That is how the 'state' began on earth . . . They do not know what guilt, responsibility, respect are, these born organisers . . . It is not in *them* that the 'bad conscience' developed, that goes without saying—but it would not have developed *without them*, . . . it would be lacking if a tremendous quantity of freedom had not been expelled from the world, or at least been rendered invisible and made, as it were, *latent*, under their hammer-blows. This *instinct for freedom* forcibly made latent . . . is the beginning of the *bad conscience*. (GM II 17)

One should guard against thinking lightly of this phenomenon on account of its initial painfulness and ugliness. For fundamentally it is the same active force which is at work on a grander scale in those forceful artists and organisers and builds states which here, internally . . . in the 'labyrinth of the breast' . . . makes itself a bad conscience, it is that *instinct for freedom* (in my language: will to power); with the difference that the material upon which this . . . force operates is here man himself, his entire old animal self—and *not . . . other* men. (GM II 18)

Bad conscience is an illness, there is no doubt about that, but an illness as pregnancy is an illness. (GM II 19)

The first thing to note is that Nietzsche explains 'class' in terms of 'race'. The ruling class, he thinks, are the descendants of the conquering race, the ruled class of the conquered race; in time, racial differences vanished—partly through intermarriage, but mainly because 'race' is essentially a body of characteristics shared by people who have lived together in the same place for a long time—but the power relationship remained. The aristocracy then became racially indistinguishable from the common people—they were, in fact, one race—and the concept of 'class' appeared to explain the power relationship between the rulers and the ruled. It is by means of this power relationship that he seeks to explain the origin of opposed types of morality, 'soul', bad conscience, guilt feelings, and so on. The aim is to employ the theory of the will to power as that 'one kind of causality' demanded by logical method.

Because 'slave morality' is essentially a reaction against a life of suffering, against life conceived *as* suffering, it is a 'life-denying' morality; it is protective, it wards off, it reduces vitality; in an extreme form it becomes a Buddhistic flight from reality, a morbid sensitivity to pain that suffers from life as from an illness; he recognizes in Schopenhauer the philosopher who had taken this tendency to its furthest limits. Against this tendency he sets an opposite ideal:

. . . the ideal of the most exuberant, most living and most world-affirming man, who has not only learned to compromise and treat with all that was and is but who wants to have it again *as it was and is* to all eternity, insatiably calling out *da capo* not only to himself but to the whole piece and play . . . (J 56)

This is the emotional significance of the recurrence: it is the most extreme form of life-acceptance; acceptance, that is, not only of what is good in life but of what is bad also:

You want if possible . . . *to abolish suffering;* and we?—it really does seem that *we* would rather increase it and make it worse than it has ever been! . . . The discipline of suffering, of *great* suffering—do you not know that it is this discipline alone which has created every elevation of mankind hitherto? That tension of the soul in misfortune which transmits to it its strength, its terror at the sight of great destruction, its inventiveness and bravery in undergoing, enduring, interpreting and exploiting misfortune, and whatever of depth, mystery, mask, spirit, cunning and greatness has been bestowed upon it—has it not been bestowed through suffering, through the discipline of great suffering? In man, *creature* and *creator* are united: in man there is matter, fragment, excess, clay, mud, madness, chaos; but in man there is also creator, sculptor, the hardness of the hammer, the divine spectator and the seventh day—do you understand this antithesis? And that *your* sympathy is for the 'creature in man', for that which has to be formed, broken, forged, torn, burned, annealed, refined— that which has to *suffer* and *should* suffer? (J 225)

Only under the sign of the superman is it possible to comprehend Nietzsche's advocacy of 'aristocracy':

Every elevation of the type 'man' has hitherto been the work of an aristocratic society— . . . a society which believes in a long scale of gradations of rank and differences of worth between man and man, and needs slavery in some form or other. Without the *pathos of distance* such as develops from the incarnated difference of classes . . . that other, more mysterious pathos could never have developed, that longing for an increasing widening of distance within the soul itself, the formation of higher, rarer, more remote, tenser, more comprehensive states, in short precisely the elevation of the type 'man', the continual 'self-overcoming of man', to take a moral formula in a supra-moral sense. (J 257)

The essential thing in a good and healthy aristocracy is . . . that it does *not* feel itself to be a function (of a kingdom or of a commonwealth), but as the *meaning* and highest justification thereof—that it should therefore accept with a good conscience the sacrifice of innumerable men who, *for its sake,* have to be suppressed and reduced to imperfect men, to slaves and tools. Its basic faith must be that society should *not* exist for the sake of society, but only as foundation and scaffolding upon which a select order of beings may raise itself to . . . a higher *existence.* (J 258)

The logic of this attitude, given all that has gone before, is inescapable; so, unfortunately for Nietzsche, is its unreality. It is doubtful if he himself thought such an aristocracy was possible; certainly it is not presented as a picture of any actually existing aristocracy. The difficulty, however, is not insurmountable; it derives mainly from the archaic language which Nietzsche

191

here employs, and the outmoded state of society which it calls to mind. The *idea* behind it is that which we have seen formed the basis of all his thought: that existence is in itself not significant, and mankind can derive no significance from being a function of it; mankind must itself *become* the significance and justification of existence.

13

The Year 1888

A: You are removing yourself faster and faster from the living: soon they will strike you off their list!—B: It is the only way of sharing the privilege possessed by the dead.—A: What privilege?—B: To die no more. (FW 262)

1

The chronology of Nietzsche's travels during the year 1888 is as simple as that of previous years. He stayed in Nice until the 2nd April, when he left for Turin, arriving on the 5th and remaining in the city until the 5th June. He was delighted with it and decided it would be 'my *Residenz* from now on'. For the summer he went to Sils-Maria and stayed there until the 20th September, when he returned to Turin. Apart from a relapse in the middle of the summer, he was feeling his health had improved; his spirits were lighter, and he experienced a joy in working which exceeded anything he had known before. Had his 'medical knowledge' been what he claimed, he might have recognized the symptoms and perhaps, even at this late stage, done something to prevent or retard the ultimate consequences: but he did nothing and, in all probability, failed to realize there was anything to be done. He accepted his 'recovery' at its face value, whereas it was only the deceptive prelude to total collapse: when he left Turin on the 9th January 1889 he was incurably insane—'a ruin that only a friend could recognise'.[1]

His decline into insanity took the form of an increasingly intense feeling of euphoria culminating at last in megalomania. As early as February his letters reveal that the overcompensation of previous years was beginning to assume a

---

[1]Overbeck to Gast, 11th January 1889.

somewhat heightened colouring: writing to Seydlitz on the 12th, for instance, he says:

> Between ourselves—it is not impossible that I am the first philosopher of the age, perhaps even a trifle more than that, . . . something decisive and fateful standing between two millennia.

By May he was experiencing a sensation of well-being which sent him into cries of rapture: 'Wonder upon wonders,' he wrote to Seydlitz on the 13th, 'I have had a notably *cheerful* spring up to now. The first for ten, fifteen years— perhaps even longer!' There was no worsening of his condition until the late autumn: then the rate of decline became catastrophic. On his 44th birthday (the 15th October) he wrote the short passage '*An diesem vollkommnen Tage*' which he placed between the Foreword and the first chapter of *Ecce Homo* and which is in its exalted cheerfulness the most pathetic in his works:

> On this perfect day, when everything has become ripe and not only the grapes are growing brown, a ray of sunlight has fallen on to my life: I looked behind me, I looked before me, and never have I seen so many and such good things together. Not in vain have I buried my forty-fourth year today, I was *entitled* to bury it—what there was of life in it is rescued, is immortal.

Everything, he thought, was now going his way: soon he would be enjoying the reward of all his years of effort; and the tragic fact is that, if his collapse had not intervened, this would have been true.

The year 1888 was not only the last of his active life but the first of his celebrity. He often affected to despise fame and a large readership, but in reality he longed for them with a passion that was the fiercer for being constantly frustrated. His assertion that his works belonged to the *few*—'the very few', he says in the Foreword to *The Anti-Christ*, 'perhaps none of them is even living yet'—is an insurance against disappointment; and it is in any case too blatant and inadmissible a paradox that he, the most readable of philosophers, should have desired not to be read. There was, on the contrary, much of the publicist in him: he formulated his ideas in a manner calculated to shock and give offence, and these tactics were subsequently so successful that he was, in some quarters, blamed for the First *and* the Second World War.[1] The

---

[1] There is no space here to discuss the allegation that Nietzsche was the philosopher of German militarism and later of Nazism; if the reader accepts, even in broad outline, the construction of him offered in this book, the allegation must in any case fall to the ground. The former charge is based on a misconception of what he meant by 'power', the latter on uncritical acceptance of what Nazi writers said about him, and both involve ignorance of what he himself wrote.

misunderstanding might have saddened or maddened him—but how he would have loved the notoriety! As it was, he experienced only its beginnings: 'To all that was tragic in Nietzsche's life,' the Danish critic and literary historian Georg Brandes wrote in his obituary about him, 'was added this— that, after thirsting for recognition to the point of morbidity, he attained it in an altogether fantastic degree when, though still living, he was shut out from life.'[1]

On the 1st January 1888 the Sunday edition of the Berner *Bund* carried an article by Carl Spitteler which was the first review of Nietzsche's work as a whole to appear anywhere. Brandes had already corresponded with Nietzsche, and on the 3rd April he wrote that he intended to give a series of lectures at Copenhagen University outlining his philosophy:

> Yesterday, [he said,] when I had . . . taken up one of your books I suddenly felt a sort of vexation at the idea that nobody here in Scandinavia knew anything about you, and I soon determined to make you known at a stroke.

The lectures were a success, Brandes reported, and Nietzsche refers to them again and again in his letters of the rest of the year: he was obviously highly delighted that at last someone had taken notice of him. Brandes was, in fact, the first figure of international repute to recognize Nietzsche's quality, and the opening words of his *Essay on Aristocratic Radicalism* (1889)—'Friedrich Nietzsche appears to me the most interesting writer in German literature at the present time'—were the first adequate appreciation he had received in print.

Brandes sought to interest him in Kierkegaard and Strindberg; but it was too late in the day for Nietzsche to derive any benefit from these or any other authors, and his brief correspondence with Strindberg is marred by signs of incipient insanity on *both* sides.

In addition to this, he was beginning to take seriously in hand the question of publicizing his work. The writings of this year were all intended to be issued in several languages—he had Strindberg in mind as a translator of *Ecce Homo*—and he had the idea of becoming the sole owner of his entire output. When Fritzsch had acquired all his works up to *Zarathustra*, Nietzsche had stipulated that he himself should bring out any future books, and he entered into an agreement to this effect with C. G. Naumann; although Naumann's name appears on the title-page of the later works, the firm was in fact technically not the publisher but the printer, Nietzsche himself being the pub-

---

[1] Reprinted in Georg Brandes: *Friedrich Nietzsche* (London 1914), p. 103.

lisher. It was under these circumstances that *Beyond Good and Evil* and the *Genealogy* appeared. By the beginning of 1888 Nietzsche had all but exhausted his capital, and his friends began to rally round to assist him: Deussen sent him 2,000 marks (possibly with the help of Paul Rée), and Meta von Salis gave him 1,000 francs, and with this money he paid for the publication in September of *The Wagner Case.*

In addition to being Nietzsche's and Wagner's publisher, Fritzsch also brought out the *Musikalisches Wochenblatt,* and the edition of the 25th October carried a reply to *The Wagner Case* by Richard Pohl entitled *The Nietzsche Case.* Nietzsche was, or affected to be, incensed that Fritzsch should have permitted an attack on one of his own authors, and he wrote him a brief and stinging note:

> How much do you want for my entire literature? *In aufrichtiger Verachtung*[1] Nietzsche.

Fritzsch replied: 11,000 marks. Nietzsche decided to take the reply seriously and asked the Naumann brothers for advice; their view was that, what with Brandes's lectures and a certain amount of journalistic controversy surrounding his name, a steep rise in the sale of his books was to be looked for; if he could raise the necessary money, he would be coming into sole possession of all his work at just the right moment. As a consequence of this advice, he wrote to a Basel solicitor on the possibility of raising a loan.

This increased activity was, however, fundamentally an effect of the growing excitement he felt within. He was advancing from the kind of self-overestimation that was hardly more than an exaggeration of a trait he had borne for years to outright insanity, and the course and rapidity of this advance can be demonstrated most clearly by quoting a series of extracts from his letters between October and the end of December:

To Malwida, the 18th October (in reply to her protest at *The Wagner Case*):

> These are not things about which I permit contradiction. On questions of *décadence* I am the highest court of appeal at present upon earth.

To Overbeck, the same day:

---

[1]'In sincere contempt', instead of *In aufrichtiger Verehrung* (= in sincere respect), a conventional valediction.

I am now the most grateful man in the world—in an *autumnal* mood in every good sense of the word: it is my great *harvest-time*. Everything comes easily to me, everything I try succeeds, notwithstanding no one has yet had such great matters in hand as I have. That the *first* book of the *Revaluation of all Values* is finished and ready for the press I report to you with a feeling for which I have no words. . . . This time, as an old artillerist,[1] I am bringing out my biggest guns: I am afraid I might shoot the history of mankind into two halves.

To Gast, the 30th October:

I have just looked at myself in a mirror—I have never before appeared as I do now: in exemplary good spirits, well-nourished, and looking ten years younger than I ought to.

To Malwida, the 5th November (in reply to her reply to his letter of the 18th October):

Just wait a little, honoured friend! I am sending you another proof that *'Nietzsche est toujours haïsable'*. Beyond any doubt I have *done you wrong;* but since I suffer this autumn from a surfeit of honesty, it really does me good to do wrong . . . The 'Immoralist'.

To Overbeck, the 13th November:

. . . people here [i.e. in Turin] treat me *comme il faut,* as if I were something extremely distinguished; there is a way of opening the door for me that I have never encountered elsewhere.

To Strindberg, the 7th December:

Now five words between ourselves, very much between ourselves! When your letter reached me yesterday—the first letter to reach me in my life—I had just finished the final revision of the manuscript of *Ecce Homo*. Since there are no longer any accidents in my life, this was, consequently, no accident. Why do you write letters which arrive at such a moment!—

To Gast, the 9th December:

Now a *serious* matter. Dear friend, I want to get back *all* copies of the *fourth* [part of] Zarathustra, in order to preserve this *ineditum* against all the accidents of life and death (—I read it yesterday and was rendered almost insensible with emo-

---

[1] He is referring to his one year's military service in 1867–68.

tion). If I publish it after a couple of decades of world-historic crises—wars!—only then will it be the *proper* time. Search your memory, please, and remember *who* possesses copies.

To Carl Fuchs (a writer on music), the 18th December:

Everything is going along marvellously. I have never experienced anything like the period from the beginning of September to today. The most unheard-of tasks are as easy as playing; my health, like the weather, appears every day with irrepressible brightness and gaiety.

To his mother, the 21st December:

Happily, I am now ripe for everything my task demands of me. My health is really splendid; the heaviest tasks, for which no man has yet been sufficiently strong, come easily to me.

To Overbeck, Christmas:

Dear friend, we must get the business with Fritzsch done quickly [i.e. the purchase of Nietzsche's books], for in two months I shall be the first name on earth . . . What is remarkable here in Turin is the fascination I exercise on people . . . When I go into a large shop, every face changes; women gaze after me in the street,—the woman who serves me in the shop keeps back the sweetest grapes for me, and *lowers the price.*

To Overbeck (received the 28th December):

I am working on a memorandum to the courts of Europe suggesting an anti-German league. I want to tie up the 'Reich' in a shirt of steel and provoke it to a war of desperation. As soon as I have my hands free I shall get the young Kaiser, *together* with his accessories, into my hands.

To Gast, the 31st December:

—Ah friend! *what* a moment!—When your card arrived, *what* was I doing? . . . It was the famous Rubicon . . . I don't know my address any more: let us assume it will soon be the *Palazzo del Quirinale.*

The state of tension in which he was living was in no way reduced by the receipt of almost equally excited letters from Gast and Strindberg. Gast, who seems to have taken Nietzsche's self-proclamations at their face value, thought the title originally intended for *Götzen-Dämmerung*, 'The Idle Hours of a Psychologist', 'too modest' and urged Nietzsche to think of a 'more glittering, more splendid title'. Strindberg wrote him that he had been sending out letters to all and sundry saying: 'Carthago est delenda, lisez Nietzsche'.[1]

Final breakdown came at the turn of the year: the letter to Gast of the 31st December was probably the last Nietzsche signed with his own name alone, although Naumann received a letter from him on the 2nd January 1889 with no indication when it was written. On the 3rd he collapsed, and when he recovered consciousness he was no longer Professor Dr. Nietzsche, formerly of Basel, but an incarnation of God-the-Sufferer in his two most impressive forms: Dionysus and the Crucified.

2

During 1888 Nietzsche worked on six short books: *The Wagner Case*, written in May and published in September; *Twilight of the Idols* and *The Anti-Christ*, written during August and September; *Nietzsche contra Wagner*, the Foreword to which is dated Christmas; the *Dithyrambs of Dionysus*, some of which are poems dating from the *Zarathustra* period, and the dedication of which (to Catulle Mendès) is dated the 1st January 1889; and *Ecce Homo*, written during the last quarter of the year.

It is an obvious question whether any of these works must be discounted as the product of unbalance. The answer is not a simple Yes or No, but it is, however, quite unambiguous. Firstly, the philosophical content is at one with that of the preceding works: no new ideas are introduced, and nothing of Nietzsche's already formulated philosophy is contradicted. The philosopher has not lost his grip on his material, he has tightened it; the notion that there is some defect of intelligence in these last works, that they contain 'nonsense', is quite false. Secondly, there is no decline in organizing ability; on the contrary, *The Anti-Christ* is the longest single inquiry since the *Untimely Meditations*, and several chapters of *Götzen-Dämmerung* would be equally lengthy if they were written in the manner of the *Meditations*. This leads to a third consideration, that of style. The works of 1888 represent Nietzsche's final victory over the German language: the famous brevity of these last works is an effect of absolute control over the means of expression. If there is a stylistic fault it is that the effects are too obviously consciously determined. Fourthly, however, as has already been said, where Nietzsche leaves philosophy and writes about himself his sense of his own quality passes the bounds of reasonableness and lands in

[1]In Karl Strecker: *Nietzsche und Strindberg* (Munich 1921), p. 35.

absurdity—yet even here there is no intellectual degeneration: even in *Ecce Homo* self-apotheosis is *almost* reducible to a desire to exert to the utmost the grandiloquent potentialities of *language*. The most disturbing passages are, in fact, not those containing the well-known grandiloquent claims but those in which Nietzsche quietly attributes to himself impossible abilities:

> I am possessed of a perfectly uncanny susceptibility of the instinct for cleanliness, so that I can ascertain physiologically—*smell*— . . . the 'entrails' of every soul. (EH I 8)

> My humanity is a perpetual self-overcoming. (EH I 8)

> Only I have the criterion of 'truths' in my possession. (EH–G 2)

The philosophical content of these last works is a repetition in brief and uncompromising form of the views Nietzsche has held from *Human, All Too Human* onwards. Most marked is the emphasis he places on his fundamental claim that the metaphysical world has no reality—a claim which provided the basis of his theory of the eternal recurrence:

> Heraclitus will always be right in this, that being is an empty fiction. The 'apparent' world is the only world: the 'real world' has only been *deceitfully added [hinzugelogen]*. (G III 2)

> The . . . idiosyncrasy of philosophers . . . in transposing the last and the first. They place that which comes at the end, . . . the 'highest concepts', that is to say the most general, the emptiest concepts, the last fumes of evaporating reality, at the beginning, *as* the beginning. This is . . . only an expression of their way of doing reverence: the higher *must* not grow out of the lower, it *must* not be grown at all . . . Moral: everything of the first rank must be *causa sui* . . . Thus they acquired their stupendous concept 'God' . . . The last, thinnest, emptiest is placed as the first, as cause in itself, as *ens realissimum*. (G III 4)

> The grounds upon which 'this' world has been designated as apparent establish rather its reality—*another* kind of reality is absolutely undemonstrable . . . The characteristics which have been assigned to the 'real being' of things are the characteristics of non-being, of *nothingness*—the 'real world' has been constructed out of the contradiction to the actual world . . . To talk about 'another' world than this is quite pointless, provided that an instinct for slandering, disparaging and accusing life is not strong within us: in the latter case we *revenge* ourselves on life by means of the phantasmagoria of 'another', a 'better' life . . . To divide the world into a 'real' and an 'apparent' world, whether in the manner

of Christianity or in the manner of Kant, . . . is only a suggestion of *décadence*—
a symptom of *declining* life. (G III 6)

Pure spirit is pure lie. (A 8)

The *lie* of the ideal has hitherto been the curse of reality. (EH–*Vorwort* 2)

He now sees the history of philosophy as a gradual devaluation of the metaphysical world, until in *his* philosophy the absurdity of speaking of a 'real' and
an 'apparent' world is made manifest:

HOW THE 'REAL WORLD' AT LAST BECAME A MYTH.
History of an Error.
1. The real world, attainable to the wise, the pious, the virtuous man—he
dwells in it, *he is it.*
    (Oldest form of the idea, relatively sensible, simple, convincing. Transcrip-
tion of the proposition 'I Plato, *am* the truth' [*Wahrheit*, corresponding to
wahre Welt—real world]).
2. The real world, unattainable for the moment, but promised to the wise, the
pious, the virtuous man ('to the sinner who repents').
    (Progress of the idea: it grows more refined, more enticing, more in-
comprehensible—*it becomes a woman,* it becomes Christian . . .).
3. The real world, unattainable, undemonstrable, cannot be promised, but even
when merely thought of a consolation, a duty, an imperative.
    (Fundamentally the same old sun, but shining through mist and scepticism;
the idea grown sublime, pale, northerly, Königsbergian [i.e. Kantian]).
4. The real world—unattainable? Unattained, at any rate. And if unattained
also *unknown.* Consequently also no consolation, no redemption, no duty: how
could we have a duty towards something unknown?
    (The grey of dawn. First yawnings of reason. Cockcrow of Positivism.)
5. The 'real world'—an idea no longer of any use, not even a duty any longer—
an idea grown useless, superfluous, *consequently* a refuted idea: let us abolish it!
    (Broad daylight; breakfast; return of cheerfulness and *bon sens;* Plato blushes
for shame; all free spirits run riot.)
6. We have abolished the real world: what world is left? the apparent world
perhaps? . . . But no! *with the real world we have also abolished the apparent world!*
    (Mid-day; moment of the shortest shadow; end of the longest error; zenith of
mankind; INCIPIT ZARATHUSTRA.) (G IV)

The 'abolition' of the 'real world' is of course metaphorical, just as the 'death'
of God is metaphorical: it has ceased to be a reality; the entire six-act drama
takes place on 'this side' of existence, the only side we know or can know. But
the consequences of this 'abolition' are rather graver than philosophers have

realized: if God is 'dead', the world has lost its old value; if there is no 'beyond', the pillars which have hitherto supported the moral world have collapsed; if the idea of a noumenal world belongs to the world of phenomena, the phenomenal world has been deprived of that which was supposed to produce it. The ethical, metaphysical and logical worlds lie in ruins. 'Incipit Zarathustra'—Here begins Zarathustra—defines Nietzsche's own position as the philosopher of a new dispensation: man, deprived of all the former certainties (errors) must now face the truth that there is nothing in all existence he can rely on but himself; and this is the moment of great illumination (mid-day). The third paragraph compresses into fewer than forty words the critique of Kant which Nietzsche had been conducting in this book and that throughout the previous decade and shows almost graphically where he placed the 'thing-in-itself' and the 'categorical imperative'—as a stage in the decline of the idea of a 'beyond': it is quite characteristic that the northerly situation of Königsberg should be made accountable for the pale, misty nature of Kant's 'real world'. The fifth paragraph contains a criticism of his own position at the time of *Human, All Too Human*, which is subtitled 'A Book for Free Spirits', when he was employing that term to describe himself and all who had liberated themselves from the prejudices of their day—but without, as he now says, fully appreciating the consequences.

As in *The Birth of Tragedy* the creative force is passion controlled; and as in *Zarathustra* the 'superman' is the man of strong passion who 'overcomes' himself:

There is a time with all passions when they are merely fatalities, when they drag their victim down with the weight of their folly—and a later, very much later time, when they are wedded with spirit [*Geist*], when they are 'spiritualised'. Formerly one made war on passion itself on account of the folly inherent in it: one conspired for its extermination—all the old moral monsters are unanimous that '*il faut tuer les passions*'. The most famous formula for doing this is contained in the New Testament, in the Sermon on the Mount . . . [where] it is said, with reference to sexuality, 'if thine eye offend thee, pluck it out': fortunately Christians do not follow this prescription. To *exterminate* the passions and desires merely in order to do away with their folly and its unpleasant consequences—this itself seems to us today merely an acute form of folly . . . — The church combats the passions with excision in every sense of the word: its practice, its 'cure' is *castration*. It never asks: 'How can one spiritualise, beautify, deify a desire?'—it has at all times laid the emphasis of its discipline on extirpation (of sensuality, of pride, of lust for power, of avarice, of revengefulness).— But to attack the passions at their roots means to attack life at its roots. (G V 1)

. . . what is freedom? That one has the will to self-responsibility. . . . That one has become more indifferent to hardship, toil, privation, even to life . . . Freedom means that the manly instincts that delight in war and victory have gained mastery over the other instincts—for example, over the instinct for 'happiness' . . . How is freedom measured, in individuals as in nations? By the resistance which has to be overcome, by the effort it costs to stay *aloft*. One would have to seek the highest type of free man where the greatest resistance is constantly being overcome: five steps from tyranny, near the threshold of the danger of servitude. This is true psychologically when one understands by 'tyrants' pitiless and dreadful instincts, to combat which demands the maximum of authority and discipline . . . *First* principle: one must need strength, otherwise one will never have it. (G IX 38)

I too speak of a 'return to nature', although it is not really a going-back but a *going-up*—up into a high, free, even frightful nature and naturalness. (G IX 48)

Goethe— . . . a grand attempt to overcome the eighteenth century through a return to nature, through a going-*up* to the naturalness of the Renaissance, a kind of self-overcoming on the part of that century . . . He did not sever himself from life, he placed himself within it . . . and took as much as possible upon himself, above himself, within himself. What he aspired to was *totality;* he strove against the separation of reason, sensibility, emotion, will . . . ; he disciplined himself to a whole, he *created* himself . . . Goethe conceived of a strong, highly cultured human being who, keeping himself in check and having reverence for himself, dares to allow himself the whole compass and wealth of naturalness, who is strong enough for this freedom; a man of tolerance, not out of weakness but out of strength, because he knows how to employ to his advantage what would destroy an average nature; a man to whom nothing is forbidden, except it be *weakness*, whether that weakness be called vice or virtue . . . A spirit thus *emancipated* stands in the midst of the universe with a joyful and trusting fatalism, in the *faith* that only what is separate and individual may be rejected, that in the totality everything is redeemed and affirmed—*he no longer denies* . . . But such a faith is the highest of all possible faiths: I have baptised it with the name *Dionysus*. (G IX 49)

The name *Dionysus* now stands for the life-affirmation of the man who is 'strong enough for freedom', who can allow himself every liberty because he has his passions under control, who is master of his life and not its victim and who, because joy consists in the exercise of one's will to power, enjoys life and consequently affirms it: 'Dionysus' is now the Dionysus of *The Birth of Tragedy* plus the Apollo of *The Birth of Tragedy*—the effect of strong passion, strong will to power, controlled by itself, i.e. *sublimated*.

To grasp this is to grasp what is meant by the famous last line of *Ecce Homo:* 'Have I been understood?—*Dionysus against the Crucified*' (EH IV 9). The 'Dionysian man' is the 'superman'—an actual and not merely hoped-for 'elevation of the type man':

> Mankind does not manifest a development of the better or the stronger or the higher . . . onward development is not by *any* means, by any necessity [the same thing as] elevation, advance, strengthening. In another sense there are cases of individual success constantly appearing in the most various parts of the earth and from the most various cultures in which a *higher type* does manifest itself— something which in relation to collective mankind is a kind of superman. Such chance occurrences of great success have always been possible and perhaps always will be possible. (A 4).

But, Nietzsche maintains,

> Christianity . . . has waged a *war to the death* against this *higher* type of man. (A 5)

Nietzsche formulated his first serious objections to Christianity in the chapter of *Human, All Too Human* called 'The Religious Life'. Scientific and especially psychological knowledge, he says, now forbid us to believe in its tenets:

> . . . in the present state of knowledge one can no longer have anything to do with it [Christianity] without irremediably soiling one's *intellectual conscience* . . . (MA 109)

Belief in the Christian God—

> . . . the false assertion of the priests that there exists a god who wants us to do good; who is the guardian and witness of every action, every moment, every thought; who loves us . . . (MA 109)—

in the divinity of Jesus—

> . . . a Jew crucified two thousand years ago who said he was the son of God. There is no evidence to support such an assertion. (MA 113)—

and in the Christian religion—

> . . . a god who begets children on a mortal woman; a sage who invites us no longer to work, no longer to sit in judgment, but to pay heed to the signs of the

imminent end of the world; a justice which accepts an innocent man as a vicarious sacrifice; someone who bids his disciples drink his blood; prayers for miracles; sins committed against a god atoned for by a god; fear of a beyond to which death is the gateway; the figure of the Cross as a symbol in an age which no longer knows the meaning and the shame of the Cross . . . (MA 113)—

is no longer possible for a thinking person. The influence of Christian belief has been psychologically harmful:

. . . it was Christianity which brought sin into the world. Faith in the remedies which it offered against sin has gradually been shaken down to its foundations: but faith in the *sickness* which it taught and disseminated still remains. (WS 78)

The founder of Christianity was . . . as a physician of the soul devoted to that infamous and untutored faith in a universal medicine. At times his methods seem like those of a dentist whose sole cure for pain is to pull out the teeth . . . But there is this difference, that the dentist at least attains his object, the cessation of pain in his patient . . . : while the Christian . . . who believes he has destroyed his sensuality is deceiving himself: it lives on in an uncanny vampire form and torments him in repulsive disguises. (WS 83)

The critique is continued in *Daybreak,* where St. Paul is called 'the *first Christian,* the inventor of Christianness [*Christlichkeit*]' (M 68), and the Christian church 'an encyclopaedia of prehistoric cults' (M 70).

Let us never forget, [he writes,] that it was Christianity which made of the *death-bed* a bed of torture.' (M 77)

. . . in antiquity there was still real misfortune, pure, innocent misfortune; only in Christianity did everything become punishment, well-deserved punishment . . . (M 78)

One drop of blood too much or too little in the brain can make our life unspeakably wretched and hard, so that we have to suffer more from this drop of blood than Prometheus suffered from his vulture. But the worst is when one does not even *know* that this drop of blood is the cause. But 'the Devil'! Or 'sin'! (M 83)

The Christian attitude towards sex seemed to him simply perverse:

Christianity has transformed Eros and Aphrodite . . . into diabolical kobolds and phantoms by means of the torments it introduces into the consciences of believers whenever they are sexually excited. Is it not dreadful to make necessary and regularly-recurring sensations into a source of inner misery . . . ? And ought one to call Eros an enemy? [In sexual intercourse] one person, by doing what pleases him, gives pleasure to another person—such benevolent arrangements are not to be found so very often in nature! And to calumniate such an arrangement and to ruin it through associating it with a bad conscience! To associate the procreation of man with a bad conscience! (M 76)

(Compare with this the following passage from *Ecce Homo*, written some eight years later:

And so as to leave no doubt as to my opinion, . . . I will impart one more clause of my moral code against *vice:* . . . The clause reads: 'The preaching of chastity is a public incitement to unnaturalness. Every expression of contempt for the sexual life, every befouling of it through the concept "impure", is *the* crime against life—is the intrinsic sin against the holy spirit of life.' (EH III 5))

As a philologist he was particularly hard on the Christian manner of Biblical exegesis and interpretation:

How little Christianity educates the sense of honesty and justice can be gauged fairly well from the character of its scholars' writings: . . . again and again they say 'I am right, for it is written—', and then follows an interpretation of such impudent arbitrariness that a philologist who hears it is caught between rage and laughter and asks himself: Is it possible? Is this honourable? Is it even decent? . . . But after all, what can one expect from the effects of a religion which in the centuries of its foundation perpetrated that unheard-of philological farce concerning the Old Testament?: I mean the attempt to pull the Old Testament from under the feet of the Jews with the assertion it contained nothing but Christian teaching and *belonged* to the Christians. (M 84)

What lies behind Nietzsche's enmity towards Christianity thus far is the view that this religion is unreasonable: that an informed and rational man ought not to believe in it. But an attack on Christianity on this ground is, so to speak, one that any philosopher might have made; and there seems to be general agreement that Nietzsche's attack is of a special kind. Its individuality in fact lies in this, that (in *The Anti-Christ* especially) it is rooted in his own philosophy and directed primarily against the teaching of Christ himself. For Nietzsche the key to the character of Jesus is to be found in his doctrine of non-resistance to evil:

. . . the opposite of all contending, of all feeling oneself in struggle has here become instinct: the incapacity for resistance here becomes morality ('resist not evil!': the profoundest saying of the gospel, its key in a certain sense), blessedness in peace, in gentleness, in the *inability* for enmity. (A 29)

The 'good tidings' are . . . that there are no more opposites; the Kingdom of Heaven belongs to *children*. (A 32)

Such a faith is not angry, does not censure, does not defend itself. . . . It does not prove itself, either by miracles or by rewards and promises, or even 'by the Scriptures': it is every moment its own miracle, its own reward, its own 'Kingdom of God' . . . One could, with some freedom of expression, call Jesus a 'free spirit'—he cares nothing for what is fixed: the word *killeth*, everything fixed *killeth*. . . . He speaks of only the inmost things: 'life' or 'truth' or 'light' is his expression for the inmost things. (A 32)

In the entire psychology of the 'gospel' the concept guilt and punishment is lacking; likewise the concept reward. 'Sin', every kind of distancing relationship between God and man, is abolished—*precisely this is the 'glad tidings'*. Blessedness is not promised, it is not tied to any conditions: it is the *only* reality. (A 33)

The 'Kingdom of Heaven' is a condition of the heart—not something that comes 'upon the earth' or 'after death' . . . The 'Kingdom of God' is not something one waits for; it has no yesterday or tomorrow, it does not come 'in a thousand years'—it is an experience within a heart. (A 34)

This 'bringer of glad tidings' died as he lived, as he *taught*—not to 'redeem mankind' but to demonstrate how one ought to live. What he bequeathed to mankind is his *practice:* his behaviour before the judges, before the guards, before the accusers and every kind of calumny and mockery—his behaviour on the *Cross*. He does not resist, he does not defend his rights, he takes no steps to avert the worst that can happen to him—more, *he provokes it* . . . And he entreats, he suffers, he loves *with* those, *in* those who are doing evil to him . . . *Not* to defend oneself, *not* to grow angry, *not* to make responsible . . . But not to resist even the evil man—to *love* him. (A 35)

One can see *what* came to an end with the death on the Cross: a new, an absolutely primary beginning to a Buddhistic peace movement, to an actual and *not* merely promised *happiness on earth*. (A 42)

'One has to regret,' he says, 'that no Dostoyevsky lived in the neighbourhood of this most interesting *décadent;* I mean someone who could feel the thrilling fascination of such a combination of the sublime, the sick and the childish' (A 31). Jesus taught salvation through refusal to resist, through 'turning the other cheek'—but for Nietzsche the vital force of life was conflict. Thus neither the title *The Anti-Christ* nor the challenge *'Dionysus against the Crucified'* involves Nietzsche's setting himself up as a counter-god: they are formulas for the opposition between his philosophy of power and Jesus' doctrine of non-resistance.

He has considerable respect for Jesus as a man:

> . . . in reality there has been only one Christian, and he died on the Cross. The 'gospel' *died* on the Cross . . . It is false to the point of absurdity to see in a 'belief' . . . the distinguishing characteristic of the Christian: only Christian *practice,* a life such as he who died on the Cross *lived,* is Christian . . . Even today *such* a life is possible, for *certain* men even necessary: genuine, primitive Christianity will be possible at all times. (A 39)

But he did consider that his doctrine had evolved as a consequence of a morbid sensitivity to pain:

> *Instinctive hatred of reality:* consequence of an extreme capacity for suffering and irritation which no longer wants to be 'touched' because it feels every contact too deeply. *Instinctive exclusion of all antipathy, all enmity, all feeling for limitation and distancing:* consequence of an extreme capacity for suffering and irritation which at once feels all resisting, all need for resistance, as an unbearable *displeasure* . . . and which knows blessedness . . . only in no longer resisting anyone or anything, neither the evil nor the evildoer—love as the only, the *ultimate* possibility of life . . . The fear of pain . . . *cannot* end otherwise than in a *religion of love.* (A 30)

The iife that Jesus led, however, was obviously not the life led by the everyday Christian, nor was his practice that of the church named after him: 'Christianity' must originate elsewhere than in the life and practice of Christ. Nietzsche's view as to where it originated is given in a single sentence: 'On the heels of the "glad tidings" came the *worst of all:* those of Paul' (A 42)—and when he speaks of it with contempt it is the religion of Paul he has in mind and not the gospel which died on the Cross. Paul, he maintains, reintroduced all the crude concepts of primitive religion Jesus had already overcome:

> Nothing is more un-Christian than the *ecclesiastical crudities* of God as a *person,* of a 'Kingdom of God' which *comes,* of a 'Kingdom of Heaven' in the *beyond,* of a 'Son of God', the *second person* of the Trinity. (A 34)

> That mankind should fall on its knees before the opposite of what was the origin, the meaning, the *right* of the gospel, that it should have sanctified in the concept 'church' precisely what the 'bringer of glad tidings' regarded as *beneath* him, *behind* him—one seeks in vain a grander form of *world-historical irony.* (A 36)

His critique of Christianity is therefore two-fold. Firstly, it is a critique of the teaching of Jesus himself. The heart of Jesus' doctrine, Nietzsche maintains, is the adjuration to total pacifism, and this doctrine must have been the expression of a certain state of being: a morbidly exaggerated sensitivity to suffering. If this state were at all general in men, whatever of value mankind has produced—indeed, 'mankind' itself—would never have appeared, since the evolution of the higher qualities has been brought about by conflict, *between* individuals and *within* individuals, within one 'soul'. He therefore feels entitled to call Jesus a 'decadent', partly on physiological grounds—i.e. he thinks that Jesus' nervous system must have been pathologically excitable—and partly on the more general ground that his doctrine, if universally followed, would lead to the decay of mankind. Secondly, he criticizes the Christian Church, not because it institutionalized the teachings of Jesus— which it self-evidently did not do—but because it was a reversion to a primitive miracle-and-salvation religion of the kind Jesus himself had left behind. Freed from the excessive rhetoric of *The Anti-Christ* Nietzsche's objection to the religion of the Western world can be seen to rest on rational grounds and to follow from the premises of his own philosophy. It should also be clear that—if I may revert to the opening of this book—the circumstances of his upbringing have nothing to do with the matter.

The question of 'decadence', which lies at the heart of *The Anti-Christ*, also lies at the heart of *The Wagner Case*. Discussion of this polemic has usually neglected to distinguish between the personal motives for Nietzsche's attack on Wagner and the substance of that attack—or even more often has ignored the substance altogether. Thus Newman, who devotes in all several pages of the fourth volume of his *Life of Wagner* to discussing *Der Fall Wagner*, feels entitled to dismiss it as 'venomous and fatuous', 'hobbledehoy ruffianism' and a 'lamentable pasquinade'[1] without even mentioning its main thesis—that Wagner was a 'decadent'—much less refuting it. The similarity in method between *The Wagner Case* and the *Untimely Meditation* on David Strauss— that of pin-pointing a certain 'problem' by means of an outstanding name— has not been sufficiently noted, nor that the ungentlemanly treatment accorded Wagner is the same in kind as that accorded Strauss, with whom Nietzsche was not personally involved: on the contrary it was assumed from the first that *The Wagner Case* owed its existence solely to its author's inability to forgive Wagner for once having enslaved him. Those of his friends who were still Wagnerians were offended on Wagner's behalf at the disrespectful tone of

---

[1] Newman: op. cit., pp. 525, 570 and 573, respectively.

the work: 'I have given my nearest and dearest a dreadful shock,' Nietzsche wrote to Brandes on the 20th October:

> There is for instance my old friend Baron Seydlitz of Munich, unfortunately president of the Munich Wagner Society; my even older friend *Justizrat* Krug of Cologne, president of the local Wagner Society; my brother-in-law Dr. Bernhard Förster of South America, the not-unknown anti-Semite, one of the keenest contributors to the *Bayreuther Blätter*—and my respected friend Malwida von Meysenbug, the authoress of the *Memoirs of an Idealist*, still goes on confusing Wagner with Michelangelo.

That Wagner had been dead five years—he died in February 1883—seemed to aggravate the offence, and it was to meet the charge of apostasy against a dead Master that Nietzsche prepared *Nietzsche contra Wagner*, which consists of passages drawn from each of his books from *Human, All Too Human* to the *Genealogy* designed to show that his opinions on Wagner had not changed since 1878, five years *before* Wagner's death.

It seems to me of some importance, then, to try to establish what *The Wagner Case* is about. It is, of course, an attack on Wagner, and an attack from several sides. The aspersions on Wagner's character we can deal with at once: they are justified. (Whether they are in the best of taste, coming from a former intimate, is another matter.) There is no reason now for dissembling over Wagner's failings in his dealings with the world: had he not been what he was he could not have achieved what he did, and that, I think, is the end of the matter. In 1888, however, it was the beginning: Wagner was in process of deification not simply as a great composer, or even as the creator of Bayreuth, but as a man. The 'official' biography, by Carl Glasenapp, had appeared in 1876: it is the life story of a sorely-tried saint and as fraudulent a piece of work as Elizabeth's biography of Nietzsche was to be, but with the difference that its subject was a silent collaborator. Nietzsche knew, of course, that Wagner was no saint, and in *Der Fall Wagner* he said so.

Wagner also stood in high esteem as a thinker. He himself brought out his own 'collected works', and it was not to be long before Houston Stewart Chamberlain would be proclaiming him the 'regenerator' of mankind—or at least of the Nordic portion of it. Nietzsche's protest at Wagner's 'literature' is another aspect of *The Wagner Case* with which no one today can have ground to quarrel.

A third object of attack is Wagner's ambiguity: his insistence that his music was more than music, that it contained unspeakable depths of meaning; his obfuscation where his own work was concerned. Nietzsche contrasts the world of Wagnerian music-drama with that of *Carmen* and says he prefers the latter.

The antithesis is so extreme that its polemical intent is obvious, Nietzsche's genuine admiration for Bizet notwithstanding: Wagner is of course a much 'greater' composer than Bizet—a fact Nietzsche never thinks of denying—but his god is Wotan, 'the god of bad weather' (W 10), and with all his power and genius he cannot achieve what Bizet achieves easily: '—*la gaya scienza;* light-footedness; wit, fire, grace; . . . the shimmering light of the South; a *smooth* sea—perfection' (W 10).

Fourthly, there is Nietzsche's assertion that Wagner was an *actor,* and that he represented the '*arrival of the actor in the world of music*' (W 11). The claim is debatable, but not outrageous or absurd; it is, on the contrary, one with which many today would agree. This, indeed, is what is striking about many of the criticisms of Wagner voiced in *The Wagner Case:* they sound like the objections of a Parisian composer of the 1920s, and Jacques Barzun has in fact gone so far as to see Nietzsche's break with Wagner as the first critical repudiation of the nineteenth century by a herald of the twentieth.[1]

The gravamen of Nietzsche's polemic is, however, none of these charges: it is that Wagner was 'decadent'. There is no ambiguity about what he meant by 'decadent' in this case: he meant that Wagner was part of the artistic decadence of the latter half of the nineteenth century. In a letter to Gast of the 26th February 1888 he had written:

> Today I experienced the pleasure of confirming my answer to a question which might seem extraordinarily hazardous: 'Who was best prepared for Wagner? Who would have been by nature . . . Wagnerian, despite and without Wagner?' For a long time now I would have said: . . . *Baudelaire.*

This conclusion leads straight to the key sentence of *Der Fall Wagner: 'Wagner est une névrose'* (W 5):

> The problems he brings upon the stage—nothing but the problems of hysteria—, the convulsive nature of his passions, his over-excited sensibility, his taste for sharper and sharper spices, his instability, . . . not least his choice of heroes and heroines viewed as psychological types (—a gallery of invalids!—): all this taken together represents a pathological pattern that leaves no room for doubt. *Wagner est une névrose.* (W 5)

The problems Wagner brings upon the stage, Nietzsche maintains, are neurotics' problems:

[1]Jacques Barzun: 'Nietzsche contra Wagner' in *Darwin, Marx, Wagner: Critique of a Heritage* (New York 1941, 1958).

. . . translate Wagner into the everyday, into the modern . . . What surprises one experiences! Would you believe it that, once you have stripped off their heroic trappings, the Wagnerian heroines are one and all the exact image of Madame Bovary? . . . Yes, by and large Wagner seems to be interested in no other problems than those which today interest little Parisian *décadents*. Always five steps from the hospital! Nothing but quite modern problems, nothing but problems of a *big city!* (W 9)

Wagner, the 'artist of *décadence*' (W 5), became conscious of himself through the 'philosopher of *décadence*', Schopenhauer, and thenceforward consciously followed the path he had previously been following blindly.

Nietzsche attempts to relate all the prominent characteristics of Wagner's nature and art to this basic thesis that he was neurotic: so, for example, he asserts that 'the musician now became an actor' and that 'this total transformation of art into play-acting . . . is a decided symptom of degeneration (more precisely, a form of hysteria)' (W 7). The title of the work, too, it should be noticed, refers specifically to this thesis: Wagner is a 'case'.

This attitude derives its full significance from being a direct riposte to the tenets of the growing Wagner cult, which insisted that Wagner was above all *German*, and in fact the national poet of the new *Reich:* Nietzsche counters with the assertion that Wagner was a *French décadent*. The Bayreuth movement was deeply imbued with anti-Semitism: Nietzsche counters with the suggestion that Wagner himself was a Jew. (The footnote in which he does so reads in part as follows:

> Was Wagner a German at all? There are certain reasons for asking. It is difficult to detect any German traits in him . . . His very nature *contradicts* what has hitherto been felt to be German . . . His father was an actor named Geyer. A Geyer [vulture] is almost an Adler [eagle—Adler is always and Geyer often a German-Jewish name] . . . That which has been circulated as the 'life of Wagner' is *fable convenue*, if not worse. I confess my mistrust of every point which rests on Wagner's testimony alone. (W *Nachschrift*)

The official biography gave Wagner's father as a Leipzig police actuary Carl Friedrich Wagner, and Wagner himself repeats this in *Mein Leben;* but he is known to have told several of his intimates that he thought he might actually be the son of his step-father, the actor and painter Ludwig Geyer. Nietzsche's definite statement as to Geyer's being Wagner's father suggests that Wagner told *him* that this was definitely so. Certainty is probably impossible at this late date: but Newman's investigation of the matter led him to the conclusion that 'it certainly looks now . . . as if the gallant opponents of the theory of the

Geyer paternity have been defending a lost cause.'[1] This appears to make it likely he *was* told by Wagner that Geyer was his father: but Nietzsche's purpose in mentioning the matter in *The Wagner Case* is nullified by evidence more recently unearthed that Geyer was in fact not Jewish; one of his middle names was 'Christian' and, like Nietzsche himself, he was the heir of a line of solid German Protestants.)

The virulence of *The Wagner Case* is, as I have noted, similar to that of the polemic against Strauss, and in both works Nietzsche is criticizing, by means of a prominent figure, the Germany of his day: the difference between them is that in the case of Wagner there is a background of personal association. Much too much has been made of this circumstance. It is not very difficult to see why Nietzsche developed a rancour against Wagner. His turning away from him around 1876 had the effect of making the preceding seven years seem wasted, and for this waste he came to blame Wagner rather than himself; this feeling was a consequence of the quasi-paternal role Wagner had played in his life during these years, and although its persistence is evidence of the strength of Wagner's hold its existence is in itself not particularly remarkable: every generation is unjust towards its predecessor and blames it for not having been different from what it was. His sense that Wagner had 'misled' him gained a wider application with Wagner's increasing success: he was now misleading all Germany and especially those young people who might otherwise have become 'followers' of Nietzsche, as Nietzsche had become a follower of Wagner:

> The Bayreuth cretinism also stands in my way, [he wrote bitterly to Malwida at the end of July 1888.] The old seducer Wagner is depriving me even after his death of those people upon whom I might have had some effect.

In his last year of sanity his opposition to Wagner's world-outlook changed into antipathy towards the man himself, in the same way as the critical attitude he had adopted towards the *Reich* from its foundation changed into detestation of the German people as such. The cause was similar in both cases: in the latter it was the failure of his countrymen to show the slightest appreciation of him or his work, in the former the humiliating sight of Wagner's increasing fame and popularity.

But to explain how a book may have originated is not to explain it away. It may be that when he wrote *The Wagner Case* Nietzsche 'had come to hate Wagner as he hated nothing else on earth'[2]—although I think this way of putting it a touch simplistic—but the task of the student is not over with this

[1]Newman: op. cit., vol. 3 (London 1945), p. 528.
[2]Ibid., vol. 4, p. 573.

discovery; it is then to discover if this 'hatred' of the man has led to any objective conclusions about him which may be valid independently of the emotion which prompted them. Nietzsche's claim that Wagner was a 'decadent' in the same sense as we should call Baudelaire one is a judgment capable of being discussed quite objectively, and so considered it has much to commend it.

In even so early a work as *Tannhäuser,* Baudelaire recognized in Wagner a kindred spirit, and published his brochure *Richard Wagner et Tannhäuser à Paris* in April 1861 in anger at the disgraceful reception accorded the work at the Opera on the 13th of the previous month. He was one of a number of French admirers who had seriously in mind the formation of a Wagner Theatre in Paris, an idea which was brought to nothing by the war of 1870. Other 'decadents' who admired Wagner and copied him included D'Annunzio, Gustav Moreau, Catulle Mendès, Barrès, George Moore, Aubrey Beardsley, Swinburne, and many lesser men. To Joseph Péladan, an inferior but highly typical author of the period, 'une Wagnererie' was 'practically synonymous with a Witches' Sabbath'.[1] Mallarmé paid homage to 'Le dieu Richard Wagner' in a poem to mark the foundation of the *Revue Wagneriènne* in 1885. Familiarity has blunted our sensibilities with respect to Wagner's operas, and it requires an effort of imagination to understand how they affected the 1880s and '90s and earlier. For many they were orgies of voluptuousness. To the 1850s the *Tannhäuser* Overture was the last word in the artistic representation of sensual abandon, and Baudelaire found in the opera 'Le sentiment presque ineffable, tant il est terrible, de la joie dans la damnation'. By the time *Tannhäuser* had begun to sound old-fashioned, *Tristan* was ready to take over, and many a young lady lost her sleep after hearing it: 'I know of some, and have heard of many [people], who . . . cried the night away [after *Tristan*],' Mark Twain wrote while on a visit to Bayreuth. 'I feel strongly out of place here. Sometimes I feel like the one sane person in the community of the mad.'[2] In the final decade of the century *Parsifal* was, alas, sometimes enjoyed less as a Christian drama of sin and redemption than as a wonderfully perverse and 'Byzantine' spectacle.

More than all this, Wagner's persistent association of eroticism with death was a predilection the 'decadents' knew how to appreciate: although on the deepest level a symbol for perfect sexual union, it appealed in a more literal way to a generation of writers who saw in it an expression of their own

---

[1]Mario Praz: *The Romantic Agony,* trans. Angus Davidson (Oxford 1933), V, note 65. This classic account of the romantic decadence includes many references to Wagner as an inspirer of greater and lesser authors and artists specializing in the erotic.
[2]A. B. Paine: *Mark Twain,* vol. 2, p. 922.

profound nihilism. 'Have you noticed,' Nietzsche asks, 'that the Wagnerian heroines have no children?—They *cannot* have them . . . Siegfried "emancipates woman"—but without hope of posterity' (W 9). This remark is not as irrelevant as it may perhaps seem. 'The androgyne ideal,' writes Praz, 'was the obsession . . . of the whole Decadent Movement',[1] and it was so as a symbol of sterility. Wagner's heroines do not live for love, they die for it; and their 'redemption' is to be found only in annihilation.

Many of the fundamental traits of 'romanticism' received enormous emphasis and convincing force in the hands of Wagner: the throwing-off of five centuries of development which have become too heavy to bear; bewilderment in the complex and unstable society of the present and the consequent nostalgia for a (supposedly) simpler existence in the past or the 'East'; preference of 'myth' (i.e. the simple and unreal) to 'history' (i.e. the complex and actual); predilection for extreme states of feeling because these obliterate all other feelings, all uncomfortable demands, all duties and the rights of others, and simplify existence to a single either/or; turning-away from the clear and unambiguous towards the dark, mysterious, unfathomable and 'profound'; the desire to be 'carried away' which ends in a desire for the ultimate 'carrying away', in a desire for extinction—all this was transported by Wagner into the highest reaches of art. The majority of his tragic characters, from the Flying Dutchman to Wotan, suffer from life as from a burden and in some sense will their own destruction. At last the desire to be free of the complications of life—they are knotted together as 'Alberich's curse'—brings about the destruction of the world; the next step was one which a large number of the 'decadent' romantics who followed also took: the death of desire itself, the extirpation of the passions, death *in* life, 'religion' in a Byzantine shape at once exotic and sterile: *Parsifal*. The magnificence of Wagner's art should not blind us to the end to which it is being put in *Parsifal:* a nihilism in which Christian symbols are made to speak the language of Schopenhauer.

That Wagner has survived his successors and enjoys today a reputation more solidly-based than ever before—he is no longer 'in vogue' because, like Bach, Mozart and Beethoven, he is always in vogue—is evidence of his quality as an artist, and not in itself an argument against Nietzsche's thesis that his tendency was decadent. This thesis is, as I have tried to show, quite capable of being discussed and sustained independently of whether Nietzsche 'hated' him or not. *Der Fall Wagner* is a protest *in advance* at the course art was to take during the closing decade of the century; and it should be clear why Nietzsche did not draw back from the 'tastelessness' of making it: the decadence of

---

[1]Praz: op. cit., V 14.

which he accused Wagner was the most influential expression then current of the nihilistic tendency of contemporary Europe and of the *Reich* in particular, a tendency which he saw as the gravest danger this civilization had ever faced.

Ecce Homo is Nietzsche's most enigmatic and problematic work, and the student who reads it must do so with caution. Much of it self-evidently belongs to the time Nietzsche no longer had control over his fantasies; on the other hand, much is not only rational but quite consonant with the outlook already familiar from the other post-*Zarathustra* works.

The extreme claims concerning his own importance in the history of European civilization—'One day my name will be associated with the recollection of something frightful—with a crisis such as there has never been on earth before' (EH IV 1) and so on—may be discounted as examples of the overcompensation we have already noted in his letters and personal writings of 1888 and earlier; where he is writing not about himself but about other people, or reiterating his philosophy, *Ecce Homo* shows no trace of unbalance. There is no intellectual degeneration: the mind is as sharp as ever and there is, above all, no decline in the stylistic control of language; on the contrary, the book is undoubtedly one of the most beautiful in German. Many passages are a *non plus ultra* of richness combined with economy: the only other writer remotely suggested is Heine, but his fleet-footed prose carries a far lighter burden of thought than Nietzsche's. To find a just comparison one must go outside literature altogether: *Ecce Homo* is the *Jupiter Symphony* of German letters.[1]

---

[1] The title, list of contents, Foreword, 'An diesem vollkommnen Tage' and the first chapter of *Ecce Homo* were already set up in type before Nietzsche's breakdown. As to how far the rest of the book corresponds to his intentions, see my Bibliography.

14

The Revaluation

A *Revaluation of all Values,* this question-mark so black, so huge it casts a
shadow over him who sets it up . . . (G *Vorwort*)

He who has publicly set himself a great objective and afterwards realises
he is too weak for it is usually also too weak publicly to repudiate that
objective, and then he inevitably becomes a hypocrite. (MA 540)

1

The completed works from *Beyond Good and Evil* to *Ecce Homo* stand in the
foreground of the creative period of Nietzsche's life the background of which
is the mass of unfinished material best referred to collectively as the *Revaluation.* This material has played a part in Nietzsche studies out of proportion to
its importance; indeed, discussion of his later philosophy has been haunted by
the shadow-existence of the *Revaluation,* and the practice of quoting from it
side by side with the finished works as if both possessed equal validity as
'Nietzsche's opinions' has blurred the distinction between what he himself
published, or prepared for publication, and what he rejected for publication.
Three considerations are involved: Nietzsche's own attitude towards the *Revaluation;* the question of its publication; and the quality of the material itself.

By the end of 1888 Nietzsche had been fighting against ill-health for sixteen
years. It is no romantic exaggeration but the simple truth to say that what kept
him alive during the latter half of this period was his sense of mission; and the
more desperately ill he was, the more desperately did he magnify the significance of that mission. In the sense in which he used the expression, Nietzsche's mission was a delusion. Its vehicle was the grandiose project called at
first *The Will to Power,* planned as a work to which *Zarathustra* would stand as

an introductory poem. Its scope was to be very large: a thoroughly detailed account of his philosophy. He began assembling material for it during 1884, and the *Nachlass* contains very many plans for its layout: the one dated the 17th March 1887 was arbitrarily selected by Elizabeth as the framework for her compilation called *The Will to Power*.[1]

The first mention of the projected book in Nietzsche's published writings occurs in the *Genealogy,* where he directs the reader in a parenthesis 'to a work I have in preparation: *The Will to Power. Attempt at a Revaluation of all Values*' (GM III 27). By the time these words were published, much of the assembled material had been used in *Beyond Good and Evil* and in the *Genealogy* itself. He wrote more. In May 1888 he dipped into it for *Der Fall Wagner* and then again in the early stages of *Götzen-Dämmerung.* But until at least the 26th August 1888 he was still planning to write the *Will to Power,* for a notebook page bearing that date and carrying yet another plan for the work has been preserved. Then he suddenly threw the idea overboard and drafted a plan for a quite different book: the detailed exposition of *The Will to Power* was to go; in its place he would write a concise book in which his latest philosophical position would be stated with the directness and brevity he had come to favour since the beginning of the year and which he had tried out in *The Wagner Case.* This new work, still in four 'books' but to be very much shorter than the abandoned one, was to elevate the former subtitle to the main position: *Revaluation of all Values.* The titles of the four 'books' are given in a plan of that autumn:

> Book 1: The Anti-Christ. Attempt at a Critique of Christianity. Book 2: The Free Spirit. Critique of Philosophy as a Nihilistic Movement. Book 3: The Immoralist. Critique of the Most Fatal Kind of Ignorance, Morality. Book 4: Dionysus. Philosophy of Eternal Recurrence.

The new *magnum opus* is mentioned at the end of the Foreword to *Götzen-Dämmerung,* which is dated 'Turin, the 30th September 1888, on the day the first book of the *Revaluation of all Values* was completed'. This 'first book' must be *The Anti-Christ,* and when it was published—after Nietzsche's collapse—it was with the subtitle given in the above plan. It was at first

---

[1]The plan reads: 'The Will to Power. Attempt at a Revaluation of all Values. Book One: European Nihilism. Book Two: Critique of the Highest Values Hitherto. Book Three: Principles of a New Evaluation. Book Four: Discipline and Breeding [*Zucht und Züchtung*].' About twenty-five plans for *The Will to Power* have survived: this one has no claim to be considered definitive (quite apart from the fact that Nietzsche abandoned the entire project); on the contrary, the paper on which it was written has been torn in two, the main title and the subtitle apart from the words 'of all Values' being missing.

described (by Elizabeth) as 'the first and only finished part of *The Will to Power*', but *The Anti-Christ* is not mentioned in any of the plans for that book: it first appears as the 'first book' of the *Revaluation*, and it is now generally thought to be 'the first and only finished part of the *Revaluation*'.[1] But this is still not the case. In *Ecce Homo* we read:

> Immediately after finishing the above-named work [i.e. *Götzen-Dämmerung*] and without losing so much as a single day I attacked the tremendous task of the *Revaluation* . . . The Foreword was written on the 3rd September 1888 . . . only on the 20th September did I leave Sils-Maria . . . I arrived in Turin on the afternoon of the 21st . . . Without delay and without letting myself be distracted for a moment I went on with my work: there was only the last quarter of the book still to be disposed of. On the 30th September a great victory; seventh day; a god takes his leisure on the banks of the Po. The same day I also wrote the Foreword to *Götzen-Dämmerung*. (EH–G 3)

This suggests that *The Anti-Christ* was no longer the 'first book' of the *Revaluation* but the *whole* book, that the *Revaluation* and *The Anti-Christ* were now one and the same thing. The suggestion is borne out by several letters of this time in which Nietzsche speaks of having finished the *Revaluation*. *Ecce Homo* he now considers a prelude to it:

> I have now, with a cynicism which will become world-historic, narrated my own story, [he wrote to Brandes on the 20th November.] The work is called *Ecce Homo* . . . The whole work is a prelude to the *Revaluation of all Values*, which lies completed before me: I swear to you that in two years we shall have the whole earth in convulsions. I am a fatality.

By this date, then, the four-part *Revaluation*, itself a reduction of the larger *Will to Power*, had been reduced to a single essay rather shorter than one of the *Untimely Meditations;* but some time between this date and the early days of 1889 Nietzsche blotted out the *Revaluation* altogether. The manuscript title-pages preserved in the *Nachlass* tell the story.[2] The earlier of the two reads: 'The Anti-Christ. Attempt at a Critique of Christianity. Book One of the Revaluation of all Values.' The later reads: 'The Anti-Christ. Revaluation of all Values.' The subtitle has been heavily crossed out, and underneath is written in large characters: 'Fluch auf das Christentum' ('A Curse on Christianity'). According to his final intentions, then, *The Anti-Christ* is neither the

---

[1]Kaufmann: op cit., p. 91.
[2]They are reproduced in Erich F. Podach: *Friedrich Nietzsches Werke des Zusammenbruchs* (Heidelberg 1961), Abb. IV and V.

whole *Revaluation* nor the first book of it: like *The Will to Power* before it, the *Revaluation of all Values* had been abandoned.

As the projected masterwork grew smaller Nietzsche's claims for it grew greater and reached their climax at just the time he had, it seems, decided to suppress it altogether: this was to lose touch with reality, and madness, open and undisguised, followed. To many people this last period of his sane life has seemed an uninterrupted decline into insanity, and the main evidence for this view has been his increasingly unreal assessment of the importance of himself and his work. But the fact that the *Revaluation* failed to appear makes it clear that the matter is not quite as simple as that.

Beneath the self-laudation there runs a parallel stream of self-criticism. Had this not been present it is probable that the masterpiece destined to shake the earth to its foundations would have expanded to proportions commensurate with its destiny; instead it was quietly reduced in scope and finally suppressed. This was the effect of an underlying *sanity* which recognized that the *Revaluation* was no advance upon the philosophy completed in *Zarathustra* but only a commentary on it, and that this commentary itself had already been published in the series from *Beyond Good and Evil* to *Götzen-Dämmerung*. One is justified in saying that a split in his conscious attitude towards himself and his work occurred during 1888. He had always had a rather excessive estimation of his own qualities, and in 1888 his inhibitions in this regard broke down completely: hence the mad self-laudation of *Ecce Homo*. But equally he had had a fine care for his reputation as a philosopher and stylist and would never publish anything open to criticism as bad thinking or bad workmanship; in this regard he remained as firm as ever: hence the sanity of *Götzen-Dämmerung*. The annunciation of a colossal project for the achievement of which he was fighting to preserve his life belongs to the former state of mind; the diminution and final disappearance of this project witnesses to the continuing strength of the latter.

2

The remnants of the abandoned work came into the hands of Elizabeth when, in 1895, she acquired the sole copyright of all Nietzsche's published and unpublished writings; and her decision to bring them out in the form of an almost-completed book was the fateful error which led to their overestimation. *The Will to Power: Studies and Fragments* first appeared in 1901, in volume 15 of the third collected edition of Nietzsche (i.e. the second edition of the *Grossoktavausgabe*, 1901–13); in this form it comprised 483 sections, edited by Peter Gast and Ernst and August Horneffer, with a Foreword and Postscript by Elizabeth Förster-Nietzsche. In 1906 the *Taschenausgabe* (Pocket Edition) of the works appeared, and by then *The Will to Power*, now edited by Gast and Elizabeth, had grown to 1,067 sections, arranged in four 'books'; this edition was subsequently (1910–11) transferred to the *Grossoktavausgabe* (supplanting the existing volume 15), where it was retitled *The Will to Power. Attempt at a Revaluation of all Values*.

The circumstances under which the first edition was produced have been outlined by Ernst Horneffer,[1] and they are indicative of Elizabeth's usual method of working. Editing of the *Nachlass* already carried out by the previous editor, Fritz Koegel, was, says Horneffer, valueless, because most of the material had not yet been deciphered or read, and no one could know how it was to be edited.

> We considered our first task was to read through the entire *Nachlass* so as to have at any rate a complete picture of it. This necessary preliminary, of paramount importance for a considered and planned edition, had up to then not been carried out. Undeciphered, uncopied, the manuscripts lay there in piles; no one had any idea what they contained. But the Archive had blithely gone on publishing. So we set to work to copy out the *Nachlass*. But that took far too long for Frau Förster-Nietzsche. She disliked intensely the 'monotony' of our way of working. Her idea was to get the job done as quickly as possible . . . In brief, the only object was to get volumes out quickly. We faced a difficult decision. Her desire to complete an edition of the *Nachlass*, however precipitately, was absolutely firm. That we knew. If we had withdrawn our collaboration she would have entrusted someone else with the job. She sometimes named names that made one tremble for Nietzsche's sake. So we decided to put up with it as long as we could, to prevent worse from happening.

These remarks apply *a fortiori* to the second edition, upon which Elizabeth was directly employed.

The objections to *The Will to Power* as it stands can be stated quite briefly: the compilation contains only material rejected by Nietzsche or used elsewhere in a different form and context (no distinction is made in Elizabeth's compilation between these two types of material); and the arrangement of the material under editorial headings, and the claim that the result is Nietzsche's 'chief work', is unjustified. The fact was grasped by Albert Lamm, who reviewed *The Will to Power* in September 1906,[2] and wrote: 'the book contains

---

[1] *Nietzsches letztes Schaffen*, quoted in Bernoulli: op. cit., vol. 2, pp. 348 ff.
[2] Quoted by Schlechta in vol. III of his edition of Nietzsche, p. 1404.

nothing that anyone who knows his Nietzsche does not know already: it is in fact a *Nachlass* publication; aphorisms which could stand beside others in *Beyond Good and Evil*, the *Genealogy*, the *Anti-Christ*, etc. . . . *nothing* new.' He goes on: 'while working this material over, Nietzsche discovered much more important things [i.e. the material he himself published], and the work which fate prevented him from carrying out is *not* that which lies before us [in Elizabeth's *Will to Power*]: what lies before us was *abandoned* by Nietzsche himself.' The important part of this judgment is that the *Nachlass* material is *abandoned* material: if Nietzsche did not use it, it was because he did not wish to use it; and this is the light in which one should read it, however it is presented.

As for the manner of presentation, no arrangement of the material—whether that of Elizabeth's *Will to Power*, or the compilation called *Unschuld des Werdens*, or that adopted by Gerhard Stenzel in the 'Bergland-Buch-Klassiker' selection—can be other than misleading, since it gives an impression of order where there is none, obscures the fact that the material being handled is *rejected* material, and distracts attention from the completed works of 1886–88, which come to be thought of as 'offshoots' of the 'uncompleted' work: a generation of students was directed to *The Will to Power* as Nietzsche's 'chief work' and to *Zarathustra* as his 'most personal'—Elizabeth's descriptions—and having found the one incoherent and the other baffling perpetuated the belief that their author was none too sure of what he was writing about. This conclusion might have been avoided altogether had it been remembered that Nietzsche's 'works' are the series from *The Birth of Tragedy* to *Nietzsche contra Wagner*, and that although he planned a book to be called *The Will to Power* he abandoned it (as he did the *Revaluation*, which supplanted it) and no such book exists.

The only method of publication of the *Nachlass* consistent with scholarly objectivity was already understood by Ernst Horneffer:

> How an edition ought really to be made, [he writes in the above-quoted repudiation of the edition for which he was partly responsible,] we saw . . . only when it was too late. And even if we had seen it sooner, we could never have convinced Frau Förster-Nietzsche of the necessity of adopting this form. For there is only one possible way of editing Nietzsche's *Nachlass* . . . : Nietzsche's manuscripts must be published word for word just as they are, without any arrangement or grouping by their editor.

Nietzsche's *Nachlass* has now been reproduced in this form in the Colli-Montinari *Kritische Gesamtausgabe* published between 1967 and 1978. (See the Postscript and the Bibliography.)

3

The *Nachlass* can be read with profit only by someone familiar with Nietzsche's published works, the reason being the above-mentioned fact that its
content is rejected material. In itself it is an enormous and confusing jumble of
notes, aphorisms and brief essays, some in a recognizably Nietzschean style—
although lacking the finish and the 'speaking' quality of the published
writings—but many no more than memoranda, jottings or lists of themes. To
attempt to absorb this mass of unorganized material without some guiding
principle is a lost labour, and the only principle which does not impose a
spurious order upon it is that of comparison and collation with the published
work.

It falls into two large divisions: (i) preliminary drafts or parallel formulations of something already published, and therefore rejected as superfluous;
and (ii) material set aside as being for one reason or another unacceptable. In
the former case one can with some confidence align the aphorism of the
Nachlass beside its published counterpart as an additional statement of Nietzsche's views; in the latter one must do the reverse—that is, exclude the
aphorism from any formulation of Nietzsche's philosophy, since this is precisely what Nietzsche himself did. And one must be capable, of course, of
distinguishing between the former kind of material and the latter. The basic
consideration to be kept in mind all the time is that anything in the *Nachlass*
which cannot be paralleled in the published works is *not valid*.[1]

Material of the first type includes notes touching every aspect of the
philosophy. A jotting such as:

> The properties of a thing are its effects upon other 'things': if we remove other
> 'things', then a thing has no properties, i.e. *there is no thing without other things,*
> i.e. there is no 'thing-in- itself' (WM 557)

is an unused fragment of the argument against a metaphysical world which
could be placed beside similar passages in the published works; as could these
aphorisms on conflict and the control of the passions:

> In contrast to the animals, man has developed an abundance of *contrary* drives
> and impulses within himself: it is a consequence of this synthesis that he is
> master of the earth . . . The highest man would have the greatest multiplicity of
> drives . . . In fact, where the plant Man shows himself strongest one finds the

---

[1]For more on this matter, see the Postscript.

most powerful *contrary* instinctive drives (e.g. Shakespeare), but controlled. (WM 966)

Overcoming of the emotions?—No, if what is implied is their weakening and extirpation. *But putting them into service:* which may also mean subjecting them to a protracted tyranny (not only as an individual, but as a community, race, etc.). At last they are confidently granted freedom again: they love us as good servants and go voluntarily wherever our best interests lie. (WM 384)

Mastery over the passions, not their weakening and extinction!—The greater the power of mastery of a will, the more freedom may the passions be allowed. (WM 933)

Similarly, a note such as the following is a contribution to the theory of sublimation:

Cruelty has been refined to tragic pity, so that it is *denied* the name of cruelty. In the same way sexual love has been refined to *amour-passion;* the slavish disposition to Christian obedience; wretchedness to humility; a pathological condition of the *nervus sympathicus,* e.g. as pessimism, Pascalism or Carlylism, etc. (WM 312)

and to the same sphere belongs the lengthy passage called 'What is *noble?*' (WM 943), which is a preliminary draft or offshoot of the chapter of that name in *Beyond Good and Evil.* The section of the *Genealogy* devoted to the origin of 'bad conscience' (GM II 16, quoted in Chapter 12) is prefigured in a note on the '*Verinnerlichung*'—the deepening and intensifying—of man:

Deepening and intensifying occurs when powerful drives which have been denied outward release by the establishment of peace and society attempt to keep themselves in check inwardly in concert with the imagination. The thirst for enmity, cruelty, revenge, violence turns itself back, 'is submerged'; in the desire for knowledge there is avarice and conquest; in the artist there reappears the submerged power of dissembling; the drives are transformed into demons, who are battled against, etc. (WM 376)

There are also many jottings on the eternal recurrence; e.g.:

1. The idea of the eternal recurrence: the suppositions that would have to be true if it were true. Its consequences.
2. As the *heaviest* idea: its probable effect if it were not prevented, i.e. if all values were not revalued.

3. Means of *enduring* it: the revaluation of all values. No longer joy in certainty but in uncertainty; no longer 'cause and effect' but the continually creative; no longer will to preservation but to power; no longer the humble expression 'It is all *only* subjective', but 'It is *our* work!—Let us be proud of it!' (WM 1059)

on 'nihilism'; e.g.:

> What does nihilism mean?—*That the highest values disvalue themselves.* A goal is lacking. An answer is lacking to the question 'Wherefore?' (WM 2)

and on such topics as anti-Semitism:

> The anti-Semites do not forgive the Jews for having '*Geist*'—and money. Anti-Semite—another name for the 'under-privileged'. (WM 864)

The second type of material comprises in general notes which take the philosophy in a direction for which there is no warrant in the published work. The following note on the recurrence is an example:

> *Duration,* with an 'in vain', without aim or goal, is the most *paralysing* idea . . . Let us imagine this idea in its most dreadful form: existence, just as it is, without meaning or aim, but irrevocably recurring, without a finale in nothingness: '*the eternal recurrence*'. This is the extremest form of nihilism: nothingness (the 'meaningless') eternally! European form of Buddhism: the energy of knowledge and strength compels to such a belief. It is the *most scientific* of all possible hypotheses. We deny final aims: if existence had a final aim it would already have been achieved. (WM 55)

This aphorism is at odds with the outlook presented in *The Gay Science* and *Zarathustra,* and although it is certainly a *possible* attitude towards the recurrence it is equally certainly not the one Nietzsche himself adopted: this attitude he rejected, and that is why his formulation of it is in the *Nachlass* and not *The Gay Science.* Another note on the subject:

> That everything recurs is the nearest approach a world of becoming can make to a world of being. (WM 504)

expresses something implied in the theory of the recurrence, and which I have taken into my account of it (see Chapter 9), but which Nietzsche did not arrive at explicitly: the idea remained in his notebooks.

The same must be said for the passage placed in the Preface to *The Will to Power* of 1906 which reads like the opening of an abandoned study of nihilism:

What I narrate is the history of the next two centuries. I describe what is coming, what can no longer come otherwise: *the rise of nihilism.* This history can be told already: for necessity itself is here at work. This future is already speaking in a hundred signs, this fate is already announcing itself everywhere; for this music of the future every ear is already cocked. For long now our entire European culture has been moving, with a tormenting tension that grows greater from decade to decade, as if towards a catastrophe: restless, violent, precipitate: like a river that wants to reach its *end.* (WM *Vorrede* 2)

Again, something of this is implied in the whole tenor of his thought, but 'the history of the next two centuries' is something he did not write: the project is one of those abandoned.

The need to remember the rejected character of the *Revaluation* notes is even more urgent when considering those that seem not a contradiction of published opinions but a development of them. The following remark on Napoleon, for instance, is famous:

The Revolution made Napoleon possible: that is its justification. For the sake of a similar prize one would have to desire the anarchical collapse of our entire civilization. (WM 877)

This has been quoted as evidence that Nietzsche's mind had toppled when he wrote it, or at the mildest that his passion for 'great men' had got the better of his sense of proportion. But one must again point out that the 'experimental' method of philosophy—the adoption of many points of view, including the extremest, in an effort to arrive at a reasonable point of view—is bound to produce abortive 'experiments': answers that are premature, inferences that are ill-founded, formulations that carry a valid insight to the point of absurdity; and that the acumen of an 'experimental' philosopher is shown in his ability to judge whether an 'experiment' has failed. (The whole philosophy of power was, from Nietzsche's point of view, an experiment that succeeded.) The publication of the above aphorism in *The Will to Power* is not evidence that Nietzsche was insane, but rather the reverse: he wrote it, but he rejected it.

More subtly misleading is the rhapsody on the universal will to power published as section 1067 of *The Will to Power:*

And do you know what 'the world' is to me? Shall I show it to you in my mirror? This world: a monster of energy, without beginning, without end; an immovable, brazen enormity of energy, which does not grow bigger or smaller, which does not expend itself but only transforms itself; as a whole of unalterable size, a household without expenses or losses, but likewise without increase or income;

enclosed by 'nothingness' as by a boundary; not something flowing away or squandering itself, not something endlessly extended, but as a definite quantity of energy set in a definite space, and not a space that might be 'empty' here or there, but rather as energy throughout, as a play of energies and waves of energy at the same time one and many, increasing here and at the same time decreasing there; a sea of energies flowing and rushing together, eternally moving, eternally flooding back, with tremendous years of recurrence, with an ebb and a flood of its forms; out of the simplest form striving towards the most complex, out of the stillest, most rigid, coldest form towards the hottest, most turbulent, most self-contradictory, and then out of this abundance returning home to the simple, out of the play of contradiction back to the joy of unison, still affirming itself in this uniformity of its courses and its years, blessing itself as that which must return eternally, as a becoming that knows no repletion, no satiety, no weariness—: this my *Dionysian* world of the eternally self-creative, the eternally self-destructive, this mystery-world of the two-fold delight, this my 'Beyond Good and Evil', without aim, unless the joy of the circle is itself an aim; without will, unless a ring feels goodwill towards itself—do you want a name for this world? A *solution* for all your riddles? A *light* for you too, you best concealed, strongest, least dismayed, most midnight men?—*This world is the will to power—and nothing beside!* And you yourself are also this will to power—and nothing beside!

Superficially, this appears to complete the philosophy of power by extending its principle to the furthest heavens; in reality, it negates that philosophy by taking it outside the field of observable phenomena. What distinguishes Nietzsche's will to power from Schopenhauer's will radically and fundamentally is that the former is an induction from observation, the latter a postulate founded on the premises of German metaphysics; but in the above passage Nietzsche succeeds in reducing the will to power to a universal substratum distinguishable from Schopenhauer's only by its 'materialist' character.

These few examples of the two types of material of which the *Nachlass* is composed will, I hope, indicate how it should be employed. Quoted without caution or a proper knowledge of the published works it can be a source of confusion and error; read intelligently it can provide a valuable insight into Nietzsche's method of working and processes of thought.

15

The Poet

Artists continually *glorify*—they do nothing else: they glorify all those conditions and things which have the reputation of making men feel good or great or intoxicated or merry or happy or wise. (FW 85)

Throughout the years of his maturity Nietzsche never ceased to write poetry, and although his achievements in verse cannot compare with his achievements in prose they are of interest as a parallel expression of the two sides of his personality I have called the Socratic and the Heraclitean. At one extreme are the little epigrammatic pieces the best known of which are those prefixed to *The Gay Science;* at the other, the formless *Dionysos-Dithyramben.* Mediating between these two extremes is a strongly rhythmic and rhymed form, a development of the style of his early years and capable of expressing both the Socratic and Heraclitean attitudes.

The epigrammatic verses are essentially an intensification, by means of metre and rhyme, of the single-sentence titled aphorisms which first appeared in *Human, All Too Human* and its sequels; e.g.:

Test of a good marriage. A marriage proves itself a good marriage by being able to endure an occasional 'exception'. (MA 402)[1]

Enemies of truth. Convictions are more dangerous enemies of truth than lies. (MA 483)

[1]This aphorism appears to have been suggested by, and to derive its full meaning from a couplet in the finale of *Die Meistersinger:*

> Der Regel Güte daraus man erwägt,
> dass sie auch 'mal 'ne Ausnahm' verträgt.
>
> (One can tell that rules are good rules
> if they can endure an occasional exception.)

The noble hypocrite. Never to talk about oneself is a very noble form of hypocrisy. (MA 505)

Bad memory. The advantage of having a bad memory is that one can enjoy the same good things for the first time *several* times. (MA 580)

Modesty of man. How little pleasure suffices most people to make them find life good; how modest man is! (WS 15)

Premises of the Machine Age. The printing press, the machine, the railway, the telegraph are premises whose thousand-year conclusions no one has yet had the courage to draw. (WS 278)

The most dangerous party-member. The most dangerous party-member is he whose defection would destroy the entire party: therefore the best party-member. (WS 290)

The object of aphorism is memorability through conciseness, and in the concisest of all his works, *Götzen-Dämmerung,* Nietzsche reduces the wordage of his aphorisms to an all-but-absolute minimum; e.g.:

Even the bravest of us seldom has the courage for what he really *knows.* (G I 2)

From the military school of life. What does not kill me makes me stronger. (G I 8)

'German spirit [*Geist*]': for eighteen years a *contradictio in adjecto.* (G I 23)

Formula for my happiness: a yes, a no, a straight line, a *goal.* (G I 44)

But memorability is also served by metre and rhyme, and it is to this fact that we owe the dozens of tiny metric aphorisms of the 1880s; e.g.:

Für Tänzer

Glattes Eis
Ein Paradeis
Für den, der gut zu tanzen weiss.

(*For dancers.* Smooth ice [is] a paradise for him who knows how to dance well. FW *Vorspiel* 13)

Aufwärts

'Wie komm ich am besten den Berg hinan?'—

Steig nur hinauf und denk nicht dran!

(*Upwards.* 'How can I best get up the mountain?'—Just climb upwards and don't think about it! FW *Vorspiel* 16)

Der Nächste
Nah hab den Nächsten ich nicht gerne:
Fort mit ihm in die Höh und Ferne!
Wie würd er sonst zu meinem Sterne?—

(*My Neighbour.* I don't like my neighbour near me: away with him into distant heights! How otherwise could he become my star? FW *Vorspiel* 30)[1]

The urbanity of the epigrams is also evident in the poems of a more conventional style, early examples of which are 'Ohne Heimat' and 'Dem unbekannten Gott'.[2] A good example from the 1880s is 'Unter Freunden' (Among Friends), annexed to the second edition of *Human, All Too Human:*

Schön ists, miteinander schweigen,
Schöner, miteinander lachen,—
Unter seidnem Himmels-Tuche
Hingelehnt zu Moos und Buche
Lieblich laut mit Freunden lachen
Und sich weisse Zähne zeigen . . .

(It is fine to be together in silence, better to laugh together—lying back against moss and beeches under the silken covering of the sky to laugh pleasantly with friends, showing our white teeth.)

During the period of *The Gay Science,* however, Nietzsche began to employ this kind of verse more and more as a vehicle for the expression of his wilder emotions: the rhapsodic, ecstatic note enters most markedly in the *Idylls from Messina* (1882, incorporated into the appendix of the second edition of *The Gay Science*) and other poems of the same date; as, for example, in 'Nach neuen Meeren' (To New Seas):

Dorthin—*will* ich; und ich traue
Mir fortan and meinem Griff.
Offen liegt das Meer, ins Blaue
Treibt mein Genueser Schiff.

---

[1] See also 'Meine Härte', quoted in Chapter 2, and 'Ecce Homo', quoted in Chapter 5.
[2] Quoted in Chapter 2.

> Alles glänzt mir neu und neuer,
> Mittag schläft auf Raum und Zeit—;
> Nur *dein* Auge—ungeheuer
> Blickt mich's an, Unendlichkeit!

(I *will* away—and henceforth I trust in myself and in my own hands. Open lies the sea, my Genoese ship surges onward into the blue.

Everything glitters new and newer, noontide sleeps on space and time: *your* eye alone—dreadfully it gazes upon me, infinity! FW *Anhang* 12)

and in 'An den Mistral' (To the Mistral), which has become a text-book example of fast-running rhythm:

> Mistral-Wind, du Wolken-Jäger,
> Trübsal-Mörder, Himmels-Feger,
> Brausender, wie lieb ich dich!
> Sind wir zwei nicht eines Schosses
> Erstlingsgabe, eines Loses
> Vorbestimmte ewiglich?
>
> Hier auf glatten Felsenwegen
> Lauf ich tanzend dir entgegen,
> Tanzend wie du pfeifst und singst:
> Der du ohne Schiff und Ruder
> Als der Freiheit frei'ster Bruder
> Über wilde Meere springst . . .

(Mistral wind, you hunter of clouds, killer of affliction, scourer of the skies, blusterer, how I love you! Are we two not the first fruit of one womb, eternally predestined for one fate?

Here on smooth rocky paths I run, dancing, towards you, dancing to your piping and singing: you who, as freedom's freest brother, leap across turbulent seas without ship or rudder . . . FW *Anhang* 14)

The tendency discernible in these verses grew more accentuated through the *Zarathustra* years until it culminated in the half-mystical ecstasies of 'Auf hohen Bergen' (From High Mountains):

> O Lebens Mittag! Zweite Jugendzeit!
> O Sommergarten!
> Unruhig Glück im Stehn und Spähn und Warten!
> Der Freunde harr ich, Tag und Nacht bereit,
> Der *neuen* Freunde! Kommt! 's ist Zeit! 's ist Zeit!

Dies Lied ist aus—der Sehnsucht süsser Schrei
    Erstab im Munde:
Ein Zaubrer tat's, der Freund zur rechten Stunde,
Der Mittags-Freund—nein! fragt nicht, wer es sei—
Um Mittag war's, da wurde Eins zu Zwei . . .

Nun feiern wir, vereinten Sieg gewiss,
    Das Fest der Feste:
Freund *Zarathustra* kam, der Gast der Gäste!
Nun lacht die Welt, der grause Vorhang riss,
  Die Hochzeit kam für Licht und Finsternis . . .

(O noontide of life! Second youth! O summer garden! Restless joy in standing and watching and waiting! Ready day and night I await the friend, the *new* friend! Come! It is time! It is time!

    This song is over—the sweet cry of desire has died in the mouth: a magician did it, the friend at the right time, the noontide-friend—no! do not ask who he is—it was noontide, when one became two . . .

Now, certain of united victory, we celebrate the feast of feasts: Friend *Zarathustra* has come, the guest of guests! Now the world rejoices, the dreadful curtain is rent, the wedding day has come for light and darkness . . . J *Nachgesang*, closing lines.)

The pressure of feeling in 'Aus hohen Bergen' is almost ready to break out of metric form and the trammels of rhyme into free verse, and in fact Nietzsche's final poetic style is characterized by the abandonment of every organizing principle except cadence:

    Still!—
    Von grossen Dingen—ich *sehe* Grosses!—
    soll man schweigen
    oder gross reden:
    rede gross, meine entzückte Weisheit!

    Ich sehe hinauf—
    dort rollen Lichtmeere:
    o Nacht, o Schweigen, o totenstiller Lärm! . . .
    Ich sehe ein Zeichen—,
    aus fernsten Fernen
    sinkt langsam funkelnd ein Sternbild gegen mich . . .

(Soft!—Of great things—I *see* something great!—one should not speak, or speak greatly: speak greatly, my enraptured wisdom! I look up—there seas of light are rolling: O night, O silence, O deathly-silent uproar! . . . I see a sign—

from the farthest distance a constellation of stars sinks glittering slowly towards me . . . 'Ruhm und Ewigkeit', 3: DD 8)

> Zehn Jahre dahin—,
> kein Tropfen erreichte mich,
> kein feuchter Wind, kein Tau der Liebe
> —ein *regenloses* Land . . .
> Nun bitte ich meine Weisheit,
> nicht geizig zu werden in dieser Dürre:
> ströme selber über, träufle selber Tau;
> sei selber Regen der vergilbten Wildnis! . . .

(Ten years have passed—not a drop of water has reached me, no moist wind, no dew of love—a *rainless* land . . . Now I ask my wisdom not to grow niggardly in this aridity: you yourself must overflow, you yourself must shower down dew, you yourself must be rain for this yellowed wilderness! . . . From 'Von der Armut des Reichsten'; DD 9)

This blurring of the distinction between prose and verse is, however, no late appearance. Passages of heightened, 'poetic,' prose occur in all Nietzsche's works, as, for example, in section 292 of *Human, All Too Human:*

> If your sight has grown sufficiently strong to see down to the bottom of the dark well of your nature and your knowledge, then there may perhaps also appear to you in its reflection the distant constellations of future cultures. Do you think such a life, with such a goal, too wearisome, too devoid of all that gives pleasure? Then you have not yet learned that no honey is sweeter than the honey of knowledge, nor that you will have to turn the clouds of affliction which lour above you to udders from which to milk the milk for your refreshment.

and in the peroration of *Daybreak:*

> *We aeronauts of the spirit!* All those brave birds which fly out into the distance, into the farthest distance—it is certain! somewhere or other they will be unable to go on and will perch down on a mast or a bare cliff-face—and they will even be thankful for this miserable accommodation! But who could venture to infer from that, that there was *not* an immense open space before them, that they had flown as far as one *could* fly? All our great teachers and predecessors have at last come to a stop . . . ; it will be the same with you and me? But what does that matter to you and me! *Other birds will fly farther!* This insight and faith of ours vies with them in flying up and away; it rises above our heads and above our impotence into the heights and from there surveys the distance and sees before it the flocks of birds which, far stronger than we, still strive whither we have

striven, and where everything is sea, sea, sea!—And whither then would we go? Would we *cross* the sea? Whither does this mighty longing draw us, this longing that is worth more to us than any pleasure? Why just in this direction, thither where all the suns of humanity have hitherto *gone down?* Will it perhaps be said of us one day that we too, *steering westward, hoped to reach an India*—but that it was our fate to be wrecked against infinity? Or, my brothers? Or?—(M 575)

Zarathustra, which is often called a 'prose poem', is written in a diversity of styles, from the prosiest prose to rhymed metric verse;[1] and many passages, and some whole chapters, produce the feeling of free verse: not only is it possible to arrange them as free verse without incongruity, but their cadence becomes more clearly audible when they are so arranged:

> Die Feigen fallen von den Bäumen, sie sind gut und süss;
> und indem sie fallen, reisst ihnen die rote Haut.
> Ein Nordwind bin ich reifen Feigen.

(The figs are falling from the trees, they are fine and sweet;/and as they fall their red skins split./I am a north wind to ripe figs. Z II 2)

> Nacht ist es:
> nun reden lauter alle springenden Brunnen.
> Und auch meine Seele ist
> ein springender Brunnen.
>
> Nacht ist es:
> nun erst erwachen alle Lieder der Liebenden.
> Und auch meine Seele ist
> das Lied eines Liebenden.

(It is night:/now do all leaping fountains speak louder./And my soul too is/a leaping fountain.

It is night:/only now do all songs of lovers awaken./And my soul too is/the song of a lover. Z II 9)

> 'Dort ist die Gräberinsel, die schweigsame;
> dort sind auch die Gräber meiner Jugend.
> Dahin will ich einen immergrünen Kranz des Lebens tragen.'
>
> Also im Herzen beschliessend,
> fuhr ich über das Meer.—

---

[1]The first part of the 'Second Dance Song' (Z III 15 1) is in the bizarre form of *rhymed prose.*

('Yonder is the grave-island, the silent island;/yonder too are the graves of my
youth./I will bear thither an evergreen wreath of life.'
Resolving thus in my heart/I fared over the sea. Z II 11)

> O du mein Wille! Du Wende aller Not,
> du *meine* Notwendigkeit!
> Bewahre mich vor allen kleinen Siegen!
>
> Du Schickung meiner Seele, die ich Schicksal heisse!
> Du In-mir! Über-mir!
> Bewahre und spare mich auf zu *einem* grossen Schicksale!

(O my Will! My essential, *my* necessity,/dispeller of need!/Preserve me from all
petty victories!
O my soul's predestination, which I call destiny!/In-me! Over-me!
Preserve and spare me for *one* great destiny! Z III 12 30)

> Still! Still! Ward die Welt nicht eben vollkommen?
> Was geschieht mir doch?
>
> Wie ein zierlicher Wind, ungesehn,
> auf getäfeltem Meere tanzt,
> leicht, federleicht: so—
> tanzt der Schlaf auf mir.

(Soft! Soft! Has the world not just become perfect?/What has happened to me?
As a delicate breeze, unseen,/dances upon the smooth sea,/light, light as a
feather: thus—/does sleep dance upon me. Z IV 10)

The step from prose of this kind to the free verse of the *Dionysos-Dithyramben*
is a short one. The excessive freedom which Nietzsche allowed himself is
probably the reason most of them are not as successful as the two from which I
have quoted: those included in the fourth part of *Zarathustra* in particular
show a lack of control, and the poor quality of the mass of fragments in a
similar style published after his breakdown suggests that he was missing the
restraining influence of metre. Yet one of his finest poems is also one of his
last: a firmly-controlled free-verse lyric in which he tells us more of the
essential truth about himself than in all the wish-dreams of Dionysus put
together:

> An der Brücke stand
> jüngst ich in brauner Nacht.

Fernher kam Gesang;
goldener Tropfen quoll's
über die zitternde Fläche weg.
Gondeln, Lichter, Musik—
trunken schwamm's in die Dämmrung hinaus . . .

Meine Seele, ein Saitenspiel,
sang sich, unsichtbar berührt,
heimlich ein Gondellied dazu,
zitternd vor bunter Seligkeit.
—Hörte jemand ihr zu?

(Lately I stood at the bridge in the brown night. A song came from afar; a golden drop, it welled over the quivering surface. Gondolas, lights, music—drunken it swam out into the twilight . . .

My soul, a stringed instrument, invisibly touched, sang to itself a gondola song thereto, quivering in many-coloured happiness.—Did anyone listen to it? EH II 7)

16

The Collapse

But to reveal my heart entirely to you, friends: *if* there were gods, how could I endure not to be a god! *Therefore* there are no gods. I, indeed, drew that conclusion; but now it draws me. (Z II 2)

As he was leaving his lodgings on the morning of the 3rd January 1889 Nietzsche saw a cabman beating his horse at the cab rank in the Piazza Carlo Alberto. With a cry he flung himself across the square and threw his arms about the animal's neck. Then he lost consciousness and slid to the ground, still clasping the tormented horse. A crowd gathered, and his landlord, attracted to the scene, recognized his lodger and had him carried back to his room. For a long time he lay unconscious. When he awoke he was no longer himself: at first he sang and shouted and thumped the piano, so that the landlord, who had already called a doctor, threatened to call a policeman too; then he quietened down, and began writing the famous series of epistles to the courts of Europe and to his friends announcing his arrival as Dionysus and the Crucified. How many he wrote is not known for certain. Those directed to public figures announced that he, 'the Crucified', would be going to Rome 'on Tuesday' (the 8th January), where the princes of Europe, together with the Pope, were to assemble: a notice to this effect went to the secretary of state of the Vatican. The Hohenzollerns, however, were to be excluded, and the other German princes were advised to have nothing to do with them: even now the *Reich* is still the enemy of German culture.

To Peter Gast went a single line:

To my maestro Pietro. Sing me a new song: the world is transfigured and all the heavens rejoice. The Crucified.

To Brandes a slightly longer epistle:

237

After you had discovered me it was not difficult to find me: the difficulty now is to lose me . . . The Crucified.

Letters also went to (among others) Strindberg, Malwida, Bülow, Spitteler and Rohde. Cosima received a single line:

Ariadne, I love you. Dionysus.

Burckhardt also received a Dionysus-letter, and later (the 6th January) a much longer one of four pages, with additions in the margins:

In the last resort I would much rather have been a professor at Basel than God; but I did not dare to carry my private egoism so far as to neglect the creation of the world on its account. You see, one must make sacrifices, however and wherever one lives . . . I walk around in my student's coat, slap this or that man on the shoulder and say: *siamo contenti? son dio, ho fatto questa caricatura* . . . The *remainder* for Frau Cosima . . . Ariadne . . . There is magic from time to time . . . I have had Caiaphas put in chains; and last year I was crucified by the German doctors in a very long drawn-out manner. Wilhelm, Bismarck and all anti-Semites abolished. You can make any use of this letter that will not lower me in the esteem of the people of Basel.

Burckhardt took this letter to Overbeck, whom he knew to be a close friend of Nietzsche's, and Overbeck recognized that it was a product of unbalance, if not of insanity. He at once wrote to Nietzsche, begging him to come to Basel. The following day, the 7th, Overbeck himself received a letter from Turin:

Although you have hitherto showed a poor opinion of my ability to pay, I hope still to prove that I am one who pays his debts—for example, to you . . . I have just had all anti-Semites shot . . . Dionysus.

He went straight to the Basel psychiatrist Wille, who read the two letters and advised that Nietzsche be brought to his sanatorium as soon as possible. Overbeck left the same day for Turin. On the afternoon of the 8th he arrived at Nietzsche's lodgings, which he found in a state of chaos: Nietzsche had again been singing and playing the piano and creating such a disturbance that his landlord was in the very act of going for the police when Overbeck appeared. Overbeck had arrived, he says, 'at the last moment in which it was still possible to get him away without any hindrance apart from his own condition'.[1] He was in a corner reading the proofs of *Nietzsche contra Wagner*—or appearing to

[1] Letter to Gast of the 15th January, in Bernoulli: op. cit., vol. 2, pp. 231 ff.

read them—when Overbeck came in; on recognizing his friend, Nietzsche embraced him violently and burst into tears.

The following day Overbeck and an attendant escorted him to the railway station and by means of persuasion and deception got him onto a train without incident. On arrival in Basel on the 10th he was taken to Wille's nerve clinic, where he stayed until the 17th. His behaviour demonstrated complete mental breakdown, although physically he was more robust than for many years. Wille's diagnosis was: 'Paralysis progressiva'—a diagnosis which proved to be correct.[1]

On the 14th Nietzsche's mother visited him. He recognized her and conducted a perfectly rational conversation about family matters until he suddenly cried: 'Behold in me the tyrant of Turin!' and the interview had to be cut short. His mother wanted to take him with her back to Naumburg, but Wille was totally opposed to this: Nietzsche required the kind of supervision and, occasionally, restraint, that could be provided only in an institution. As a compromise he suggested removal to a clinic nearer home, and Overbeck wrote to the director of the university clinic of Jena, Otto Binswanger, asking if it were possible for Nietzsche to be received there. Binswanger agreed, and on the 17th Nietzsche was transferred to Jena by train in the care of a doctor, an attendant and his mother. He was very calm at first, but before they reached Frankfurt he had broken out into a storm of rage against his mother, and for the remainder of the journey was restless and noisy. He arrived in Jena on the 18th and was admitted to the psychiatric clinic there the same afternoon.

Back in Basel, Overbeck was profoundly pessimistic about his friend's future. 'I have never seen so dreadful a picture of collapse,' he had written to Gast on the 11th. Now, on the 20th, he says that 'it would have been a far more genuine act of friendship' to have taken Nietzsche's life than to have handed him over to an asylum.[2]

> I have no other wish than that it may soon be taken from him, [he goes on.] I feel not the slightest uncertainty in saying this, and I think no one who had been with me during these days would feel otherwise. It is all up with Nietzsche!

---

[1] The record of Nietzsche's stay as a patient at Basel is reproduced in full in Erich F. Podach: *Nietzsches Zusammenbruch* (Heidelberg 1930), pp. 109 ff.

[2] Overbeck to Gast, in Bernoulli: op. cit., vol. 2, p. 238.

IV

1889–1900

Only the day after tomorrow belongs to me. Some are born post-humously. (A *Vorwort*)

17

Nietzsche's Death

> . . . he will be misunderstood and for a long time thought an ally of
> powers he abhors. (UIII 4)

1

To the story of Nietzsche's life must be added the story of his death. He took
eleven years to die, and in that time he became a figure of legend: living yet
dead, existing in a world beyond human reach, he excited to a dangerous
degree the myth-making powers of a nation increasingly addicted to fantasy
and irrationalism. The Nietzsche for whom the Nazis built the museum at
Weimar was, in all strictness, a madman: the Nietzsche of the last eleven years,
transformed from a rational philosopher and writer of genius into a man
without qualities upon whom any characteristics might be put. The reality—
that the philosopher had succumbed to an infection, most probably syphilitic,
and was declining into a condition usually called general paralysis of the
insane—disappeared in the fog of confusion, self-deception and gobble-
degook which had been drifting down upon the *Reich* since its inception and
against which Nietzsche himself had constantly and vociferously warned; so
that at last Ernst Bertram, a prominent member of Stefan George's 'Circle',
called Nietzsche's insanity an 'ascent into the mystic' and a 'proud transition'
to a higher state.[1] The content of Nietzsche's life-work was abolished, his
breach with Wagner healed, his enmity towards the *Reich* explained away: he
was made into 'an ally of powers he abhors' (UIII 4). The process was taken so
far that he became identified with the ultimate heirs of the movement against
which he had from the first set his face: with anti-Semitic, race- and state-
worshipping, anti-rationalist Nazism. 'His followers,' wrote Bertrand Russell

[1]Bertram: *Nietzsche: Versuch einer Mythologie* (1918), pp. 361–62.

towards the end of the Second World War, 'have had their innings':[1] the phraseology is as English as the misapprehension was universal.

It cannot be denied that Nietzsche was in some degree infected by the word- and myth-spinning tendencies of his nation and age; but it must also be asserted that he fought them, and that his anti-Germanism was, at bottom, the outward sign of an inward struggle. He foresaw the danger and warned against it in the first of his *Untimely Meditations,* in which he expressed the fear that the recent victory over France would result in 'the defeat if not the extirpation of the German *Geist* for the benefit of the "German *Reich*"' (UI 1); in the end he thought his fears had been realized:

> '*Deutschland, Deutschland über alles*' was, I fear, the end of German philosophy. (G VIII 1)

Helpless after his collapse, he fell into the hands of Elizabeth—who had always been more Förster than Nietzsche—and subsequently those of the whole tribe of Teutonic myth-manufacturers. In the Nazi era, the search for 'good ancestry', extended into the cultural and ideological field, lighted upon the 'solitary of Sils-Maria' the more easily since Elizabeth had already prepared him; and the Ninevite structure erected at Weimar to house the Nietzsche Archive was a tribute not only to her work but to the silence and collusion of most of the German academic world.[2] With all this Nietzsche himself had, of course, nothing to do: it is part of the story, not of his life, but of his death.

The condition in which he entered the clinic at Jena is revealed in the physician's report for the 19th January (1889):[3]

> The invalid followed us to his quarters with many polite bows. He paced his room with majestic tread, gazing at the ceiling, and thanked us for the 'magnificent reception'. He does not know where he is. Sometimes he believes himself to be in Naumburg, sometimes in Turin . . . He gesticulates and speaks constantly in an affected tone and with bombastic expressions . . . While speaking he makes constant grimaces. At night too his disconnected chatter goes on almost unceasingly.

For the remainder of 1889 he persisted in much the same state: sometimes almost rational, often talking nonsense, occasionally violent, but physically

---

[1]Russell: *History of Western Philosophy* (1946), p. 800.
[2]See Podach: *Friedrich Nietzsches Werke des Zusammenbruchs,* pp. 11–12 and 412 ff. for a commentary on this. Karl Löwith (*Von Hegel bis Nietzsche*) wittily calls the building 'Wagner's revenge on Nietzsche'.
[3]Reproduced in Podach: *Nietzsches Zusammenbruch,* p. 120.

fairly fit. At the beginning of 1890 Gast came to Jena, and he describes his meeting with Nietzsche in a letter to Carl Fuchs:

> He recognised me straightaway, embraced and kissed me and was tremendously pleased to see me; he shook my hand again and again as if he couldn't believe I was really there.[1]

He accompanied the patient on long walks and observed him closely. Sometimes he felt a cure was near at hand; at other times, he says, 'it seemed—horrible!—as if Nietzsche was feigning madness, as if he was glad to have ended like this!' Overbeck records having had a similar feeling the previous year, but in both cases it must have been the consequence of some otherwise unaccountable facial expression of Nietzsche's, or possibly of that 'feigning to feign' which is an accompaniment of some forms of insanity. Overbeck was also in Jena during February of 1890, and took turns with Gast in escorting Nietzsche on his exercise: he reports that for much of the time conversation was normal, except that Nietzsche could remember nothing of what had happened to him after the end of 1888 and was not aware of his condition or of where he was.

During all this time Franziska had been visiting her son when his condition allowed, and in mid-February she took a small house in Jena in order to be near him. Her sole desire was to get him away from the clinic and into her own care, but the clinic of course resisted this until it was clear that no improvement could be expected and that there was no risk to his mother involved in releasing him to her. This they did on the 24th March, and Nietzsche lived with her in Jena until, on the 13th May, they went back to Naumburg—back to the house at No. 18 Weingarten, which he had first left as a boy of 14 to go off to Schulpforta. By this time he had become very calm and docile, following his mother about like a child, but in need of constant surveillance. When in company he was well behaved, but what could happen if he went off alone is illustrated by an incident in May, when he left the house one morning in advance of his mother. Once in the street he immediately attracted attention by the violence of his gestures and the strangeness of his behaviour; and when he began to undress on the pavement the police were called and he was taken into custody. It was soon realized who he was, and he was being escorted back home by a policeman, to whom he was chattering gaily, when his distracted mother next saw him.

Back at Naumburg he entered into the sole care of his mother. She looked after him with great devotion, and seems to have drawn some of her courage

[1] Ibid., p. 135.

from the idea that God had given him back to her. In a letter to Overbeck she wrote: 'Again and again my soul is filled with gratitude to our dear, good God that I can *now care for* this child of my heart'.[1] On one occasion she spoke of someone who had died, and Nietzsche remarked: 'Blessed are those who die in the Lord.' She calls this evidence of the 'religious mood' into which he had been falling more and more, and expresses naive surprise at the extent of his knowledge of the Bible.[2] Gabriele Reuter was told that Franziska had considered burning her son's godless writings (*The Anti-Christ* was probably meant), but had been dissuaded by Elizabeth, who had said that 'the work of a genius belongs to the world, not to his family'. Nonetheless, says Gabriele, she was proud of her son's fame, and would heatedly defend his reputation.[3]

The history of the next two years is one of a decline into increasing apathy, with occasional bouts of liveliness. Hopes that Nietzsche might in the end be cured were reluctantly but at last completely abandoned, and Franziska's efforts were bent upon keeping him as happy as possible and guarding against any untoward incidents which might lead to his being taken back to Jena—a fate she dreaded more than anything else. Her letters to Overbeck, published in 1937 as *Der kranke Nietzsche,* give us a detailed account of these almost-eventless years. On the 1st October 1893 she wrote that he was still looking healthy and spent much of his time sitting on the veranda; he did not give the impression of suffering in any way and he 'even makes little jokes and laughs at them with us [i.e. herself and Elizabeth] in a perfectly natural way'. He was well for Christmas of that year but in March 1894 he was very sick, shouting and singing for hours on end, although again he appeared to be suffering no pain—'he looks quite pleased with himself' (letter of the 29th March). In the same letter she says that the daily walks have now had to be given up: as soon as they turn the street corner, Nietzsche asks 'Where is our house?' and is not happy until he is back there.

At Easter 1894 Rohde paid his first visit to the invalid, at Elizabeth's invitation.

I saw the unhappy man himself, [he wrote to Overbeck on the 27th December (visitors were usually dissuaded from seeing Nietzsche himself)]: he is totally apathetic, recognises no one but his mother and sister, speaks hardly a single sentence for a month at a time; his body has become shrivelled up and weak, although his face has a healthy colour . . . But he clearly feels nothing more, neither happiness nor unhappiness.

[1]See Erich F. Podach: *Der kranke Nietzsche* (Vienna 1937), p. 141.
[2]Ibid., p. 87.
[3]See Podach: *Gestalten um Nietzsche,* p. 31.

By the autumn he was hardly able to leave the house, having grown almost totally apathetic. Gast, who saw him in October, wrote to Overbeck:

> Nietzsche lies upstairs all day dressed in a flannel gown. He does not look bad, has grown very quiet and gazes ahead with a dreamy and very questioning expression . . . He hardly recognised me any more.

On his fiftieth birthday (the 15th October 1894) Paul Deussen visited him:

> His mother led him in, I wished him a happy birthday, told him he was fifty years old, and gave him a bouquet of flowers. Of all this he understood nothing. Only the flowers seemed to engage his attention for a moment, then they too lay unnoticed.[1]

Overbeck saw Nietzsche for the last time one day towards the end of September 1895. He describes his appearance in a letter to Rohde of the 31st December:

> Five and a half years before I had been able to walk with him for hours alone through the streets of Jena, when he was able to talk about himself and knew quite well who I was; now I saw him only in his room, half crouching, like a mortally-wounded wild animal that desires only to be left in peace, and he made literally not one sound while I was there. He did not look as if he was suffering or in pain, apart perhaps for the expression of profound distaste which was visible only in his lifeless eyes. Moreover, every time I went in he seemed almost always to be struggling against falling asleep. He had been living for weeks in a condition in which a day of dreadful excitability, which rose to the pitch of roaring and shouting, alternated with a day of total prostration. It was on a day of the latter kind that I saw him.

2

When Nietzsche collapsed he left behind him a large mass of unpublished material, some of it with him in Turin, some at Genoa and some—of a kind to be described later—at Sils-Maria. Of the writings of 1888 only *The Wagner Case* had been published; *Twilight of the Idols* was ready for publication, *Ecce Homo* and *Nietzsche contra Wagner* were partly printed, and *The Anti-Christ* and the *Dionysos-Dithyramben* were in manuscript. His immediate 'heirs', so far as his writings were concerned, were Overbeck, who felt responsible for

[1]Deussen: op. cit., p. 97.

their preservation, Gast, who counted himself Nietzsche's only 'disciple', and the firm of Naumann, whose business had come to be to a large extent tied up with Nietzsche. On the 20th January 1889 Overbeck wrote to Gast that the *Nachlass*—strictly speaking it was not that yet, since Nietzsche was still living—was being sent to him from Turin: apart from the finished books it is, he says, a 'wilderness of writings', some completely unreadable. On the 27th, after reading the finished work, Overbeck wrote again, saying that in his opinion, *Nietzsche contra Wagner* ought to be kept back, but there seemed to be no decisive reason for withholding *Götzen-Dämmerung*—'this truly astonishing cornucopia of intellect and insight'. *Ecce Homo* he has not yet seen. On the 4th February Overbeck says that Nietzsche's remaining papers are now with him in Basel. He has read the two printed parts of *Ecce Homo* and has been shaken by them. Naumann themselves thought that the autobiography ought not to be proceeded with and Overbeck agrees, 'however exceptionally valuable it will be later'. Upon the remaining papers he does not comment, except to say, in a letter of the 23rd February: 'I am not at all happy about what may happen to Nietzsche's literary *Nachlass* if we, I mean you and I, lose control over it.'

He was no doubt thinking, as Gast must have been when he read these words, of Elizabeth. It was well known to both of them that brother and sister had fallen out hopelessly, and that Elizabeth had come to represent to Nietzsche everything he disliked in the Germany of his time; and they must have thought things would go ill with Nietzsche's remains if they fell into Elizabeth's hands. At this time, she was still out in Paraguay. Förster committed suicide in June 1889, and after his death Elizabeth stayed on until the end of 1890 when, desperate for money, she returned to Germany to seek some out: one of her appeals was for funds to build a church for the spiritual needs of New Germania; another took the form of a short book in which Förster figures as a tragic hero.

Her brother's collapse and her husband's suicide had robbed her in one year of the only men who had ever been of any real consequence in her life, and the double loss brought out both the best and the worst in her: the best, in that it determined her to stand on her own feet and to show of what stern stuff she was made; the worst, in that the need to do so robbed her of what scruples she still had left. Her first intervention in the publication of Nietzsche's remaining works was to delay the public issue of the still-unpublished fourth part of *Zarathustra*. She considered much of it, and particularly the 'Ass Festival' chapter, blasphemous, and she convinced Franziska that they would stand in danger of prosecution if it were published. Franziska then wrote in anxiety to Overbeck (on the 24th and 29th March 1891) and to Gast, who had prepared it for printing by Naumann (the 1st April), urging it should be kept back, as Nietzsche himself had often said he did not want it to become public.[1] Gast was convinced that this was not Nietzsche's serious wish, but out of deference to the mother the work was for the moment set aside.

In August 1892 Elizabeth left Germany for New Germania just in time to miss the publication, by one of her colonists, Fritz Neumann, of a critique of her colonizing methods. According to Neumann, the jungle had won in New Germania: utterly inadequate preparations had been made to combat this elemental enemy of the La Plata colonist, and work was virtually at a standstill. Förster is accused of 'thoughtlessness', Elizabeth of 'crime' in continuing to lure people out there. The newspaper devoted to colonial interests in South America, the *Südamerikanische Kolonial-Nachrichten*, decided that Neumann was telling the truth, asked for more evidence, and at length itself accused the organizers of New Germania of incompetence and double-dealing: the whole concern, it said in the edition of September 1892, was 'more of a plundering of inexperienced and credulous people, performed without conscience and in a most ruthless way'. Klingbeil's allegations, it admitted, had been correct in every particular.[2] During the following year the paper published an 'open letter' to Elizabeth from a former ally of hers, one Paul Ullrich, who minced no words and called her a liar and thief and a calamity for the colony, upon which she was adjured to turn her back for good. The paper echoed this demand and urged the colonists to turn her out if she would not leave voluntarily. That summer Elizabeth liquidated what assets she had left and returned to Germany.

During 1892, with the agreement of Franziska and after discussion with C. G. Naumann, Gast had begun the preparation of a collected edition of Nietzsche's published works; also to be included were the fourth part of *Zarathustra*, a selection from the *Nachlass*, and prefaces by Gast. The work proceeded for about a year; then, on the 19th September 1893, Gast wrote to Overbeck: 'An event has occurred which is bound to disrupt both me and the whole Nietzsche cause: Frau Förster has come back from Paraguay. There followed a couple of dreadful days in which I would have liked to have chucked up my editorship.' But Gast had no need to chuck up his editorship: he was kicked out of it shortly afterwards. 'I handed over the *Nachlass* to Frau Förster on the 23rd October in Leipzig,' he told Overbeck on the 13th November. '"Who appointed you editor, then?" she demanded of me. My prefaces are to be set aside. In a notice to be written by Dr. Koegel [Elizabeth's substitute for

---

[1] See Podach: *Der kranke Nietzsche*, pp. 111 ff.
[2] See Chapter 12 for the allegations of Julius Klingbeil.

Gast] it is to be said: Gast's prefaces were printed in Nietzsche's works "in error".'

Gast's edition was terminated at the beginning of 1894 and a second collected edition begun under Koegel; but this too was subsequently interrupted by quarrels over method.[1] In February Elizabeth founded the 'Nietzsche Archive' at 18 Weingarten: two upstairs rooms were made into one, and filled with memorials of Nietzsche's life and work. The chief—if concealed—exhibit was Nietzsche himself. By the summer this accommodation had become too small, and the Archive was taken to a larger house nearby. With the foundation of the Archive a new figure appeared upon the stage of history: Elizabeth Förster-Nietzsche, the former Eli Förster (as she was known in her Paraguay days) transformed into the priestess of a new mystery cult. In an article in the *Bayreuther Blätter* of the 15th January 1895 she bade farewell to colonization; New Germania, the brain-child of her sainted husband from which she had been driven by calumnies unspeakable, would have to struggle on as best it could without her: 'another great life-task: the care of my dear and only brother, the philosopher Nietzsche, the tending of his works and the description of his life and thought, claims from now on all my time and strength'.[2] She had lost one colony, but found another.

In the meanwhile, she had been trying to lay her hands on everything that had belonged to Nietzsche, and especially, of course, everything he had written. Her idea of a 'manuscript' was, however, peculiar, and fateful for the concept *'Nachlass'* when applied by her to Nietzsche. I have remarked that she made no distinction between unpublished material which he had used in a different form and unpublished material which he had rejected; but, worse than this, she made no distinction either between material he had kept and material he had actually thrown away. The *'Nachlass'* rescued from Sils-Maria was of this last kind.

When Nietzsche departed from Sils-Maria for the last time he left behind in his room not only a quantity of books but also a heap of paper. He expected to return the following summer, but he specifically told his landlord, one Durisch, that the paper was waste: notes and jottings for which he had no further use, and which he asked Durisch to burn when he got round to clearing the room out. Durisch did, in fact, not burn it, but collected it together from Nietzsche's waste-paper basket and from the floor nearby and put it into a cupboard. Later, when tourists came to see the house Nietzsche had lived in and asked for some memento of the philosopher, he brought out

---

[1] See also Chapter 14.
[2] Quoted in Podach: *Gestalten um Nietzsche*, p. 176.

armfuls of this paper and invited them to help themselves. The fact became known through a news item in the *Magazine für Literatur* for autumn 1893, and Durisch was approached and asked what he was doing with 'Nietzsche's manuscripts'; unwilling to risk trouble, he at once sent the whole load of refuse to Elizabeth, who subsequently placed it in the 'Archive'—when the *Will to Power* was prepared, it was among the 'manuscripts' from which selection was made.

At the end of 1895 Elizabeth became Nietzsche's 'guardian' and the owner of his copyrights. From the time of his breakdown his legal guardian had been his mother, and it was perhaps natural that this guardianship should in time pass to his sister; but Elizabeth was not disposed to wait for their mother to die before making herself the 'heir' and inheritor of Nietzsche's works—which were fast increasing in monetary value. During December 1895 she persuaded Franziska to sign over to her the ownership of the Archive, of the works and, indeed, of Nietzsche himself; and this she did by means of a lie: according to Franziska's letter to Overbeck of the 27th, she was told that 'friends' of her son had offered to give 30,000 marks to the Archive provided Elizabeth became the official guardian of the Nietzsche 'heritage'; but even then she delayed four weeks before finally signing the necessary papers. Later she discovered that the money was merely a *loan*, which, she says, she had half-suspected all along.[1]

With Elizabeth in full possession, the Nietzsche 'cause' took on an added impetus. In the summer of 1896 the Archive was removed from Naumburg to Weimar—the Mecca of German culture, some of whose glamour she hoped would rub off onto the sombre figure of her brother. The hollowness of the 'cause' she was propagating had already been apprehended even by Rohde, who, as we have seen, had become quite unsympathetic: he wrote to Overbeck on the 17th March 1895:

> There really has been enough bellows-blowing about Nietzsche by now. Now they should complete the edition [of his works], write the biography, and then let the cause take care of itself.—Oh, *cause* I say: but there *is* no 'cause'; it is *only* and nothing but a *person*.

This made the soundest sense; but it was uttered in a country where sense of this kind was no longer of interest to a large body of influential opinion. For the prosaic facts as described by Erwin Rohde they had no time: they were living in the hope and expectation of a 'New *Reich*' and listening out for its heralds; and in Nietzsche they thought they had heard one. In reality, how-

---

[1] See Podach: *Der kranke Nietzsche*, pp. 193 and 200.

ever, the Nietzschean 'cause' lacked all content. All that was real was the unique individual Nietzsche, who had died in the first days of 1889, and his philosophy; and the activities of the Archive were, its publications of Nietzsche's writings apart, of little consequence.

3

Franziska Nietzsche died on the 20th April 1897 at the age of 71. She had been caring for her son, night and day, for seven years, and her devotion was often the object of admiring comment even during her lifetime. She had watched him decline into almost total apathy, and during the closing months of her life she had been increasingly the prey of anxiety about what would happen to him after she was gone. Her task had been lightened by the assistance of her maid Alwine, who had been with the family for thirty years, and it was Alwine who took charge of Nietzsche when his mother was no longer there to do so.

Elizabeth had already left Naumburg to go, with the Archive, to Weimar, where she installed herself and it in the Villa Silberblick, a house which a Swiss woman admirer of Nietzsche had rented for the purpose. Thither Nietzsche himself was taken after his mother's death and lodged in a room on the upper floor. His arrival was noted as an event in the town and has been recorded by his former pupil Ludwig von Scheffler, who was living there at the time. The Villa Silberblick, he says,[1] was an ugly building standing in a spot so isolated and unprotected from the hot summer sun that it was accorded the nickname 'Villa Sonnenstich'—Villa Sunstroke.

> One day my small son came home excitedly from school, [Scheffler writes], and said: 'Papa, what do you think? A mad philosopher has moved in up there!' [Scheffler went up to the Villa Sunstroke.] Nietzsche's sister led me into a sort of salon. It was piously dedicated to mementoes of her great brother: his pictures on the walls, books, manuscript collections . . .

Many visitors were received into this salon in the ensuing years; but if they hoped to see Nietzsche himself they were usually disappointed. Clad in a white dressing gown, he remained upstairs hidden away and silent, save for the occasional sound of a footfall as he paced the floor. Elizabeth herself saw him less and less, his care being entrusted to the faithful Alwine.

We can see from contemporary accounts how a half-mystical cult came to develop around this tragic-pathetic figure. A natural awe at the completeness

[1] Quoted in Bernoulli: op. cit., vol. 2, p. 379.

of his collapse and at the terrible contrast it presented to the vivid life of his books gradually changed into an awe of the man himself, as if he had become not something less than human (which was the case) but something more. Even before he left Naumburg those visitors who saw him and who had not known him in his sane years were often seized by an almost superstitious dread of the suffering and broken figure—a dread which some did little to curb but rather cultivated within themselves and spread abroad among those for whom Nietzsche was a new and exciting experience. Gabriele Reuter recorded how he impressed her in language which, while perhaps objective in intention, is sufficiently emotive to be dangerously exciting to the sensibilities of Germany in the 1890s:

> I stood trembling beneath the power of his glance, which seemed to rise from unfathomable depths of suffering . . . It seemed to me that his spirit dwelt in boundless solitude, endlessly distant from all human affairs. Who can tell how much of that great, unhappy soul still lived on in the secluded body?[1]

From this kind of dramatization it is not very far to the total unreality of the attitude represented by Rudolf Steiner, who wrote of the

> wonderful sensation that—while we were busy downstairs arranging his manuscript treasures for the world—he sat enthroned on the veranda above in solemn awfulness, unconcerned with us, like a god of Epicurus. Whoever saw Nietzsche at this time, as he reclined in his white, pleated robe, with the glance of a Brahman in his wide- and deep-set eyes beneath bushy eye-brows, with the nobility of his enigmatic, questioning face and the lionine, majestic carriage of his thinker's head—had the feeling that this man could not die, but that his eye would rest for all eternity upon mankind and the whole world of appearance in this unfathomable exultation.[2]

4

But Nietzsche did die: on the 25th August 1900, six weeks before his 56th birthday. During the previous two years he had known nothing, felt nothing, thought nothing. So far as we can tell he did not know that his mother was dead or that he was in Weimar. He did not know that he was famous, or that his fame rested upon a distortion of almost everything he had taught. When he died he did not know that for nearly eight months he had been living in the

[1]Quoted in Podach: *Der kranke Nietzsche*, pp. 251–52.
[2]Quoted in Bernoulli: op. cit., vol. 2, p. 370.

twentieth century, so much of whose subsequent history he had foreseen: the century of the 'rise of nihilism' and the collapse of the old world-order; the 'classic age of war' and of 'politics on a grand scale' which would draw conclusions from the 'death of God' and the disappearance of any sanction for morality; and in which the will to power, unsublimated and unchecked by the constraints which still imposed upon the nineteenth century, would everywhere seize the levers of power, 'this accursed anti-Semitism' would provide the occasion and motive for the ultimate in nihilistic crime, and his theory that a people of strong will to power deprived of outward satisfaction will will its own destruction rather than not will at all was to be demonstrated with terrible thoroughness by the desperate and frustrated *Reich*.

During the previous year—the last of the old century—a third collected edition of his works had been begun: Gast had become reconciled with Elizabeth and was collaborating with her on the new edition, in the Archive and with the defence of the 'cause'; and it was Gast who spoke the funeral oration when Nietzsche was buried beside his father in the churchyard at Röcken. He was obviously very much moved, but his words, which were in the spirit of the quotation from Rudolf Steiner above, reveal a dreadful misunderstanding of his 'Master'. He closed his address by declaiming: 'Peace be with thine ashes! Holy be thy name to all future generations!' In *Ecce Homo* Nietzsche had written: 'I have a terrible fear that one day I shall be pronounced "holy".' This too he had foreseen.

5

He was to be called 'holy'—and, rather more frequently, 'unholy'—for a century after his death. Today all this is, or should be, a part of the past: 'Nietzscheanism' is as dead as 'Wagnerism', and what we are left with is not a doctrine that might be preached and stand in need of defence but a human individual, an artist in language of great skill and power, and a philosopher of compelling insight and strictness of principle; we are left with the man and his philosophy. His life and thought were both in a sense 'experiments', and in so far as they were both carried through to a logical end they are self-justified and require no defending.

Postscript 1999

1

The most important events in the domain of the study of Nietzsche since this book first appeared, in 1965, have been the publication of the Colli-Montinari editions of Nietzsche's works and letters and the enormous enlargement of interest in him both within and beyond the academic world.

In 1965 the most recent edition of the works advertised as being complete was the *Musarionausgabe*, which appeared in 23 volumes from 1920 through 1929; but the text of that edition, though it was arranged differently, differed hardly at all in substance from that of the self-styled 'standard' edition, the *Gesamtausgabe in Grossoktav*, the second version of which was published in 19 volumes from 1901 through 1913. It was a product of the Nietzsche Archive in Weimar, the keys of which were still in the custody of Elizabeth, where they remained until her death in November 1935 at the age of 89. A new, 'historical-critical' edition was begun in 1933 but was halted by the war when it had advanced no further than the juvenilia; and partial publication of his writings between the appearance of the *Musarionausgabe* and the beginning of the Colli-Montinari edition failed, with one exception, to augment further the quantity accessible to the reader. This exception, Erich Podach's *Friedrich Nietzsches Werke des Zusammenbruchs* which appeared in 1961, was based on original research in Weimar—seemingly the only foray into the German Democratic Republic to eventuate in the publication of new material. The upshot of all these considerations was that in the 1960s Nietzsche's text, especially the text of the writings and notes unpublished at the time of his collapse—the so-called *Nachlass*—was still almost in the state in which it was presented in Elizabeth's edition of the first decades of the century.

The Colli-Montinari edition is an improvement on this in every respect: in conjunction with a publication I shall mention in a moment it enables us for the first time to speak of a definitive edition of Nietzsche's work. What has excited most interest in this edition has been its publication of the *Nachlass* in something approaching the order in which it was written so far as this can be ascertained, and while this is obviously of consequence for the student of his philosophy it is also of a distinct and peculiar interest to his biographer. For a biography of those men whose significance for us lies chiefly in what they produced rather than in what they did in any other sense contains the paradox that what is of the greatest significance to us about them finds almost no place in it. Consider in this regard Newman's life of Wagner: it could hardly be more detailed or in the conventional sense complete, yet that activity through which Wagner acquires his greatest interest for us, namely the composition of music, hardly occurs in it. We see him doing a hundred and one things, but we hardly ever see him composing music. The same consideration applies, of course, to Nietzsche, and for the same reason: the activity through which he acquires command of our interest is the thousand times repeated one of writing, and with this the biographer can do nothing. In the case of Nietzsche, however, we now possess in the Colli-Montinari edition of the *Nachlass* something that affords us an insight into how he thought and how he assessed his own performance; it enables us to watch him at work; so that, while all this newly accessible material might not require a reassessment of him as a philosopher, it can certainly provide matter of the first importance for his biography: when at some future time it comes to be employed to this end, it can form the basis of an intimate and closely observed biography of Nietzsche's thinking.

The Nietzsche-biographer of the future will be indebted even more to the Colli-Montinari edition of the letters. Here the biographical connection is obvious; what is not so obvious, perhaps, unless you have tried to use Nietzsche's letters in a biography of him, is how enormous an improvement this edition is over everything that came before. In 1965 the one existing edition of the letters that purported to be complete was *Friedrich Nietzsches Gesammelte Briefe*, published in six volumes from 1900 through 1909. It was arranged, in accordance with the custom of the time but very unhelpfully nonetheless, not chronologically but by recipients: Nietzsche's letters to Rhode, Nietzsche's letters to Gast, Nietzsche's letters to his mother and sister, and so on. The edition was supervised by Elizabeth and was therefore unreliable. Other letters by and to Nietzsche had also appeared in isolated volumes, though they were mostly unobtainable, and what was possibly the most interesting of them—Bernoulli's edition of the correspondence with Overbeck—was disfigured by extensive opaquing in black: the outcome of a court order obtained by Elizabeth when she was frustrated in her endeavour to have the publication banned outright. An attempt at a chronological publication of the letters begun in 1933 came to a halt the following year because of her refusal to allow their would-be editor, Karl Schlechta, to see, read or in any other way molest the documents he was supposed to be editing.

Such, more or less, was the state of things when the Colli-Montinari edition was begun. 'New' letters would see the light of publication from time to time, and there were creditable attempts at constructing a 'life' out of a chronologically arranged selection from letters already published; a large selection had appeared in Schlechta's edition of the 1950s, and you could read many letters from Nietzsche and be sure they were all right; but the situation produced by the Colli-Montinari edition nonetheless amounts to a revolution for the better in this field. It enables us to follow the course of Nietzsche's life often day by day, not only through the quantity and chronological ordering of the letters, but also by integrating letters by Nietzsche with the volumes of letters to him. Each of Nietzsche's letters is, where appropriate, followed by a reference to any letter in the companion volume to which it is a reply or which is a reply to it: the result is a continuous chain of correspondence in which every nuance of meaning is preserved.

The 150th anniversary of Nietzsche's birth saw the republication of the juvenilia assembled for the abortive *Historisch-kritische Gesamtausgabe* begun in 1933: comprising nearly three thousand pages in five volumes, it collects together his surviving writings from the years 1854 through 1870, only a small part of which was available in print elsewhere. The writings are accompanied by copious commentary. Without for a moment wishing to doubt the desirability, indeed necessity, of this publication, I question whether anyone is likely to stay the whole course from page 1 to page 2909: its intrinsic interest is too slight for that. Its value as biography, however, is considerable, for both the light it throws on Nietzsche's early intellectual evolution and the first-hand evidence it furnishes as to the kind and, above all, quantity of work a schoolboy and student was expected to do in the higher reaches of German education in the late nineteenth century.

The excellence of the Colli-Montinari works and letters and the edition of the *Frühe Schriften* is equalled by the excellence of C. P. Janz's edition of Nietzsche's musical compositions, which appeared in 1976. The composer himself published only one of them—the *Hymnus an das Leben*—and it is easy to see why: they are mostly juvenile or novice work, and all lack individual distinction. The *Hymnus* itself, for chorus and orchestra with the orchestration done by Gast, could have been composed by anyone with a background of Protestant hymnody; and the most celebrated critique of another of Nietzsche's styles of composition is surely that contained in a letter by Hans von

Bülow of the 24th July 1872 written in response to the receipt from Nietzsche of the score of his *Manfred Meditation* in which Bülow describes the work as 'the most fantastically extravagant, the most unedifying, the most anti-musical thing I have come across for a long time in the way of notes put on paper. Several times', he goes on, 'I had to ask myself whether it is all a joke', and gives Nietzsche a brief lecture on the rationale of the employment of dissonance and other 'advanced' procedures in the music of Wagner, of which he clearly thinks the *Manfred Meditation* to be an unwitting parody. (An English translation of this letter appears in the fourth volume of Newman's life of Wagner.) Because they are by Nietzsche, some of these compositions have been publicly performed and commercially recorded—which would hardly have happened if they had been composed by someone you have never heard of.

2

The efflorescence of Nietzsche scholarship, explication and interpretation in the interval that has passed since the publication of the initial edition of the present book has been awe-inspiring. Expansion of interest in academia has been such that any student of philosophy, 'cultural studies' or an allied discipline who is taught nothing at all about him must now feel short-changed, and there have been few intellectual or artistic movements that have not laid a claim of some kind to him. The recent decline of Marxism has been shadowed by a renewal of that interest in the politically leftist possibilities in Nietzsche which was a decisive element in the enthusiasm for him prevalent a hundred years ago. The existentialist Nietzsche has been succeeded by the deconstructionist Nietzsche, and the irrational, fascist Nietzsche—never more than a phantom—by an acceptance of him as the pivotal philosopher in the transition to post-modernism. There is a feminist Nietzsche and a post-feminist Nietzsche, representing movements sufficiently convincing to have provoked a counter-attack (i.e. by feminists who don't like him). There is the Nietzsche held responsible for the existence of the ethical relativism which is allegedly infecting contemporary (mainly American) society and causing its moral disintegration (Bloom's Nietzsche). There is the Nietzsche who stands at our end of the road to moral nihilism inaugurated by the Enlightenment (MacIntyre's Nietzsche). And there is, as a concomitant of all this serious involvement with him, Nietzsche the cultural icon whose high visibility has induced in many the illusion they know far more about him than they do.

I have not the space, knowledge or presumption to attempt to assess the value of all that has been written about him over the past thirty years: I have not read it all (no one could have done that), and I have not understood all of it I have read (this may be a generation problem, but it may equally be the case that some exegeses, explications and elucidations of Nietzsche are in fact incomprehensible). I therefore limit myself to saying that the more recent tendencies in thinking about Nietzsche which appeal to me most are those which view him as a philosophical paradigm or starting-point in relation to modes of thought characteristic of the twentieth century, and of these the one that seems the most securely based is the deconstructionism associated chiefly with Derrida: the critique and overcoming of binary thinking which can now be seen to constitute a large part of Nietzsche's philosophical project. If I had been able to read Derrida before writing *Nietzsche: The Man and His Philosophy*, parts of my exposition of his thought would have borne a different emphasis.

With these qualifications I would add that I have experienced nothing over the past thirty years that has led me to think that the account of Nietzsche's life and philosophy I give here is in need of correction except in a few small details. As I made clear in the original edition, the construction of the philosophy I offer is grounded in Walter Kaufmann's, and especially in his 'rehabilitatory' work of 1950; I was and am aware that Kaufmann makes of Nietzsche more of a humanist than he in fact was, and I tried to take that into account. By the time I came to write the book, in 1963 and 1964, the only comprehensive attempt to understand Nietzsche I knew of which seriously challenged Kaufmann's was that of Heidegger, especially in the volumes published in 1961. Although they differ in almost every other respect, Kaufmann and Heidegger are at one in regarding the will to power as Nietzsche's central tenet, without consideration of which he cannot be understood, and to this extent I found in Heidegger a confirmation of the line I had taken, but the rest of his Nietzsche interpretation I found incommensurate with my own. What principally stood in the way of my taking Heidegger into consideration was the fact that my account of Nietzsche relies almost wholly on the works he himself published, whereas Heidegger famously rejects the published works and relies entirely on the *Nachlass,* of which I make much less use than even Kaufmann does. I agreed, and still agree, with Karl Schlechta when he says, 'It seems to me a requirement of intellectual propriety [*geistigen Taktes*] to understand an author primarily in the way he wished to have himself publicly understood'. And when it was borne in upon me that, according to Heidegger's reading, 'Nietzsche's philosophy' is not explicitly present in his writings at all, published or unpublished, but must be educed by the interpreter, I came to think that Nietzsche himself would have failed to recognize Heidegger's Nietzsche. That Heidegger's interpretation has exercised a deep and wide influence seems to me no ground for objecting to this conclusion: the influence of Heidegger's own philosophy has been as deep and wide as that of any philosopher of the twentieth century, and has been in part responsible for the dissemination of interest in Nietzsche; but that has meant that many have been introduced to Nietzsche as a serious philosopher through the importance Heidegger accords him and have thus come to see him as Heidegger does. But to those whose involvement with Nietzsche predates any real understanding of Heidegger, it must almost inevitably seem that Heidegger's Nietzsche is precisely that: a construct no one but he would or could have devised.

It was not so much Heidegger's treatment of the *Nachlass* as the Colli-Montinari edition which led me to think for a time that I may have been too absolute in my rejection of it as a constituent of a valid presentation of Nietzsche's philosophical position. Although they are certainly harder to read and make sense of than the published works, the fragmentary notes of the 1880s contain so much of interest that to confine oneself to the published works alone might seem unwarrantably austere and self-denying. This consideration notwithstanding, however, I was always driven back to the fact (and it appears to me to be a fact) that the unemployed matter that constitutes the *Nachlass* was not left unemployed by accident, that what Nietzsche felt able to present as philosophy was what he himself published or demonstrably intended to publish; so I was still able to contend that anything in the *Nachlass* of the 1880s that cannot be paralleled in the published work is not valid as a statement of his considered view.

3

There are two small points I should like to discuss at slightly greater length than can be accommodated in a footnote.

1. Messina (see Chapter 10), at the north-east tip of Sicily, is the most southerly place Nietzsche visited, and conjecture as to why he went there has given rise to the suggestion he did so because he had learned that Wagner was in Sicily and hoped they might meet. While Nietzsche was in Messina, Wagner and his family were staying at Acireale, whence they undertook excursions to nearby resorts; from the 10th to the 14th April they were in Messina itself. If the two did meet, the fact would certainly have been recorded, by Nietzsche and probably by Cosima if by no one else, and we must therefore assume they did not. That there has been speculation on the matter is ulti-

mately due to the difficulty people experience in accepting the fact of co-incidence.

2. Long after the present book was published, an American scholar demonstrated that most of Nietzsche's essay on Hölderlin was lifted word for word from a volume in a popular series of 'modern classics' (*Moderne Klass-iker: Deutsche Literaturgeschichte der neueren Zeit in Biographien, Kritiken und Proben,* Cassel, 1853). This revelation inspired solemn and sensorious comment, and a quantity of schadenfreude was uncorked when it was observed how highly the essay had been commended by some famous commentators who had been unaware it was a product of plagiarism. (It also emerged that the *Moderne Klassiker* text plagiarized by Nietzsche was itself in large part lifted without attribution from a biography of Hölderlin by C. T. Schwab and a critical analysis of his work by Alexander Jung.) None of this is to my mind of great consequence: any youth can commit an act of folly, and an expert in any subject can be caught out if he has not been alerted. It is more interesting to reflect on what might have happened to Nietzsche if the deception had been detected, as it easily could have been. Would he have been expelled? And if so, what would have happened to him then? Or was cribbing quite common at Pforta in Nietzsche's day?

Selective Bibliography

The Nietzsche literature is by now so large and increasing so fast that a complete bibliography of it is probably no longer desirable and even if it were desirable would certainly be incomplete before it was printed. This bibliography is confined to book publications and even in this respect is very selective indeed. Many of the books listed, however, possess their own bibliographies, some of them extensive. The list which follows is divided into (1) collected editions in German, (2) English translations and (3) the secondary literature.

1

Kritische Gesamtausgabe: Werke. Ed. Giorgio Colli and Mazzino Montinari. (30 vols., Berlin: de Gruyter, 1967–78) *Sämtliche Werke. Kritische Studienausgabe.* Ed. Giorgio Colli and Mazzino Montinari. (15 vols., Berlin: de Gruyter, 1980) *Werke auf CD-ROM. Historisch-Kritische Ausgabe.* (Berlin: de Gruyter, 1994 / Charlottesville, Va.: InteLex, 1995).

Kritische Gesamtausgabe: Briefwechsel. Ed. Giorgio Colli and Mazzino Montinari (24 vols., Berlin: de Gruyter, 1975–84) *Sämtliche Briefe. Kritische Studienausgabe.* Ed. Giorgio Colli and Mazzino Montinari (8 vols., Berlin: de Gruyter and DTV, 1975–84).

Werke in drei Bänden. Ed. Karl Schlechta (3 vols. plus index vol., Munich: Hanser, 3rd edn., 1965).

Frühe Schriften. Ed. Hans Joachim Mette, Karl Schlechta and Carl Koch. (5 vols., Munich: Beck, 1994).

Der musikalische Nachlass. Ed. Curt Paul Janz. (Basel: Bärenreiter, 1976).

2

Complete Works. Ed. Bernd Magnus. (20 vols., Stanford, Calif.: Stanford University Press, 1995 onwards).

The Birth of Tragedy. Trans. Walter Kaufmann. (New York: Vintage, 1966).

Untimely Meditations. Trans. R. J. Hollingdale. (Cambridge: Cambridge University Press, 1983).

Human, All Too Human. Trans. R. J. Hollingdale. (2 vols. in 1, Cambridge: Cambridge University Press, 1986).

Daybreak. Trans. R. J. Hollingdale. (Cambridge: Cambridge University Press, 1982).

The Gay Science. Trans. Walter Kaufmann. (New York: Vintage, 1974).

Thus Spoke Zarathustra. Trans. Walter Kaufmann. (in *The Portable Nietzsche*, New York: Viking, 1954). Trans. R. J. Hollingdale (Penguin, 1961).

Beyond Good and Evil. Trans. Walter Kaufmann. (New York: Vintage, 1966). Trans. R. J. Hollingdale (New York: Penguin, 1973).

On the Genealogy of Morals. Trans. Walter Kaufmann and R. J. Hollingdale. (New York: Vintage, 1967). Trans. Carol Diethe. (As *On the Genealogy of Morality*. Cambridge: Cambridge University Press, 1994).

The Case of Wagner. Trans. Walter Kaufmann. (New York: Vintage, 1966).

Twilight of the Idols. Trans. Walter Kaufmann (in *The Portable Nietzsche*, New York: Viking, 1954). Trans. R. J. Hollingdale. (New York: Penguin, 1968).

The Antichrist. Trans. Walter Kaufmann. (In *The Portable Nietzsche*, New York: Viking, 1954). Trans. R. J. Hollingdale (New York: Penguin, 1968).

Nietzsche contra Wagner. Trans. Walter Kaufmann (In *The Portable Nietzsche*, New York: Viking, 1954).

Ecce Homo. Trans. Walter Kaufmann. (New York: Vintage, 1967). Trans. R. J. Hollingdale (New York: Penguin, 1979).

Dithyrambs of Dionysus. Bilingual edn., trans. R. J. Hollingdale. (London: Anvil Press Poetry, 1984).

The Will to Power. Trans. Walter Kaufmann and R. J. Hollingdale. (New York: Vintage, 1967).

Philosophy in the Tragic Age of the Greeks. Trans. Marianne Cowan. (South Bend, Ind.: Gateway, 1962).

Philosophy and Truth: Selections from Nietzsche's Notebooks of the Early 1870s. Ed. and trans. Daniel Breazeale. (Atlantic Highlands, N.J.: Humanities Press, 1979).

The Poetry of Friedrich Nietzsche. Ed. and trans. Philip Grundlehner. (New York: Oxford University Press, 1986).

A Nietzsche Reader. Ed. and trans. R. J. Hollingdale. (New York: Penguin, 1977).

Nietzsche Selections. Ed. Richard Schacht. (New York: Macmillan, 1993).

Selected Letters of Friedrich Nietzsche. Ed. and trans. Christopher Middleton. (Chicago: University of Chicago Press, 1969).

Nietzsche: A Self-Portrait from His Letters. Ed. and trans. Peter Fuss and Henry Shapiro (Cambridge, Mass.: Harvard University Press, 1971).

3

ALDERMAN, Harold: *Nietzsche's Gift*. (Athens: Ohio University Press, 1977).

ALLISON, David (ed.): *The New Nietzsche*. (Cambridge, Mass: MIT Press, 1985).

ANSELL-PEARSON, Keith: *An Introduction to Nietzsche as Political Thinker*. (Cambridge: Cambridge University press, 1994).

Selective Bibliography

ANSELL-PEARSON, Keith, and Howard Caygill (eds.): *The Fate of the New Nietzsche.* (Aldershot: Avebury Press, 1993).

ASCHHEIM, Steven E.: *The Nietzsche Legacy in Germany, 1890–1990.* (Berkeley and Los Angeles: University of California Press, 1993).

BABICH, Babette E.: *Nietzsche's Philosophy of Science.* (Albany: SUNY Press, 1994).

BINION, Rudolph: *Frau Lou: Nietzsche's Wayward Disciple.* (Princeton, N.J.: Princeton University Press, 1968).

BRANDES, George: *Friedrich Nietzsche.* (London: Heinemann, 1914).

BRANN, H. W.: *Nietzsche und die Frauen.* (Leipzig, 1931; Bonn, 1978).

BRINTON, Crane: Nietzsche. (Cambridge, Mass.: Harvard University Press, 1941).

CARR, Karen L.: *The Banalization of Nihilism.* (Albany: SUNY Press, 1991).

CHAMBERLAIN, Lesley: *Nietzsche in Turin.* (London: Quartet, 1996).

CLARK, Maudmarie: *Nietzsche on Truth and Philosophy.* (Cambridge: Cambridge University Press, 1990).

DANTO, Arthur: *Nietzsche as Philosopher.* (New York: Macmillan, 1965).

DELEUZE, Gilles: *Nietzsche and Philosophy.* Trans. Hugh Tomlinson. (New York: Columbia University Press, 1983).

DERRIDA, Jacques: *Spurs: Nietzsche's Styles.* Trans. Barbara Harlow. (Chicago: University of Chicago Press, 1979).

DEUSSEN, Paul: *Erinnerungen an Friedrich Nietzsche.* (Leipzig: Brockhaus, 1901).

DIETHE, Carol: *Nietzsche's Women.* (New York and Berlin: de Gruyter, 1996).

FOUCAULT, Michel: 'Nietzsche, Genealogy and History', in *Language, Counter-Memory, Practice.* (Ithaca, N.Y.: Cornell University Press, 1977).

FUKUYAMA, Francis: *The End of History and the Last Man.* (New York: Free Press, 1992).

GILLESPIE, M. A., and T. B. Strong (eds.): *Nietzsche's New Seas.* (Chicago: University of Chicago Press, 1988).

GILMAN, Sander: *Conversations with Nietzsche.* Trans. David J. Parent. (New York: Oxford University Press, 1987).

GRAYBEAL, Jean: *Language and 'The Feminine' in Nietzsche and Heidegger.* (Bloomington: Indiana University Press, 1990).

HAYMAN, Ronald: *Nietzsche: A Critical Life.* (London: Weidenfeld, 1980).

HEIDEGGER, Martin: *Nietzsche.* Trans. David Farrell Krell. (4 vols., New York: Harper & Row, 1979–86).

'Who Is Nietzsche's Zarathustra?', in David Allison (ed.): *The New Nietzsche.* (Cambridge, Mass.: MIT Press, 1985).

'The Word of Nietzsche: "God Is Dead" ', in *The Question Concerning Technology and Other Essays.* (New York: Harper & Row, 1977).

HIGGINS, Kathleen: *Nietzsche's Zarathustra.* (Philadelphia: Temple University Press, 1987).

HIGGINS, Kathleen, and Bernd Magnus (eds.): *The Cambridge Companion to Nietzsche.* (Cambridge: Cambridge University Press, 1996).

HIGGINS, Kathleen, and Robert Solomon (eds.): *Reading Nietzsche.* (New York: Oxford University Press, 1988).

HOLLINGDALE, R. J.: *Nietzsche.* (London: Routledge, 1973).

IRIGARAY, Luce: *Marine Lover of Friedrich Nietzsche.* Trans. G. C. Gill. (New York: Columbia University Press, 1991).

JANZ, Curt Paul: *Friedrich Nietzsche Biographie.* (3 vols., Munich: Hanser, 1978).

JASPERS, Karl: *Nietzsche: An Introduction to the Understanding of His Philosophical Activity.* Trans. Charles Walraff and Frederick J. Schmitz. (Chicago: Regnery, 1965).

KAUFMANN, Walter: *Nietzsche: Philosopher, Psychologist, Antichrist.* (Princeton, N.J.: Princeton University Press, 1950; 4th edn. 1974).

KOELB, Clayton (ed.): *Nietzsche as Postmodernist.* (Albany: SUNY Press, 1990).

KOFMAN, Sarah: *Nietzsche and Metaphor.* Trans. Duncan Large. (Stanford, Calif.: Stanford University Press, 1993).

KÜNG, Hans: 'Nietzsche: What Christians and Non-Christians Can Learn', in *Does God Exist?* Trans. Eduard Quinn. (New York: Vintage, 1981).

LÖWITH, Karl: *Nietzsches Philosophie der ewigen Wiederkehr des Gleichen.* (3rd edn., Hamburg: Felix Meiner, 1978).

MANN, Thomas: 'Nietzsches Philosophie', in *Neue Studien.* (Stockholm: Bermann-Fischer, 1948).

Nietzsche's Philosophy in the Light of Contemporary Events. (Washington, D.C.: Library of Congress, 1947).

NEHEMAS, Alexander: *Nietzsche: Life as Literature.* (Cambridge, Mass.: Harvard University Press, 1985).

OWEN, David: *Nietzsche, Politics and Modernity.* (London: Sage, 1995).

PARKES, Graham: *Composing the Soul.* (Chicago: University of Chicago Press, 1994).

SALOMÉ, Lou: *Nietzsche.* Ed. and trans. Siegfried Mandel. (Redding Ridge, Conn.: Black Swan, 1988).

SANTANIELLO, Weaver: *Nietzsche, God and the Jews.* (Albany: SUNY Press, 1994).

SCHABERG, William: *The Nietzsche Canon.* (Chicago: Chicago University Press, 1996).

SCHACHT, Richard: *Nietzsche.* (London: Routledge, 1983).

(ed.): *Nietzsche, Genealogy, Morality.* (Berkeley and Los Angeles: University of California Press, 1994).

SCHRIFT, Alan: *Nietzsche and the Question of Interpretation.* (London: Routledge, 1990).

SCHUTTE, Ofelia: *Beyond Nihilism.* (Chicago: University of Chicago Press, 1984).

SEDGWICK, Peter (ed.): *Nietzsche: A Critical Reader.* (Oxford: Blackwell, 1995).

STATEN, Henry: *Nietzsche's Voice.* (Ithaca, N.Y.: Cornell University Press, 1990).

STERN, J. P.: *A Study of Nietzsche.* (Cambridge: Cambridge University Press, 1979).

STERN, J. P., and M. S. Silk: *Nietzsche on Tragedy.* (Cambridge: Cambridge University Press, 1981).

STRONG, Tracy B.: *Friedrich Nietzsche and the Politics of Transfiguration.* (Berkeley and Los Angeles: University of California Press, 2nd edn. 1988).

WILCOX, John T.: *Truth and Value in Nietzsche.* (Ann Arbor: University of Michigan Press, 1974).

Index

Note: Because the whole of the index refers to him in one way or another, Nietzsche himself is not accorded a separate entry. If he or she wishes, the user may insert 'Nietzsche, Friedrich Wilhelm' at the head of the index and regard all the following entries as sub-headings.

267

Cab
0818371175